T3-BIE-627

TOOLS

Icon	Name	Use
	Selection	Selects and moves points, lines, objects or groups of objects
	Direct Selection	Selects parts of grouped objects without the need to ungroup the object
	Object Selection	Selects all of a path or graphic by clicking on any part of it
	Zoom in	Magnifies the scale of the view on the desktop
	Zoom out	Reduces the scale of the view on the desktop
	Scroll	Scrolls the view around the desktop
	Type	Places type into your Illustrator document
	Area type	Enters text inside any closed path
	Path type	Places text along any path
	Freehand	Draws curves or lines by tracing with cursor
	Autotrace	Provides automatic tracing of a template or part of a template

BOOKS THAT WORK JUST LIKE YOUR MAC

As a Macintosh user, you enjoy unique advantages. You enjoy a dynamic user environment. You enjoy the successful integration of graphics, sound, and text. Above all, you enjoy a computer that's fun and easy to use.

When your computer gives you all this, why accept less in your computer books?

At SYBEX, we don't believe you should. That's why we've committed ourselves to publishing the highest quality computer books for Macintosh users. Externally, our books emulate the Mac "look and feel," with powerful, appealing illustrations and easy-to-read pages. Internally, our books stress "why" over "how," so you'll learn concepts, not sequences of steps. Philosophically, our books are designed to help you get work done, not to teach you about computers.

In short, our books are fun and easy to use—just like the Mac. We hope you find them just as enjoyable.

For a complete catalog of our publications:

SYBEX

SYBEX Inc.
2021 Challenger Drive, Alameda, CA 94501
Tel: (510) 523-8233/(800) 227-2346 Telex: 336311
Fax: (510) 523-2373

 SYBEX is committed to using natural resources wisely to preserve and improve our environment. As a leader in the computer book publishing industry, we are aware that over 40% of America's solid waste is paper. This is why we have been printing the text of books like this one on recycled paper since 1982.

This year our use of recycled paper will result in the saving of more than 15,300 trees. We will lower air pollution effluents by 54,000 pounds, save 6,300,000 gallons of water, and reduce landfill by 2,700 cubic yards.

In choosing a SYBEX book you are not only making a choice for the best in skills and information, you are also choosing to enhance the quality of life for all of us.

The Adobe Illustrator 3.2
DESIGNER'S GUIDE

The Adobe Illustrator® 3.2
DESIGNER'S GUIDE

DAVID A. HOLZGANG

San Francisco   Paris      Düsseldorf   Soest

SYBEX®

Acquisitions Editor: *Dianne King*

Developmental Editor: *Kenyon Brown*

Editors: *David Krassner, Guy Hart-Davis, and Abby Azrael*

Technical Editor: *Len Gilbert*

Word Processors: *Ann Dunn and Susan Trybull*

Chapter Art: *Claudia Smelser*

Screen Graphics: *Arno Harris*

Page Layout and Typesetting: *Claudia Smelser and Len Gilbert*

Proofreader: *Rhonda Marie Holmes*

Indexer: *Anne Leach*

Cover Designer: *Ingalls + Associates*

Cover Illustrator: *Mark Fox, BlackDog Studio*

SYBEX is a registered trademark of SYBEX Inc.

TRADEMARKS: SYBEX has attempted throughout this book to distinguish proprietary trademarks from descriptive terms by following the capitalization style used by the manufacturer.

SYBEX is not affiliated with any manufacturer.

Every effort has been made to supply complete and accurate information. However, SYBEX assumes no responsibility for its use, nor for any infringement of the intellectual property rights of third parties which would result from such use.

Copyright ©1992 SYBEX Inc., 2021 Challenger Drive, Alameda, CA 94501. World rights reserved. No part of this publication may be stored in a retrieval system, transmitted, or reproduced in any way, including but not limited to photocopy, photograph, magnetic or other record, without the prior agreement and written permission of the publisher.

Library of Congress Card Number: 92-61124
ISBN: 0-7821-1002-9

Manufactured in the United States of America
10 9 8 7 6 5 4 3 2

CONTENTS AT A GLANCE

TABLE OF CONTENTS

INTRODUCTION

ABOUT THIS BOOK

This introduction and overview will help you understand how to use this book and how it was set up to help you master Illustrator. The first section talks about the objectives that this book is designed to meet and relates those to the reader's expected needs and background. There is also a discussion of what this book expects you to know already, and what experience you might want to have before starting the exercises here. The second section discusses the book's structure.

PURPOSE

The purpose of this book is to teach you to understand and use Illustrator. Illustrator is an extremely powerful tool. Unfortunately, the power of any computer tool is directly related to its complexity. Illustrator is not inherently difficult to use; it is only unfamiliar and, in some aspects, complex. This book is structured to minimize the complexity by introducing you to Illustrator operations step by step. You will become familiar and comfortable with Illustrator through doing and discussing many examples, covering a whole range of Illustrator tools and techniques.

Objectives

The first objective is to teach you to use Illustrator's tools. The intention is not only to acquaint you with the Illustrator Toolbox, but also to make you fluent in the use of these tools. You should be able to choose and use tools for most ordinary work without reference to any additional materials. As an integral part of this process, you should also understand the basic processes of creation and modification of artwork, whether beginning with a template or starting from a blank Illustrator drawing surface.

The second objective is to teach you techniques that produce results. This means that, besides facility with tools, you should develop a working knowledge of the processes that generate the effects essential to making graphic images: layering, shadowing, color use, and so on. These techniques are the basis of the most spectacular Illustrator output that you see, and here you will learn how to use them to your advantage.

Requirements

To begin with, you should be willing to work through the examples. Illustrator really is like any other toolkit in that ease and proficiency come from practice. So you should do the exercises and examples. I encourage you to try alternative approaches and to print out your variations to see how you are progressing. One of the most interesting things about Illustrator, in my experience, has been how much pure fun it is to play with. You can generate an amazing variety of graphics, just by trying options and tools. Please enjoy this experience; it will make the learning process more satisfying for you.

One thing that is not covered here is general computer concepts. Although I try to define precisely all terms that are intrinsic or even related to using Illustrator, there are certainly a number of concepts that apply to computers generally and Macintosh operations specifically that are understood. I'm not going to tell you how to turn on your computer or printer. Things like what a file is, or what pull-down menus are, and how the mouse works, are taken for granted.

This book also doesn't tell you how to install or start up your program. Illustrator installs quite easily, using the Installer application provided with it. The assumption in this book is that you have installed all the Illustrator defaults into a separate folder, as recommended in the Illustrator installation. You start Illustrator, like any other Macintosh application, either by double-clicking on the application itself or by double-clicking on a document prepared by it.

In addition, there is very little information about printer operations or other output devices. The entire issue of output processing is particularly complex for Illustrator. Since Illustrator can drive a wide range of output devices, it is impossible to give much consistently applicable advice regarding output problems that may crop up. Generally, all of the output in this book should come out approximately the same on any PostScript or PostScript-compatible device.

Finally, as you will see by the figures in this book, I have used System 7 for all the work here. This isn't a limitation. Illustrator 3.2 works perfectly under earlier versions of Apple's system software (at least back to 6.0.1). I have chosen System 7 because of the advantages that it provides in both application control and in printing; I expect that most readers will either already be using System 7 or will soon migrate to it.

Book STRUCTURE

The book follows a regular pattern that grows naturally out of the objectives that we discussed above. It includes in its structure three proven techniques that can help you build your understanding of Illustrator. First, the book follows a course of study, a plan that is designed to present the various operations in Illustrator in a natural way. The book also proceeds in a cumulative manner, with each topic and exercise building on the previous ones. Finally, the book provides ample exercises and examples to help you practice the concepts presented in a concrete setting and allow you sufficient drill to make these concepts and operations really familiar.

Task Orientation

The basic orientation of the book is to *do* first and *talk* after. Although there are some things that you must do before you can reasonably start an exercise, the general approach is to present only as much material as is necessary to understand the exercise and then to let you do the work. Any discussion that may be required follows the examples and exercises. For much of the book, however, the examples really are the text. By that I mean that you are learning techniques, not technical material. This is the same issue as learning to, say, scramble an egg. Once the cookbook has lead you through the process, there really isn't much more commentary that is necessary or appropriate.

Exercises and Examples

Both the exercises and examples are to some extent cumulative. To begin with, the techniques and tools that are covered earlier in the book are not explained when you use them again. Also, there are several images that are taken up repeatedly and enhanced or modified to demonstrate certain points of technique. This is a useful approach since it minimizes the continual duplication of basic information, allowing you to concentrate on the new and unfamiliar.

Of course, there is a certain amount of repetition that is both useful and necessary. Sometimes you cannot reuse the same graphic; even when you can, you often have to redo some things that you have learned and practiced before. This can be valuable as a reinforcement for certain processes and as a review of techniques. Believe me, there is no repetition in this book that is unnecessary; it is all essential to accomplishing the goals of the exercise. Where certain techniques unavoidably require repeated use, you will find that the demonstrations and discussion become very brief to avoid boring you. Therefore, if you come across a technique that you don't feel comfortable with, try looking back in the chapter or use the index to find a previous reference that contains the full explanation.

Software and Hardware Used

The work in the book is based solely on Illustrator. No other software was used to prepare the output pages. All the output images were produced on a standard Apple LaserWriter, which is the most common PostScript output device. The color images referred to in *Chapter* 10 and in the Appendix were created in Illustrator and separated using the Abode Separator utility program, then imaged on a Scitex Dolev and printed on high-speed presses.

But there are a wide variety of output devices that understand and support PostScript, and more are announced every week. We cannot guarantee that all the various output devices available will produce the same results as shown here. In particular, use of an imagesetting system for output may well cause some changes, due to higher resolutions and so on.

CHAPTER ONE

ONE

Introducing
Adobe Illustrator

WHAT IS ILLUSTRATOR?

The Illustrator software provides powerful tools for artists and designers. It enables you to create complex drawings that incorporate both graphics and text. However, as you will see in this book, the program is also useful for making simple forms and logos. Illustrator's tools allow you to manipulate images in much the same way that a word processor's tools allow you to manipulate text.

Illustrator can generate output of the highest quality on a wide variety of output devices—from dot-matrix printers to laser printers to high-resolution imagesetting machines. In each case, Illustrator will adapt to the selected device and generate the image you see onscreen. The high quality of the output is a result of the *PostScript* language. PostScript allows you to produce images that are impossible to generate with earlier graphics-processing technologies.

Illustrator provides tools for electronic drawing analagous to those of a traditional paper artist, including rulers, palettes, and brushes. Your images may consist of straight and curved lines or closed shapes that are clear, white, black, or any shade of gray. If you have a color monitor, you can assign and display colors. In addition to creating and displaying color images, you can use the Adobe Separator utility to produce color separations.

You can also magnify, reduce, and move images around on the drawing surface. Illustrator provides methods for transforming graphic images into new shapes and forms in a number of unusual ways. In short, the software not only automates the more routine and repetitive aspects of generating artwork, but also promotes creativity by allowing the designer to develop images in exciting new ways.

Illustrator Terminology

In this book, I am going to use terms such as *draw* and *trace* to describe the creation and manipulation of graphics. These terms translate quite naturally from their usual pencil-and-paper context to the computer environment of mouse, cursor, and screen image. I'm assuming that you are already familiar with mouse operations—clicking, dragging, and so on.

The specific Illustrator terms used throughout this book are *template, artwork, tools,* and *menus.* It is essential that you understand how these items relate to Illustrator and to one another.

The terms *template* and *artwork* as used in Illustrator denote two different states of graphic objects. A *template* is a bitmapped image that acts as a guide for an Illustrator drawing; templates are typically scanned images or images created by painting programs, such as SuperPaint or MacDraw, and they cannot be manipulated or changed within Illustrator.

Artwork is the term for images you've created using the Illustrator tools. Artwork, which may be generated by tracing a template or even created from scratch, is a creation of Illustrator and can be manipulated within the program. In this context, *tracing* a template means using the various Illustrator tools to create an artwork outline that overlays and matches the template image to whatever degree of precision you want.

Illustrator provides two ways to access its facilities: *tools* and *menus.* *Tools* are objects used to create, display, and manipulate artwork. *Menus* are lists of commands that govern source and destination files as well as modes of operation within Illustrator. *Chapter 2* provides a quick overview of both of these basic features.

Graphic Processing

Illustrator offers the same exciting techniques for the processing of graphic images that spreadsheets provide for handling numbers and word processors provide for handling text. Word-processing and page-composition software can make allowances for graphics, but their handling and processing of graphics is limited.

Ideally, the graphic designer and artist should be free to develop images from external sources, such as photographs or other artwork, or create new images directly on the computer. Any of these basic sources should produce electronic images that can be used in the same way and with the same flexibility that paper images can be used, retaining the ease of revision that is essential in computer-based applications.

The vast majority of the devices available to output graphics fall into the broad, general class of *raster-output devices*. They form all characters and images out of a series of dots that are activated in some way. These dots— which may in fact be square or oval—each represent one picture element, or *pixel*. The number of pixels-per-unit area is a measure of a device's ability to render images in greater or less detail; this is called the *resolution* of the device.

One common method of producing images on raster-output devices is to "paint" the image onto the device by setting each pixel explicitly *on* or *off*. An image produced by such a process is called a *bitmapped* image. This process introduces certain problems. First, because different devices have different numbers of pixels-per-inch, a bitmapped image that is adequate for one device will have too little (or too much) information for another of different resolution. Second, a bitmapped image cannot be separated into component parts and handled uniformly.

The alternative to bitmapped processing is a common, device-independent language. PostScript provides just such an independent and flexible method for graphic processing.

Illustrator and PostScript

PostScript provides a way to describe both text and graphic output independently of any specific device limitations, while allowing the output to take full advantage of available device characteristics. PostScript is both a programming and a page-description language; its special characteristics derive directly from this dual nature. It is

- Dynamic
- Device-independent

> ▶ Graphically powerful

> ▶ Page-oriented

If all of us were PostScript programmers, the matter would end there and graphic processing would be easy. Unfortunately, PostScript is not very accessible to the ordinary user—and is certainly not a natural way for an artist to deal with graphic concepts. Providing a language to do the processing is, in fact, only the first step in making graphic processing accessible to a wide range of users.

Illustrator provides a great interface that uses graphic methods to generate PostScript output. Its tools and functions translate graphic elements into PostScript code, which can be immediately displayed on the screen to show you what you have done. You can then produce these images on any PostScript device.

EARLY ILLUSTRATOR VERSIONS

When Illustrator 1.0 was released in 1987, it was the first program of its type. When I saw the prototype version, I was impressed: It seemed to me that Illustrator was the perfect tool to harness the inherent graphic flexibility and power of the PostScript language. The program could provide creative people who would not want to spend a lot of time learning a programming language the facilities to expand their creativity in new and unexpected ways. The remarkable success of Illustrator and all its offspring is clear proof that the creative impulse is not hampered by an electronic interface.

New Features in Illustrator 3.0 and 3.2

Illustrator 3.0, the immediate predecessor to 3.2, added a number of features lacking or poorly integrated in previous releases. Version 3.2 further improves upon these and other features.

The entire toolbox has been restructured. In response to user requests, the new toolbox adds new text tools and improves the availability of other tools.

For example, the Zoom in tool had previously been available only as a combined key and mouse selection. Other new or improved tools include the following:

- New selection tools to access an entire object at once or just a section of a grouped object without ungrouping

- A Zoom out tool directly available in the toolbox

- An additional rectangle tool to allow you to create rounded-corner rectangles

- Centered rectangle and oval tools directly available from the toolbox

- Dialog box versions of the scale, reflect, rotate, and shear tools directly available from the toolbox

- New path adjustment tools to make adding or deleting anchor points clearer and to change a direction point from a corner to a smooth point and back

- New text tools to add text to an area of any shape, whether regular or irregular, or to any arbitrary path

Handling Text

In addition to these new tools, Illustrator has completely overhauled its text-handling facilities. You can now enter text directly onto a drawing, without using menus and dialog boxes. This is both more natural and faster than the previous methods. The new type handling also allows you to set tracking, kerning, indentation, and other important text variables. Illustrator now comes with the latest version of Adobe Type Manager (ATM), which provides improved letter placement and visibility onscreen. If you use ATM, you can access the character outlines of ATM fonts for use as graphic elements in your artwork (see the upcoming section *TrueType and PostScript Fonts*).

The Improved Desktop

Illustrator has also restructured its desktop to match how artists work. In the first versions of Illustrator, the entire desktop (18"×18") was tiled with a drawing surface that was divided into several pages. This was equivalent to using the current version of Illustrator with the Tile imageable areas setting selected in the Artwork board radio group, found in the Preferences dialog box. While this worked perfectly well, it placed artwork by default on the fifth page of the tiles, which often caused some consternation in first-time users. The new version of Illustrator automatically creates only one page of drawing surface, centered on the desktop. This better reflects the typical use of Illustrator and is much easier to understand. If you still need to tile the entire desktop, you can do so using the Preferences dialog box as described above.

Using Previous Formats

Illustrator 3.2 allows you to both read and edit Illustrator artwork files made with earlier versions of Illustrator.

Artwork that was prepared with Illustrator 88 or earlier versions will not show up as an Illustrator document type icon in the Finder. That means that you cannot double-click on the document and have it automatically find and open the application. However, if you start Illustrator and choose File ➤ Open, you will see the documents listed in the Open dialog box, where you can open them correctly. The only difficulty you may have with these files is with their page location on the desktop. Illustrator defaults to a single page in the middle of the desktop when you open a new document. The information in older files produced with the tiling mechanism, however, is coded in such a way that the page appears at the top of the desktop, and the artwork is usually not on the page at all. This can be corrected easily using the Page tool as described in *Chapter 2*. Alternatively, you can set the Preferences back to the tiling option, which places the pages and artwork together in the center of the desktop.

You can also *save* artwork in a format that is compatible with earlier versions. Illustrator uses PostScript language procedures to create the effects that you have drawn on screen in your printer or other output device. The current version uses an expanded and improved version of these routines—collectively known as a *header*—to implement your artwork. Earlier versions used similar, but not identical, routines for their output. If you want to transfer artwork to earlier versions for editing or displaying, select the correct header version in the Compatibility pop-up menu item on the Save dialog box (File ➤ Save).

Illustrator and System 7

Adobe Illustrator 3.2 fully supports Apple's System 7 software. It runs under System 7 and allows you to use System 7 features such as aliases, balloon help, and so on. Here is a brief review of the System 7 features, as implemented in Illustrator 3.2.

▶ Illustrator 3.2 supports standard balloon help, but does not provide additional balloon help for the program itself. (Personally, I find balloon help more annoying than helpful and never turn it on for ordinary processing.)

▶ Illustrator 3.2 supports all the new file features, such as aliasing.

▶ Illustrator 3.2 is 32-bit clean; that is, you can run it on a 32-bit Macintosh (the IIci, IIsi, LC, LC II, and the IIfx) without getting a warning message.

▶ Illustrator 3.2 supports Apple Events and Publish and Subscribe functions, using the Publishing menu selection, when running under System 7.

In general, Illustrator 3.2 is completely compatible with System 7 and makes good use of its new features.

TrueType and PostScript Fonts

There is one feature of System 7 that we have not yet discussed in relation to Illustrator: TrueType fonts. TrueType is Apple's outline font technology that is built into System 7. These outline fonts replace the previous bitmapped fonts that were used for screen display in earlier system versions of the Macintosh.

Outline fonts are a great improvement over bitmapped fonts for two reasons. First, they provide better and clearer representation of text on the screen at all text sizes. Second, they take up less space on your disk. Outline fonts have always been used in PostScript output devices because they are so much better than simple bitmapped fonts. In earlier versions of the Macintosh system, the LaserWriter driver translated bitmapped fonts that you saw on the screen to

PostScript outline fonts when you printed. This gave rise to occasional problems when artists and designers were laying out type on artwork, particularly if the type was used as a graphic element, where precise placement and control of the exact edges of the characters was essential. Using such features in Illustrator required a lot of test prints to get the correct placement for the type in relation to other graphic elements.

Then Adobe released a program called Adobe Type Manager (ATM), which solved these problems. ATM intercepts all calls for type in your documents and automatically selects, scales, and draws the correct characters by using the PostScript fonts in your printer. ATM fonts are stored in your System folder, in the Extensions folder in System 7, and loose in the System folder in earlier Macintosh system versions.

With TrueType and System 7, you can use built-in outline fonts on the screen as well as on the printer. However, the font outlines that TrueType uses are not the same as those used in your PostScript printer, resulting in possible conflicts between your printouts and what you see onscreen. System 7 comes with the following fonts automatically stored in your System file: Helvetica, Times, Courier, and Symbol.

There are several reasons why you should use PostScript fonts and ATM with Illustrator instead of using the TrueType fonts built into System 7.

▶ Using ATM allows you access to the font outlines for the characters in all your PostScript fonts. This can be very useful when you are designing artwork and want to use type as a graphic element. You can stretch, bend, distort, and generally transform the characters of your text in any way that you want. This feature is available in Illustrator only if you have ATM loaded and in operation.

▶ TrueType fonts add a substantial amount of additional code to your artwork. This is unnecessary, since the PostScript form of the fonts is already built into most PostScript devices. Downloading the TrueType version does nothing for your output, but it does create the possibility of transmission errors and other problems.

▶ TrueType fonts have been found to cause problems in some circumstances when creating output on PostScript devices.

I strongly recommend that you do not use TrueType fonts with your Illustrator documents. Indeed, if you are creating output for high-resolution imagesetting devices, I recommend you consult with your service bureau or run tests before using TrueType fonts on any documents. Since you have ATM available, you can remove the TrueType fonts from your system and still have the same matching between screen and printed output with none of the worries over compatibility.

Summary

Illustrator offers the tools and methods to draw and manipulate graphics onscreen and to translate those images into PostScript. With these tools and methods, Illustrator provides all the desirable qualities for graphics processing in a form that is much more accessible than PostScript itself. All in all, Illustrator is a remarkable and powerful product that you will find fascinating to use.

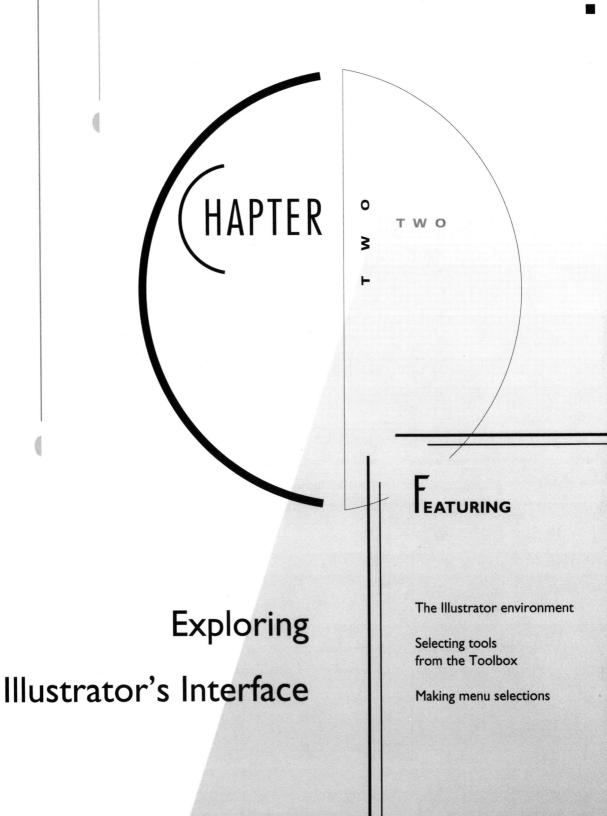

CHAPTER TWO

TWO

Exploring
Illustrator's Interface

FEATURING

The Illustrator environment

Selecting tools
from the Toolbox

Making menu selections

STARTING ILLUSTRATOR

You are now ready to start using Illustrator. This discussion will set the groundwork for creating your first Illustrator artwork, which we'll do in *Chapter 3*.

To start Illustrator, double-click its program icon in the Finder. You will see the standard Adobe startup screen. The first time you start the program, you will be given an opportunity to personalize the Illustrator screen with your name and company. After the startup screen is displayed, you'll see a blank desktop like Figure 2.1. Let's look at this for a moment.

Figure 2.1

The blank Illustrator desktop displays its Toolbox and other controls found in most Macintosh applications.

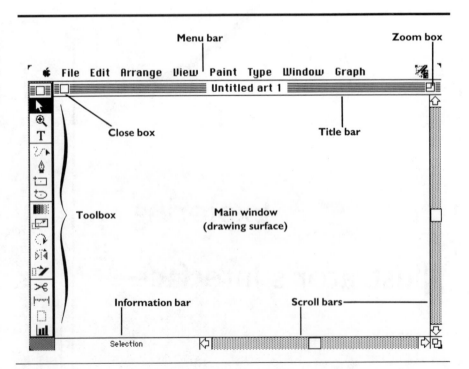

The starting desktop contains a blank screen with two bars of information across the top and a Toolbox along the left side. The first bar contains a series of menu choices; it is called the *menu bar*. Below that is the *title bar*, which shows you the name of the current document. When you begin your work, the current document will be *Untitled art 1*, as shown in Figure 2.1. Other features of the window, such as the *close box*, *zoom box*, and *scroll bars*, perform the same functions as they do in any other Macintosh application. The only other unusual feature of the Illustrator window is the *information bar* in the lower-left corner. This bar gives you information about the selected tool or provides a short description of what you are doing.

When you work in Illustrator, you generally draw in the main window. You have two ways to draw and change your work: using tools from the Toolbox and making selections from the menu bar. Because you are likely to use the Toolbox more than the menu items, after a quick review of the interface, we'll explore tools that you can use.

The Mouse and the Keyboard

Like all Macintosh applications, Illustrator has a graphic interface that requires the use of a pointing device, such as a mouse. Throughout the book, I will use the word *mouse* to mean any pointing device compatible with the Macintosh. Although Illustrator works best with a mouse, you can access many features and menu options equally well with keyboard controls. Where such alternatives are available, I will provide them in the text. If you feel more comfortable using one method exclusively, feel free to substitute it for my recommendations.

THE ILLUSTRATOR TOOLBOX

When you start Illustrator, you will see a narrow window called the *Toolbox*, which contains the default set of available tools, as shown in Figure 2.2. The selected tool is highlighted.

You access additional tools simply by clicking on a default tool and holding down the mouse button. Generally, these additional tools complement the default tool. For example, the Zoom out tool is accessed through the Zoom in tool.

Figure 2.2

*The Illustrator Toolbox
displays the default
tool set.*

To access one of these alternate tools, click on the default tool and hold down the button until the alternate tools appear. Then drag the pointer to the alternate tool you want to select. That tool will replace the default tool in the Toolbox. This procedure essentially allows you to customize the Toolbox. To return to the default tool, follow the same steps you used to choose the alternate tool, or hold down Shift and double-click on the alternate tool. If you have changed several tools, hold down Option along with Shift while you double-click any tool. This restores *all* tools in the Toolbox to their defaults.

A very useful feature in Illustrator is its *dialog tools*. These are tools that bring up dialog boxes, where you can enter precision settings. Each of these tools is described below.

The Selection Tools

The *Selection* tool

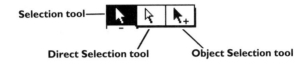

Selection tool ——

Direct Selection tool   **Object Selection tool**

enables you to select points, lines, objects, or groups of objects. The level of selection that you perform depends on the nature of the object you are pointing to when you click the mouse button. This tool is also used to move selected objects around the desktop. You can access the Selection tool while you have another tool selected by pressing the ⌘ key. This action changes the cursor to the selection arrow, showing you that your current tool has been changed into the Selection tool.

The *Direct Selection* tool allows you to select *portions* of grouped objects. The regular Selection tool selects a grouped object as a unit, but the Direct Selection tool allows you to access individual portions of a group without having to ungroup the objects. Pressing the ⌘ key and Tab at the same time allows you to access the Direct Selection tool when you have another tool selected. Note that you must hold down both keys to get to the Direct Selection tool even if you are already using the Selection tool.

The *Object Selection* tool allows you to select all of a path or graphic by clicking on any part of it. When you use the Object Selection tool, any object you click on behaves as if its elements were grouped. You can access the Object Selection tool by holding down Option when you are using the Selection tool. Pressing Option and ⌘ at the same time allows you to use the Object Selection tool when you have selected some other tool from the Toolbox.

The Zoom Tools

The *Zoom in* tool

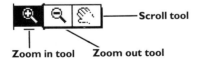

—— **Scroll tool**

Zoom in tool   **Zoom out tool**

magnifies the scale of the view on the desktop. The view is magnified around the position of the tool when you click. Each click magnifies the view by a factor of 2; when you reach the limit of magnification, the plus (+) in the center of the tool cursor disappears. To access the Zoom in tool while you have another tool selected, press the spacebar and the ⌘ key at the same time.

The *Zoom out* tool reduces the scale of the view on the desktop. Analogous to the Zoom in tool, the view is reduced around the position of the tool when you click. Each click reduces the view by a factor of 2; when you reach the limit of reduction, the minus (−) in the center of the tool cursor disappears. You can change the Zoom in tool to the Zoom out tool by pressing Option while you have Zoom in selected. Pressing Option along with ⌘ and the spacebar allows you to use the Zoom out tool when you have selected some other tool.

The *Scroll* tool enables you to shift the view around on the desktop. The Scroll tool cursor looks like a hand. You can most easily understand how this tool works if you think of it as an extension of your own hand moving the art-work drawing surface around the desktop. The Scroll tool is most useful for moving the artwork in a diagonal direction; the scroll bars are most useful for moving in the horizontal and vertical directions. To access the Scroll tool while you have another tool selected, press the spacebar.

The Type Tools

The *Type* tool

allows you to place text in your Illustrator document. When you select the Type tool, the cursor changes to an I-beam surrounded by a dotted square with a cross-line that marks the position of the baseline for the text.

The *Area Type* tool allows you to enter text inside any closed path. The text that you enter is flowed to match the shape of the path. The Area Type tool cursor is similar to that of the Type tool, but is surrounded by an oval.

The *Path Type* tool allows you to place text along any path. Text that you enter is shaped to match the path. The Path Type tool cursor displays the I-beam cursor with a slanted line behind it.

The Freehand and Autotrace Tools

The *Freehand* tool

Freehand tool————————Autotrace tool

allows freehand drawing on the desktop.

The *Autotrace* tool provides automatic tracing of a template or part of a template.

The Pen Tools

The *Pen* tool

is the standard Illustrator drawing tool. It allows you to draw both straight and curved lines.

Illustrator has two basic drawing modes: one uses the Pen tool and one uses the Freehand tool. Although both of these employ the mouse as a drawing mechanism, they are quite different in how they use the mouse and generate graphics. Because the Pen tool is the more basic and precise of the two modes, it will be the first one you learn to use. You will use the Freehand tool for exercises later in the book. I mention the differences here because the Freehand tool uses the mouse in a more natural way than the Pen tool does, using it in a way similar to bitmapped painting programs with which you may be familiar, such as MacPaint.

The Rectangle Tools

The *Rectangle* tool

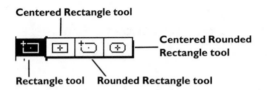

allows you to draw rectangles and squares. This tool draws a rectangle from the top-left corner to the bottom-right corner. To force a square, hold down Shift as you draw the rectangle.

The *Centered Rectangle* tool allows you to draw rectangles and squares from the center point instead of the top-left corner.

The *Rounded Rectangle* allows you to draw rectangles that have rounded corners instead of square corners. The corner radius is set in the Preferences dialog box (choose Edit ➤ Preferences).

The *Centered Rounded Rectangle* allows you to draw a round-cornered rectangle or square from the center point.

The Oval Tools

The *Oval* tool

enables you to draw ovals and circles. This tool draws an oval from the upper-left to the lower-right of the oval. To force a circle, hold down Shift as you draw the oval.

The *Centered Oval* tool allows you to draw ovals from the center point of the oval instead of the upper-left.

The Blend Tool

The *Blend* tool

allows you to automatically transform one selected shape or color into another in a definable number of steps.

The Scale Tools

The *Scale* tool

allows you to change the size of selected objects on the desktop.

The *Scale dialog* tool performs the same function, but presents you with a dialog box for the scaling process. This tool allows you more precise control over the scaling. To access the Scale dialog tool, press Option when the Scale tool is selected.

The Rotate Tools

The *Rotate* tool

allows you to rotate selected objects on the desktop.

The *Rotate dialog* tool performs the same function, but presents you with a dialog box for the rotation. This allows you more precise control over the rotation. To access the Rotate dialog tool, press Option when the Rotate tool is selected.

The Reflect Tools

The *Reflect* tool

Reflect tool —————— Reflect dialog tool

allows you to mirror a selected object across a given plane.

The *Reflect dialog* tool performs the same function, but presents you with a dialog box for the reflection. This allows you more precise control over the reflection. You can access the Reflect dialog tool by pressing Option when the Reflect tool is selected.

The Shear Tools

The *Shear* tool

Shear tool —————— Shear dialog tool

allows you to distort a selected object in a nonuniform fashion along a given axis.

The *Shear dialog* tool performs the same function, but presents you with a dialog box for the shearing process. This allows you more precise control over the shearing. You can access the Shear dialog tool by pressing Option when the Shear tool is selected.

The Path and Point Tools

The *Split Path* tool (also called the *Scissors* tool, for obvious reasons)

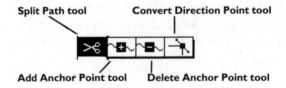

Split Path tool   Convert Direction Point tool

Add Anchor Point tool   Delete Anchor Point tool

enables you to cut a line into two pieces at a given point.

The *Add Anchor Point* tool adds an anchor point to a line at a given point.

The *Delete Anchor Point* tool deletes an anchor point from a line. The resulting line will pass directly from the anchor point before the deleted point to the one after it.

The *Convert Direction Point* tool allows you to change an anchor point from a straight-line anchor point to a curved-line anchor point, or to convert an anchor point to a corner anchor point by individually changing its direction points.

The Measure Tool

The *Measure* tool

allows you to measure the distance and angle between any two points on the desktop. The results are displayed in a small dialog box.

The Page Tool

The *Page* tool

lets you alter the page grid used for tiling large documents.

The Graph Tools

All the *graph* tools

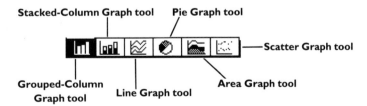

allow you to define particular types of graphs. These graph types are also available by choosing Graph ➤ Graph Style.

It isn't important that you learn all of these tools and their names right now. As you work through the exercises and examples in this book, you will learn to use them. I've included this list to show you what the tools are and how they are named. If you have any questions when tools are referenced in the text, you may want to return here to look at the names and descriptions again.

Toolbox Display Options

If you need the entire screen for drawing, you can hide the Toolbox. Either click on the close box at the top of the Toolbox or select Window ➤ Hide Toolbox.

The current tool does not change when you hide the Toolbox. However, when the Toolbox is hidden, you cannot select tools from it directly. Instead you must use a keyboard alternative. Here is a list of the shortcuts for commonly used tools. You can also use these keys to access tools when you don't want to return to the Toolbox to make another selection.

Tool	Key Access
Selection tool	⌘
Object Selection tool	⌘–Option
Direct Selection tool	⌘–Tab
Scroll tool	spacebar
Zoom in tool	⌘–spacebar
Zoom out tool	⌘–Option-spacebar

In addition, some tools allow you to access their alternates when they have been selected by pressing the Option key, even when the Toolbox is hidden. The list below shows you these tools and their alternates. In all cases, you can access the alternate tool with the Option key if you have the base tool selected.

Alternate	Base Tool
Object Selection tool	Selection tool
Zoom out tool	Zoom in tool
Centered Rectangle tool	Rectangle tool
Centered Oval tool	Oval tool
Scale dialog tool	Scale tool
Rotate dialog tool	Rotate tool
Reflect dialog tool	Reflect tool
Shear dialog tool	Shear tool
Add Anchor Point tool	Split Path tool

To restore the Toolbox once you have hidden it, you must select Window ➤ Show Toolbox.

ILLUSTRATOR'S MENUS

When you work in Illustrator, you will use the commands in the menus as well as the tools in the Toolbox to create and save your artwork. In some cases—graphs are the most notable example—the menu items provide you with an alternate method of performing the same function as the Toolbox. In most cases, however, menu commands supplement or extend the action of the tools. In this section, we'll take a look at each of the menus.

As you read these descriptions, you may come across words or descriptions that are not clear to you. They refer to specialized Illustrator processes that will be covered in later chapters. The discussion here is intended as a quick reference and brief introduction to all of the Illustrator commands. If you have any questions, look up the command name in the index and review the exercise or example that uses that command. In many cases, you can also look up the command in your Illustrator documentation.

Menu Items and Options

Illustrator provides two methods for accessing menu commands. The first and most common is to click on a menu and then drag down the list of commands to highlight the desired selection. When you release the mouse button, the highlighted menu item executes. As you know, we are noting this as *Menu* ➤ *Command*. The second method is the keyboard shortcut. These are key combinations that execute menu commands without accessing the menu. For example, if you wanted to quit Illustrator, you could press the ⌘ key and the q key at the same time. This is the same as choosing File ➤ Quit. In the following section, as we discuss the menu items, I'll specify any keyboard shortcuts in parentheses; for example, Quit would have (⌘-Q) after it. For our purposes, we will use capital letters, although this doesn't mean that you need to use Shift for the letter. If accessing a command requires that you press Shift, I will indicate that explicitly. Most of these shortcuts are listed in the menus next to their commands.

The File Menu

The *File* menu is shown in Figure 2.3.

New (⌘-N) provides a new, clean drawing surface for your work. You may also optionally associate and display a template with your new drawing.

Figure 2.3

The File menu displays commands for handling Illustrator documents.

File	
New...	⌘N
Open...	⌘O
Place Art...	
Close	⌘⌥W
Save	⌘S
Save As...	
Page Setup...	
Print...	⌘P
Quit	⌘Q

Open (⌘-O) opens an existing document. If you have previously associated a template with this artwork, the template will open as well.

Place Art imports EPS (encapsulated PostScript) graphics files as a unit into your Illustrator artwork. You can transform a placed graphic—for example, you can rotate it, shear it, and so on—but you cannot alter the components within it.

Close (⌘-Option-W) closes the current window with its associated artwork. This action is the same as clicking on the close box in the upper-left corner of the window. If you have made changes to the artwork that you have not saved, you will be prompted to save the artwork before you close it. If you don't save, the changes will be lost.

Save (⌘-S) saves the current artwork under the name shown in the title bar. If the artwork is unnamed, you are prompted to provide a new name when you save it.

Save As allows you to save the current artwork under a different name than that shown in the title bar. If you save the artwork under a new name, the new name replaces the old name in the title bar. The original artwork remains unchanged under the old name on your disk.

Page Setup brings up the standard Macintosh Page Setup dialog box. This dialog box allows you to set the page size and other important information for your printed output. Note that you must select a printer using the Chooser before you can access the Page Setup dialog box. You should always review the page setup when you change printers in the Chooser. See your Macintosh and Illustrator documentation for a complete description of the options in this dialog box.

Print (⌘-P) brings up the standard Macintosh Print dialog box, which allows you to print your artwork to your chosen output device. See your Macintosh and Illustrator documentation for a complete description of the options in this dialog box.

Quit (⌘-Q) terminates the Illustrator program. If you have changed your artwork and not yet saved it, you will be prompted to save it before quitting.

An Important Word on Safety

You should always make backup copies of your work. For maximum safety, you should do two things.

First, as you work, occasionally save your work to ensure that you don't waste substantial time and effort in the event of a mistake or power outage. Some people advocate saving at some regular interval, such as every quarter or half hour. I prefer to save when I have finished a major section. This means that I may save very often or not at all, depending on how fast I'm working. The choice is up to you; just be sure to save your work as you proceed.

Second, make *complete backup copies of all your work* to floppy disks on some regular schedule. Determine how often you should back up by how much you work with the program. For example, an artist who uses Illustrator several hours a day would probably be wise to back up daily; someone else who uses the program only a few times a week can probably back up less frequently. The essential point here is to make backup copies, and make them regularly enough so they will serve as a safety net in case you lose or damage your original work.

The Edit Menu

The Edit menu is shown in Figure 2.4.

Undo (⌘-Z) reverses your last action. For this reason, the Undo entry will generally be followed by a descriptive word about what you can undo. For example, if you rotate an object, the Undo command will say *Undo Rotate*. Once you have used the Undo feature, the menu item changes to Redo.

Cut (⌘-X) removes the current selection. The cut selection disappears from your drawing and is stored in the Clipboard. You can retrieve the cut selection from the Clipboard by using the Paste selection or one of its variants.

Figure 2.4

The Edit menu contains commands for selecting and ordering portions of your document.

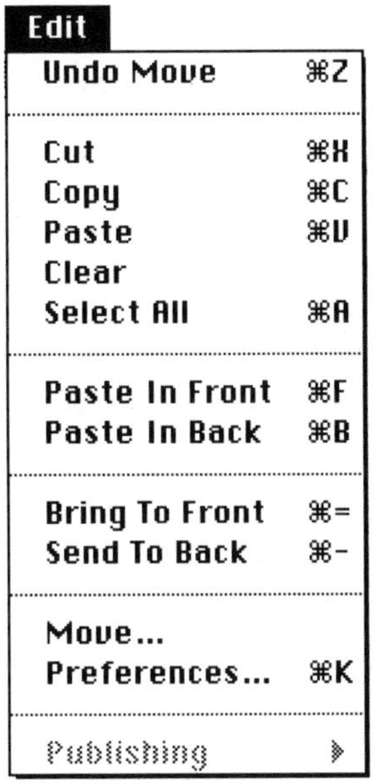

```
┌─────────────────────────┐
│ Edit                    │
│  Undo Move        ⌘Z    │
│ ·······················  │
│  Cut              ⌘H    │
│  Copy             ⌘C    │
│  Paste            ⌘U    │
│  Clear                  │
│  Select All       ⌘A    │
│ ·······················  │
│  Paste In Front   ⌘F    │
│  Paste In Back    ⌘B    │
│ ·······················  │
│  Bring To Front   ⌘=    │
│  Send To Back     ⌘-    │
│ ·······················  │
│  Move...                │
│  Preferences...   ⌘K    │
│ ·······················  │
│  Publishing        ▶    │
└─────────────────────────┘
```

Copy (⌘–C) duplicates the current selection. The selection is retained on the desktop *and* copied to the Clipboard.

Paste (⌘–V) places the Clipboard's contents into your illustration. If you Cut or Copy and then Paste immediately, the resulting item is positioned just where it was when it was moved to the Clipboard. If you move the cursor, however, the pasted material is placed in the center of the window.

Clear (Delete) removes any selected items from your artwork. These items are discarded and are not available from the Clipboard.

Select All (⌘–A) selects all the items in the current document. This command is useful when you need to move or change the entire document at once.

Paste In Front (⌘–F) places the Clipboard's contents in front of all the other items in the current document. This means that the item will paint and display *after* all other items.

Paste In Back (⌘-B) places the Clipboard's contents behind all the other items in the current document. This means that the item will paint and display *before* all other items.

Bring To Front (⌘-=) moves the selection in front of the other items in the document. This command is equivalent to Cut followed by Paste In Front.

Send To Back (⌘--) moves the selection behind the other items in the document. This command is equivalent to Cut followed by Paste In Back.

Move brings up the Move dialog box, where you can move or copy the selection by an exact amount in any direction. It provides a precise substitute for dragging. The Move dialog box is shown in Figure 2.5.

Preferences (⌘-K) allows you to set a variety of Illustrator parameters according to your personal work habits and tastes in the Preferences dialog box, as shown in Figure 2.6. This dialog box also allows you to access two additional dialog boxes: Type Preferences and Progressive Colors. You use these dialog boxes to specify additional information. In general, you will find that the default values of the preferences are quite satisfactory for most operations. As you proceed through the exercises in this book, you will be introduced to some alternate settings as they become necessary.

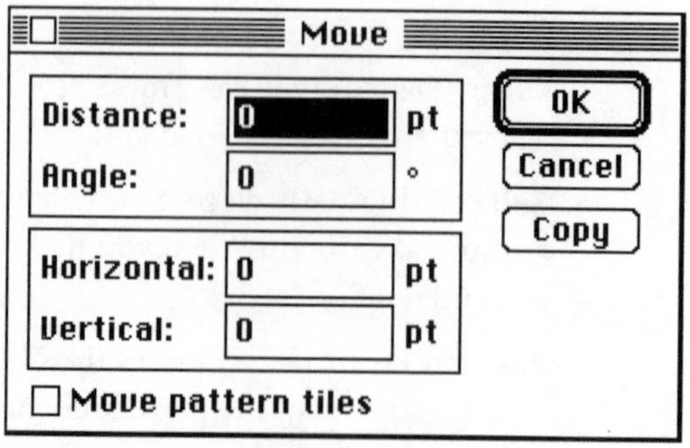

Figure 2.5

The Move dialog box allows you to move a selected item a precise distance.

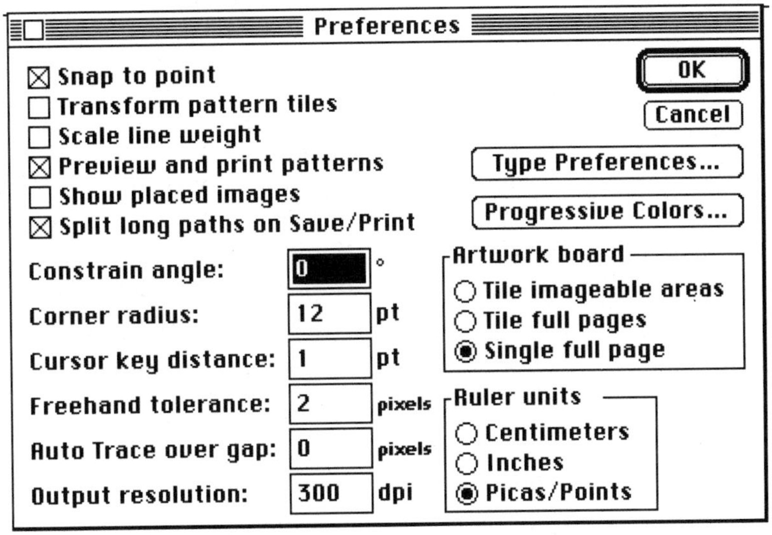

Figure 2.6
*The Preferences
dialog box allows you to
customize the Illustrator
working environment.*

```
┌─────────────────────────────────────────────────────────────┐
│ ▤▤        ═══════ Preferences ═══════                         │
│                                                               │
│  ☒ Snap to point                         ┌──────────┐        │
│  ☐ Transform pattern tiles               │    OK    │        │
│  ☐ Scale line weight                     └──────────┘        │
│  ☒ Preview and print patterns            ┌──────────┐        │
│  ☐ Show placed images                    │  Cancel  │        │
│  ☒ Split long paths on Save/Print                            │
│                                      ┌─────────────────────┐ │
│  Constrain angle:    [0]    °        │ Type Preferences... │ │
│                                      └─────────────────────┘ │
│                                      ┌─────────────────────┐ │
│  Corner radius:      [12]  pt        │ Progressive Colors..│ │
│                                      └─────────────────────┘ │
│  Cursor key distance:[1]   pt    ┌Artwork board──────────┐   │
│                                  │ ○ Tile imageable areas│   │
│  Freehand tolerance: [2]  pixels │ ○ Tile full pages     │   │
│                                  │ ◉ Single full page    │   │
│  Auto Trace over gap:[0]  pixels └───────────────────────┘   │
│                                  ┌Ruler units─────────┐      │
│  Output resolution:  [300] dpi   │ ○ Centimeters      │      │
│                                  │ ○ Inches           │      │
│                                  │ ◉ Picas/Points     │      │
│                                  └────────────────────┘      │
└─────────────────────────────────────────────────────────────┘
```

The Arrange Menu

The *Arrange* menu is shown in Figure 2.7.

Transform Again (⌘-D) repeats a transformation on a selected graphic without resetting the parameters or tools. This command can be especially useful when you are making repeated versions of a graphic.

Group (⌘-G) collects all of the selected items into a single group. Once items are grouped, clicking on any part of the group selects the entire group. As noted in the tools section, the Direct Selection tool allows you to select a part of a group.

Ungroup (⌘-U) removes the grouping attribute from the selected group. At that point, you can select any part of the group in the ordinary way by using the Selection tool.

Join (⌘-J) connects two endpoints with a straight line. There are two important points to note about Join. First, you can join only an endpoint of a path; you cannot join interior points. Second, unlike Average, Join does not move the two selected points; it simply connects them.

Average (⌘-L) moves any two or more points to a new position that is the average of the current positions. The Average command brings up the Average dialog box, which allows you to control how the averaging is done: along both axes or along only the horizontal or vertical axis. When you average along both axes, the selected points will move to one common point. When you constrain the average along either axis, the points will align only on that axis.

Lock (⌘-1) "bolts down" the current selection so it cannot be selected. This can be very helpful when dealing with overlapping objects.

Unlock All (⌘-2) removes the lock function from any locked objects in the current artwork.

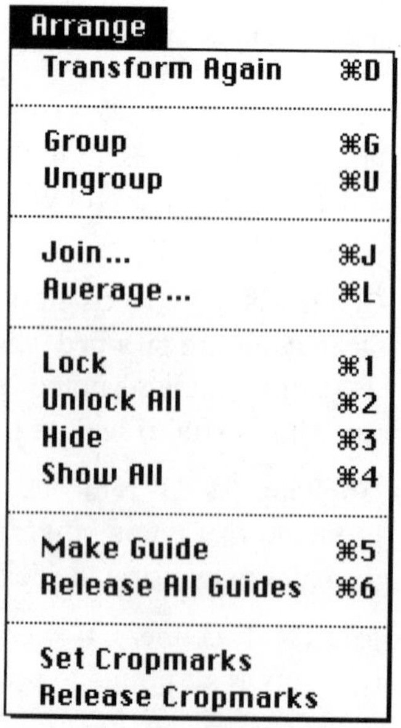

Figure 2.7

The Arrange menu allows you to set display and group parameters for selected objects.

Arrange	
Transform Again	⌘D
Group	⌘G
Ungroup	⌘U
Join...	⌘J
Average...	⌘L
Lock	⌘1
Unlock All	⌘2
Hide	⌘3
Show All	⌘4
Make Guide	⌘5
Release All Guides	⌘6
Set Cropmarks	
Release Cropmarks	

Hide (⌘-3) removes any selected objects from view. Objects that are hidden do not appear in either the artwork or the preview views. However, they are still part of the artwork and they will print.

Show All (⌘-4) restores all hidden objects to the desktop. When the objects reappear, they are automatically selected.

Make Guide (⌘-5) makes a selected path or object into a *guide object*. A guide is an object that is visible as a dotted outline on the artwork desktop. Although visible, a guide object cannot be selected in the ordinary way. To select a guide object, use the Selection tool and hold down ⌘ and Shift while you click on the guide—notice that the information bar changes to *Move guide*.

Release All Guides (⌘-6) turns all guide objects in the current artwork into standard Illustrator paths. The new paths are automatically selected; if you want to remove the guides, press Delete.

Set Cropmarks adds standard *cropmarks* to your artwork. If you want cropmarks to appear on the current page, click on a blank area away from all your artwork (so that nothing is selected), and choose Set Cropmarks. If you want to set cropmarks for a smaller area, use the Rectangle tool to place a rectangle around the area that you want included inside your cropmarks and then select Set Cropmarks. The rectangle is replaced by the cropmarks at each edge. Note that you cannot select or move cropmarks with the usual Illustrator tools, and you can have only one set of cropmarks in your artwork; any time you reset the cropmarks, the new set will automatically replace the old ones.

Release Cropmarks removes any cropmarks you have made without replacing them with other cropmarks.

The View Menu

The *View* menu controls how your screen looks and is shown in Figure 2.8.

Preview Illustration (⌘-Y) shows you the drawing of your current artwork as it will appear when you print—or as close a facsimile as is possible on screen.

Figure 2.8

The View menu controls how the artwork and drawing surface are displayed on your screen.

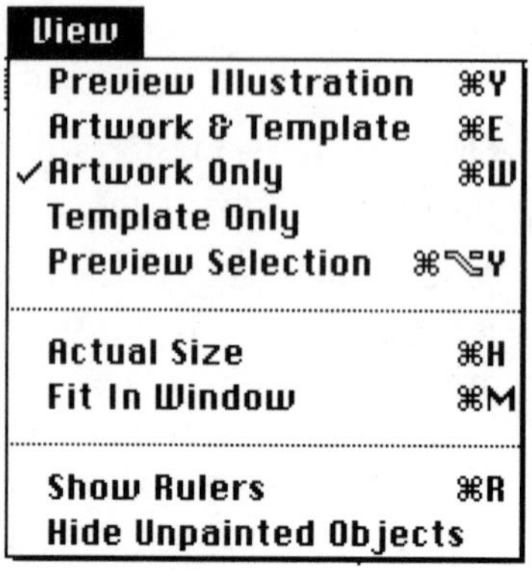

View	
Preview Illustration	⌘Y
Artwork & Template	⌘E
✓**Artwork Only**	⌘W
Template Only	
Preview Selection	⌘⌥Y
Actual Size	⌘H
Fit In Window	⌘M
Show Rulers	⌘R
Hide Unpainted Objects	

Artwork & Template (⌘-E) gives you the default Illustrator view of the desktop. This view shows your artwork and any template that you have associated with it (the template is shown in gray).

Artwork Only (⌘-W) shows only the artwork on the desktop. The template associated with the artwork is hidden from view. This view is identical to the Artwork & Template view if there is no template associated with the current artwork.

Template Only shows only the template that is associated with the current artwork. The artwork is hidden and the template appears dark.

Preview Selection (⌘-Option-Y) allows you to preview a selected part of your artwork. This view can be especially valuable when you have complex artwork and don't want to take the time to preview the entire drawing. Only the selected items appear in the preview; all other items are hidden.

Actual Size (⌘-H) returns you to the default view of the desktop. This full-size view is positioned approximately in the center of the drawing page.

Fit In Window (⌘-M) shows you the entire drawing surface on your screen. The drawing area is shown in white with an outline of the current page size on it.

Show Rulers (⌘-R) brings up the Illustrator rulers along the bottom and right edges of the drawing window. You can set the units used in the rulers in the Preferences dialog box (choose Edit ➤ Preferences). If the rulers are visible, this entry will say Hide Rulers instead.

Hide Unpainted Objects hides any artwork that will not print because the painting attributes are not set. Such objects are often helpful guides for printing in Illustrator. Hiding such objects once they have been used is very practical.

The Paint Menu

The *Paint* menu controls how your artwork looks—see Figure 2.9.

Style (⌘-I) brings up the Paint Style dialog box, shown in Figure 2.10. This dialog box allows you to set the painting attributes for your artwork. The two basic methods of painting artwork are to *Fill* the interior of the artwork with a shade or color and to *Stroke* the lines that make up the artwork with a shade or color. The dialog box allows you to set either or both of these options for a given selection. In addition, you can set other special features to establish the style of the selected artwork.

Pattern allows you to define a new pattern or edit old patterns that you use to fill objects in your artwork.

Figure 2.9

The Paint menu allows you to set display information and create patterns and colors for your artwork.

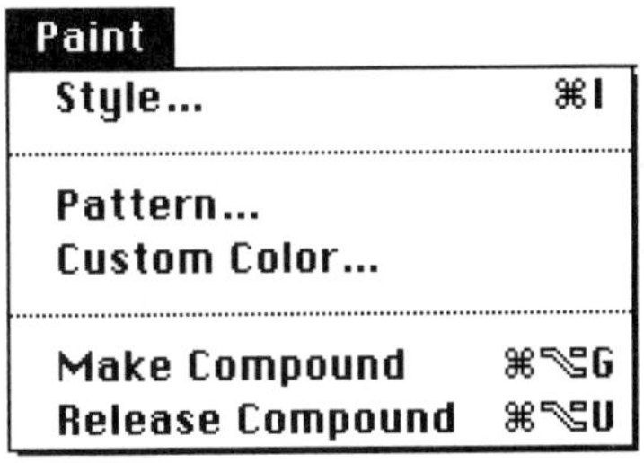

```
┌─────────────────────────────┐
│ Paint                       │
│  Style...              ⌘I   │
│ ........................... │
│  Pattern...                 │
│  Custom Color...            │
│ ........................... │
│  Make Compound       ⌘⌥G   │
│  Release Compound    ⌘⌥U   │
└─────────────────────────────┘
```

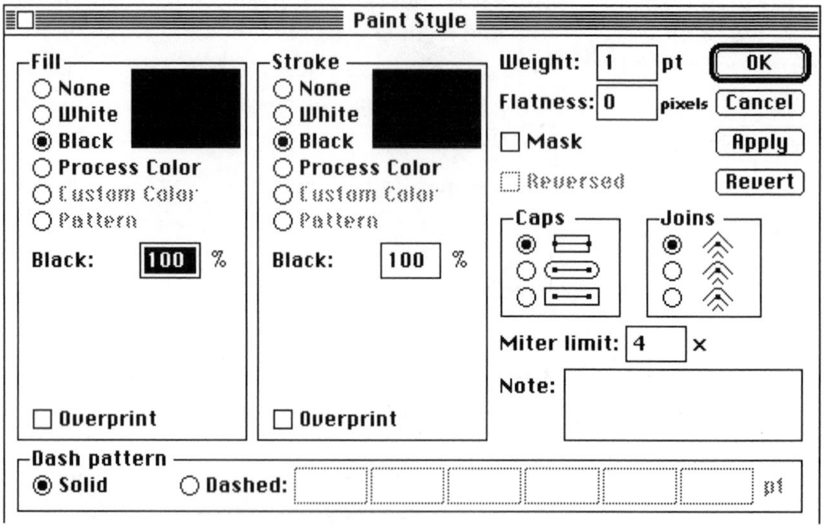

Figure 2.10

The Paint Style dialog box allows you to determine how the selected objects in your artwork will print.

Custom Color allows you to define a custom color for use in your artwork. The color is defined as percentages of the standard printing colors: cyan, magenta, yellow, and black.

Make Compound (⌘–Option-G) enables you to create compound paths. Compound paths allow you to make objects visible that fall inside the compound path.

Release Compound (⌘–Option-U) removes the compound path attribute from the selected path.

The Type Menu

The Type menu controls how your text looks. Unlike the other menus, the Type menu contains many redundant items; that is, several different menu items allow you to access the same control. You should keep this in mind as you read the following descriptions. The Type menu is shown in Figure 2.11.

Style (⌘–T) brings up the Type Style dialog box, shown in Figure 2.12. This dialog box allows you to set the type attributes for your artwork. You specify type by setting individual *Character*

Figure 2.11

The Type menu allows you to set and control all aspects of the text that you enter into your Illustrator documents.

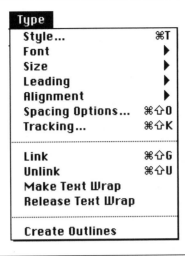

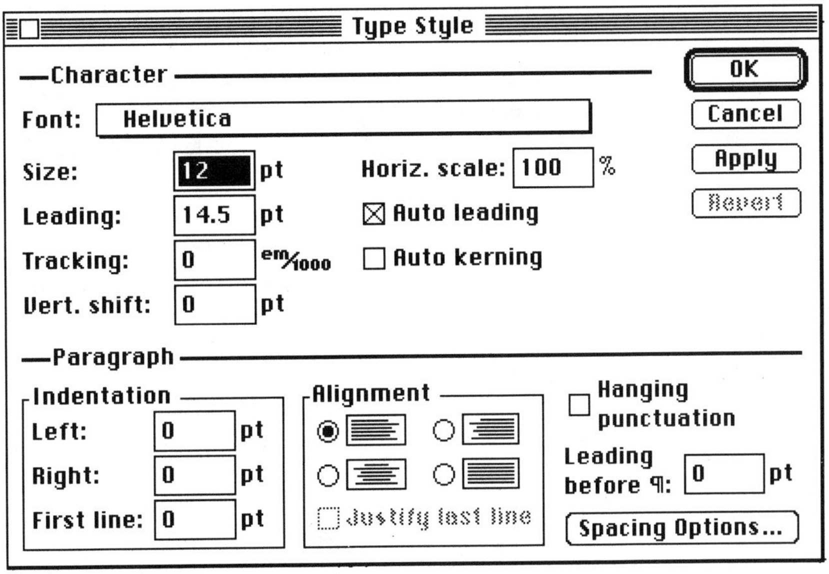

Figure 2.12

The Type Style dialog box sets font and display information for your text.

attributes and how to set *Paragraph* features. The dialog box allows you to set either or both of these options for a given selection. For characters, you can set the Font, Size, Leading, and Tracking options. You can also change these options by selecting the corresponding command from the Type menu. For paragraphs, you can set the standard margins and a standard indent for the first line. You can also set the Alignment for the text. A separate button allows you to set the Spacing Options.

The Font selection displays the current font that you are using for your text. Its submenu also lists other fonts that you have selected in the artwork. By selecting Other (⌘–Shift-F), you are presented with the Font dialog box shown in Figure 2.13. This dialog box is somewhat different than the standard Macintosh dialog box. It is also much easier to use if you have many fonts. The font families you have installed are shown in the list box on the left, and the associated font characteristics (such as Italic, Roman, Bold, and so on) are shown in the list box on the right. This arrangement makes it very easy to select the correct font and characteristic for your text. Once you have made the selection, Illustrator substitutes the full name of the selected font in the Type Style dialog box. For example, if you select Palatino and Italic, the font name that appears in the font list and in the Type Style dialog box will be *Palatino-Italic*.

Figure 2.13

The Font dialog box allows you to select fonts and font styles for your text.

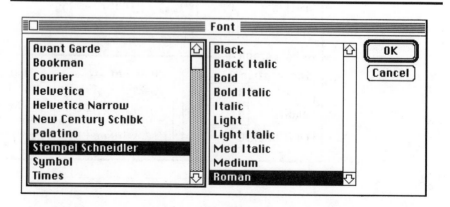

Font leads to a menu containing all the fonts you have selected. You can choose any of these fonts by selecting them from the submenu. Note however, that selecting a font that you used previously from the submenu does not select the same size, alignment, and so on that you had associated with that font. For example, if you used Helvetica 24 point previously, Helvetica will show in the Font submenu. However, if you select Helvetica in the submenu after using Palatino 12 point, the selected font will be Helvetica 12 point, not Helvetica 24 point.

Size displays a submenu that shows you the current size of your text and a selection of other sizes for the text. If you select Other (⌘-Shift-S), you get the combined Type Size/Leading dialog box, which allows you to set both of these options to any value.

Leading displays a submenu that shows you the current leading for your text and a selection of other leading values. *Leading* is the amount of space between lines of text. Generally, the spacing provided by the leading should be slightly greater than the size of the text; Illustrator will automatically set the leading in this fashion if you check Auto. For large sizes of text, setting the leading to the size of the text is best; if you are setting large text, turn off the Auto and set the leading manually. If you select Other (⌘-Shift-S), you get the combined Type Size/Leading dialog box, which allows you to set both of these options to any value you want.

Alignment displays a submenu that shows you the four possible alignment options. *Alignment* refers to how the edges of the text line up with one another. The possible choices are Left (⌘-Shift-L), which aligns the text along the left edge and leaves the right edge ragged; Centered (⌘-Shift-C), which centers each line of text and leaves both the left and right edges ragged; Right (⌘-Shift-R), which aligns the text along the right edge and leaves the left edge ragged; and Justified (⌘-Shift-J), which aligns both the left and right edges of the text by adding space between words and letters of the text. The amount of spacing is controlled by the Spacing Options you have set. Note that the Text Style dialog box also allows you to justify all lines of the text, including the last line, by selecting the Justify last line checkbox; the Justified option uses this setting to determine whether the last text line should be justified or not. The default setting is to *not* justify the last line. This can be very important, since the last line of a block of text is usually shorter than the other lines and normally should not be justified.

Spacing Options displays the Spacing Options dialog box, shown in Figure 2.14. This dialog box allows you to set the Minimum, Maximum, and Desired spacing that you want to use in your text. The settings are percentages of the current font size. Although spacing is generally applied to justified text, it can be applied to blocks of unjustified text as well. Note that spacing affects entire paragraphs. If you want to change the spacing of a single line of text, use Tracking.

Tracking changes depending on what you have selected. The default selection displays a dialog box that allows you to set the tracking value for the selected text. Tracking sets spacing between the characters of the selected text; positive values add space between letters and negative values subtract it. If you click between two letters in a text block, the menu entry changes to Kern. This allows you to move the two individual letters closer together or further apart in the same way that Tracking affects a group of letters.

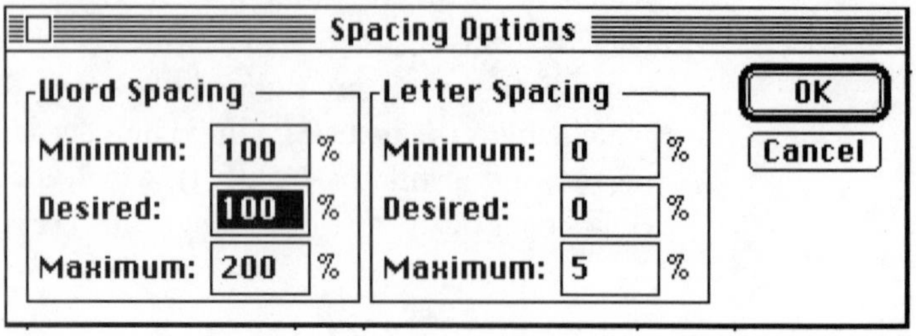

Figure 2.14

The Spacing Options dialog box allows you to determine word and letter spacing for your Illustrator text.

Link (⌘-Shift-G) allows you to link several Illustrator graphic objects so that text will flow from one object into the next based on the painting order of the objects.

Unlink (⌘-Shift-U) breaks a link established by the Link selection. However, it does not remove text that has already been flowed in the previously linked objects.

Make Text Wrap allows you to wrap selected text around a selected graphic object.

Release Text Wrap releases an existing text wrap from a selected text and graphic combination.

Create Outlines turns selected text into paths for further modification. Note that you must have Adobe Type Manager installed for this command to be active (ATM is bundled with Illustrator). Also, you must have the Type 1 font outlines for the font you are using installed and available on your Macintosh.

The Window Menu

The *Window* menu controls the Illustrator windows on your desktop and is shown in Figure 2.15.

Show Clipboard displays the Clipboard's contents on your desktop. However, the Clipboard window does not display Illustrator graphics; you will see a line of text telling you how many objects are on the Clipboard.

Figure 2.15

The Window menu selects and controls the Illustrator windows.

```
┌─────────────────────┐
│ Window              │
├─────────────────────┤
│ Show Clipboard      │
│ Hide Toolbox        │
│ Reset Toolbox       │
├·····················┤
│ New Window          │
├·····················┤
│ ✓Untitled art 1     │
└─────────────────────┘
```

Hide Toolbox hides the Toolbox. This command performs the same function as clicking on the close box at the top of the Toolbox. If the Toolbox is not visible, this command appears as Show Toolbox and will restore the Toolbox to the desktop.

Reset Toolbox sets all the tools in the Toolbox to their defaults.

New Window opens a new window, which displays the same artwork that is presently displayed. Additional windows are updated to reflect changes in any one window. The most common use of a second window is to show a Preview version of your artwork as you make changes in the drawing.

Additional lines in the Window menu give you the names of all the open drawing windows. You can select the drawing window that you want to display from this list. The selected window moves in front of any overlapping windows and becomes the active window.

The Graph Menu

The *Graph* menu is shown in Figure 2.16.

Graph Style (⌘-Shift-Option-S) displays the Graph Style dialog box shown in Figure 2.17. This dialog box allows you to set the type of graph you want, as well as options and other features of the graph. You can also set the type of graph by selecting the appropriate tool from the Toolbox.

Graph Data (⌘-Shift-Option-D) allows you to enter or import data for the selected graph.

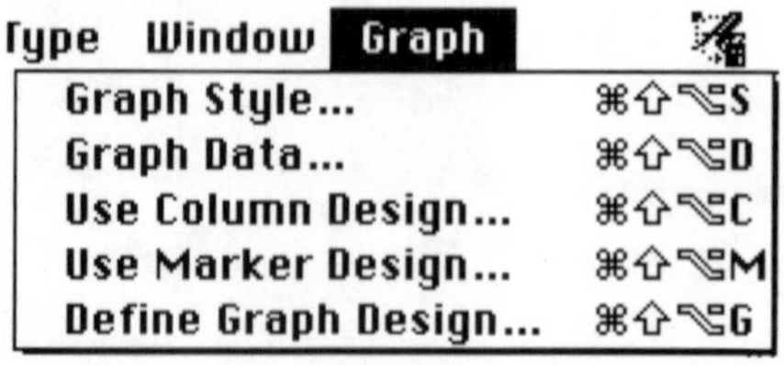

Figure 2.16

The Graph menu allows you to set up and display graphs in Illustrator.

Type	Window	Graph	
Graph Style...			⌘⇧⌥S
Graph Data...			⌘⇧⌥D
Use Column Design...			⌘⇧⌥C
Use Marker Design...			⌘⇧⌥M
Define Graph Design...			⌘⇧⌥G

Use Column Design (⌘-Shift-Option-C) allows you to use the column design you created with the Define Graph Design command for the column display in the selected graph. The selected graph must be a Grouped or Stacked column graph.

Use Marker Design (⌘-Shift-Option-M) allows you to use the marker design you created with the Define Graph Design command as the marker for data points in the selected graph. The selected graph must be a Line or Scatter graph.

Define Graph Design (⌘-Shift-Option-G) allows you to define a graphic object to display as the columns (on a column graph) or as the data points (on a graph that shows individual data points).

Figure 2.17

The Graph Style dialog box allows you to select one of the standard Illustrator graph styles.

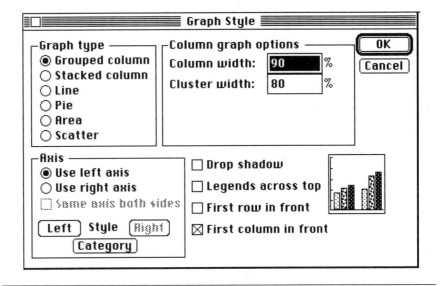

CHAPTER THREE

THREE

Illustrator at Work

THE ILLUSTRATOR ENVIRONMENT

When you start to work with Illustrator, the first step is either to select old artwork that you wish to modify or create new artwork. As your first exercise, you will create an entirely new piece of artwork. When you launch Illustrator, you get a blank drawing surface, with the title *Untitled art 1* at the top, as shown in Figure 3.1. When you save the artwork, the name you give it will replace this default name.

Illustrator's Drawing Surface

Illustrator works on a *drawing surface* that acts like a large piece of paper pinned to a desktop. The basic drawing area is a square, 18"×18". The

Figure 3.1

When you start Illustrator, you get a blank drawing surface.

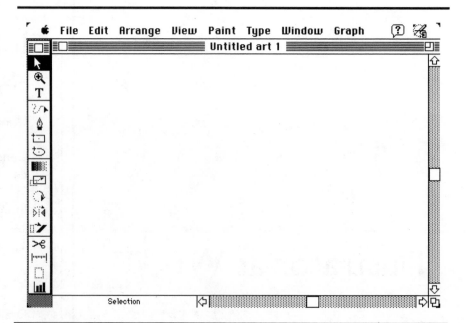

portion that you are drawing on is centered in the middle of this sheet. To see how this looks, choose View ➤ Fit In Window.

The center of the drawing surface is a standard 8½ ×11" page. The edges of the page itself are designated by solid lines, while the dotted lines are *margins* that enclose the printable area of the page as defined in the printer driver—in this case, a LaserWriter. Notice the page number in the lower-left corner of the page. Since there is only one page in this drawing, the page number is 1. Although you can see the margins and the page number on the screen, these neither print nor show up on preview.

In this exercise, as with most of the others in this book, you will use the standard 8½ ×11" page size; however, you can select any other page size that is supported by your printer. The page size is set in the Page Setup dialog box (choose File ➤ Page Setup).

As you see, the Paper radio group allows you to select several paper sizes for your output. To use these other sizes, however, your printer must support them; choosing a different size here does *not* automatically change the paper in your printer.

Illustrator's Line and Shape Tools

Illustrator provides two distinct types of drawing tools: line tools and shape tools. The former includes the *Pen* tool, which you just used, and the *Freehand* tool, which you will use in a later chapter. The latter includes the *Rectangle* and the *Oval* tools. The names of these tools denote what shapes they generate.

Both types of tool have features in common. In the next exercise, and in exercises in later chapters, you will work with both types of tool and explore their features in detail. Before you start to work, though, I would like to mention some of the common functions to help you understand and use the tools with ease and confidence.

You have already learned about constraining lines to be horizontal, vertical, or multiples of 45°; you constrain a line by holding down Shift as you create it. Similarly, you can constrain the Rectangle tool to produce only squares and the Oval tool to produce only circles, also by using Shift. Normally, rectangles and ovals are generated by drawing them from one corner to another, as you will see. However, by holding down Option as you create the shape, you can draw shapes from their center points outward instead of from the corner. Illustrator also provides special versions of each of these tools, the *Centered Rectangle* and the *Centered Oval* tools, which always draw from the center point. If you select one of these tools from the toolbox, pressing Option returns you to the standard version. These two techniques can be combined, so you can constrain an oval to a circle, for example, and also draw it from the center point outward.

As you draw each of these shapes, notice that they have anchor points, just like lines. For the rectangle, these anchor points are at the four corners and the center; for the oval, they are at the top, bottom, and both sides of the oval, as well as the center. These anchor points can be used for placement and measurement of the figure. They also, however, are indications of how the figures are generated. Both of these shapes are actually composed of four segments and a center point: for the rectangle, the four sides; and for the oval, the four matching arcs. These pieces are automatically linked together making them behave like a single unit. As you will see in the exercise that follows, you can break these groups up into their component pieces, when necessary, by using Arrange ➤ Ungroup. Once divided in this way, each part of the shape can be handled individually.

EXERCISE 3.1: BASIC DRAWING TECHNIQUES

This exercise will draw a simple but interesting figure using straight lines. The figure is an interlocked triangle. Since you do not have any template to guide you for this figure, you will use the Illustrator rulers as a guide.

Start with an empty drawing surface and choose View ➤ Show Rulers (or press ⌘–R). This will add a set of rulers at the bottom and side of your drawing surface, as shown in Figure 3.2. When you open a document in the ordinary way, the rulers are not visible.

The rulers provide precise page positions for placing artwork. We will note positions with coordinates; for example (2,3) would indicate a position of 2 on the x-axis and a position of 3 on the y-axis. The default units of measurement on the rulers are points (72 points = 1 inch) and picas (6 picas = 1 inch). If you want, you can change the units of measurement in the Ruler Units radio group in the Preferences dialog box (choose Edit ➤ Preferences).

The *origin* (point 0, 0) is on the bottom, left-hand corner of the page. You can adjust this origin if you want to; you will learn how in *Chapter 7*. Note the dotted lines on the rulers that indicate the position of the cursor; in Figure 3.2, for example, the dotted markers indicate that the cursor is at position (34, 30). The major divisions on the rulers here are picas, so the cursor is 34 picas from the left edge of the page and 30 picas from the bottom edge. The minor divisions are one-third of a pica, or four points each. If you were to move the cursor one division to the right and one division down, the new position would be (34p4, 29p8) or 34 picas, 4 points from the left edge and 29 picas, 8 points from the bottom.

For a variety of mechanical reasons, most printers cannot print out to the actual edge of the page. Therefore, there will always be some space on the output that will not be available for printing. In Illustrator, this space is bounded

Figure 3.2

Choose View ➤ Show Rulers to display the rulers as drawing guides.

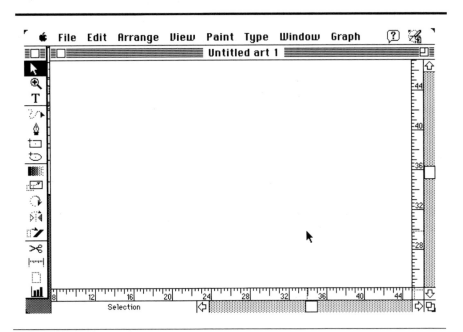

by the light lines that indicate the edge of the page and the dotted lines that indicate the margins.

The ruler origin (0, 0) is positioned at the corner of the page, while the printable margins start where the cursor is placed, at (2p6, 2p7). These margins are determined by the printer-driver software that you use for your system. If you have another type of printer, you may see slightly different margins. Also notice that the ruler's units expand with the magnification, changing to match the view. You can also see the page number in the bottom-left corner.

Select the Pen tool from the Toolbox; notice that the cursor changes into an ✕ as you move onto the drawing surface. Position the ✕ cursor at (16, 22) on the sheet. The screen should now look something like Figure 3.3. Click once at (16, 22). A small black square will appear.

This small, black square is an *anchor point*, which determines where a line segment begins or ends. In this case, you are beginning a straight line segment.

Figure 3.3

Click once to place the first anchor point.

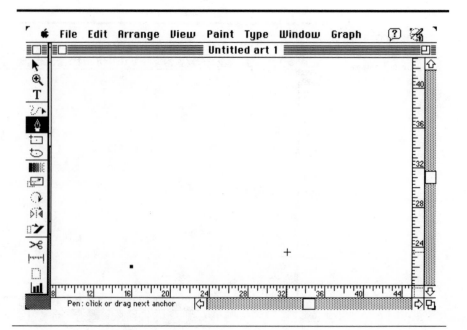

Notice also that the shape of the cursor changes from the ✕ to a +. This indicates that the next anchor point you create will be connected to the previous one. You should always be aware of the shape of the cursor to avoid unwanted results. If you *do* make an unwanted line segment or other shape, you can simply press Delete to remove it. If you really botch things up, press Delete twice to remove all the current work. This will not affect parts of a figure that you completed previously; it will remove only the lines that you have been working on. Alternatively, you can choose Edit ➤ Undo or press ⌘-Z to undo your last action, provided you haven't done anything else in the interim. The Undo menu command is *dimmed* if it is not available. In *Chapter 7*, you will learn about these and other error correction techniques in detail.

Move the + cursor to (32, 22), hold down Shift and click once. A line appears connecting the first point with a new point.

You have just created your first line in Illustrator. By holding down Shift, you forced the line to be straight. This is called *constraining* a line or movement. Illustrator allows you to constrain the position of lines and movement of figures to the vertical axis, the horizontal axis, or any multiple of 45° from the axes.

Move the cursor up to (36, 29) and click again. *Do Not* hold down Shift, since this line is not at an appropriate angle for constraining—that is, its angle is not a multiple of 45°. Click again at (28, 42p8)—that is, two minor divisions above 42 picas on your vertical ruler. This also should not be constrained, since the line is again at an arbitrary angle. Make a straight line (using Shift again to constrain the line) from (28, 42p8) to the point (20, 42p8). Continue making the border of the figure by connecting (20, 42p8) to the point (12, 29). This is not a constrainable angle. Finish the border of the figure by connecting (12, 29) with the starting point, (16, 22). At this point, your finished border should look like Figure 3.4.

Paths

The series of connected lines that you have drawn form a figure. Any set of connected lines is called a *path*. Notice that the cursor has changed back into an ✕ automatically. This means that Illustrator will not connect the next point that you make with the last point of the previous path. Since you have

Figure 3.4

The completed border

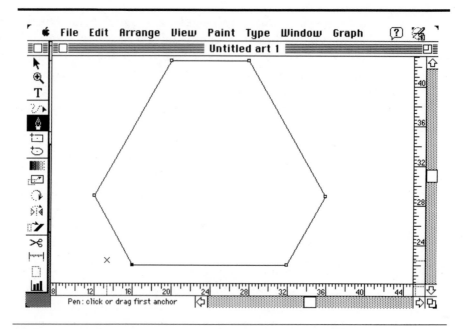

returned to the starting point, the path that you have drawn is *closed*. On the other hand, any path where the beginning and ending points are not the same is said to be *open*. Earlier, when you were adding points to an open path, Illustrator assumed that you were continuing that path, and so each point added was connected to the previous point; however, once a path is closed, the program assumes that the next point added is no longer part of the closed figure, which is normally the case. For example, the next object we draw will be a part of the interior of the figure and not part of the border. If you wanted to continue a path you've closed by returning to the starting point, you can do so by clicking on the starting point again.

Choose Paint ➤ Style. The Paint menu commands govern several characteristics of Illustrator figures, including output appearance. For now, let's paint the path that you have created.

Click on None in the box labeled Fill and then click on the radio button Black in the box labeled Stroke. As soon as you do, the default percentage of 100 shows in the box next to Black, and other boxes, previously dimmed, are now active. Change the line Weight value from the default of 1 to 4 and click on OK to record these settings. This is shown in Figure 3.5.

Fill and Stroke

Illustrator assumes that all objects are to be filled with a 100% Black interior. You can either fill an object by painting its interior a designated color or shade of gray; or you can *stroke* an object by painting only the lines that make up the object (again in any color or shade of gray) and leaving the interior empty. Objects are often both stroked and filled. Objects may be stroked in a color and then filled with white to cover parts of objects that are behind them; you will see examples of this in later exercises.

The *Weight* of a line is its thickness when painted, measured in points. The line on the actual output is drawn so that one half of the thickness, or *line width*, is on one side of the line you see on the screen and the rest on the other. For thin lines this doesn't usually cause problems, but for thick lines there can be noticeable problems in positioning.

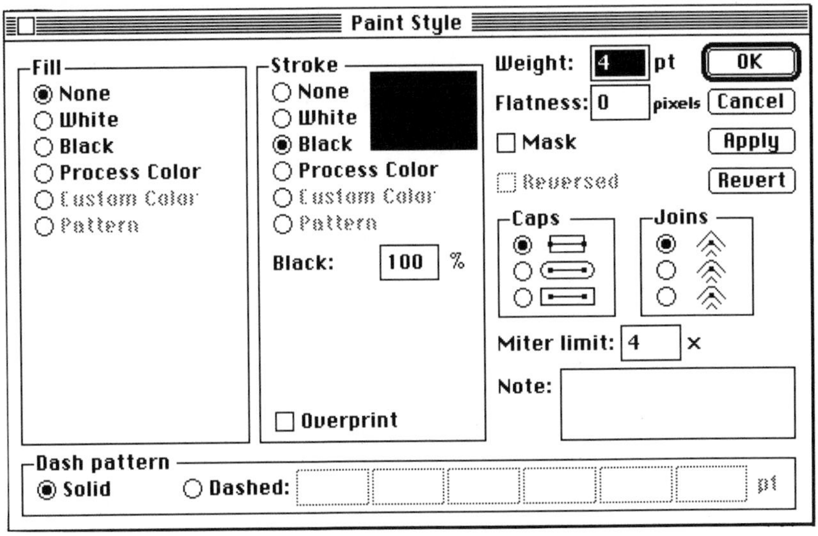

Figure 3.5

The Paint Style dialog box allows you to set the printing characteristics of your artwork.

Illustrator applies the settings that you make in the Paint Style dialog box to the currently selected object or objects. An object is *selected* if its anchor points are visible as either hollow squares or black squares. In this case, the border you just completed is automatically selected; if you look back at Figure 3.4, you will see that the last anchor point you clicked on—which was also the first anchor point you created—is a solid black square, and the remaining anchor points around the border are small, hollow squares. If the figure were not selected, you could use the selection tool to click anywhere on the border to select it. If you click on an anchor point itself, it becomes selected individually as well, so that it will show as a solid black square while the other anchor points that make up the object will be hollow.

What you have done so far is create the border of the finished figure and set it to print at a line weight of four points. The interior of the border is empty, since you chose no fill in the Paint Style dialog box. Now you need to place the interior elements of the figure within the border. The first interior elements are three identical diamonds that are placed along the short sides of the border.

Move the pen cursor to (16, 29). Draw a straight line connecting that point to (18, 25.5). That is, place the point on the y-axis, half way between the 25 and 26 markings. This will be between the two minor divisions. We could also call this 25p6, but 25.5 seems clearer, since there is no exact division at this point on the rulers. Continue the diamond with a line to (16, 22). Don't worry that this is also part of the original border; the new anchor point goes over the first one. The active one is determined by which figure is selected.

Continue with a line to (14, 25.5) and finish by closing the diamond with a line back to the starting point at (16, 29). Select Paint ➤ Style again and set the line Weight to 1. The lines that form the diamond will now paint at one-quarter of the thickness of the lines that form the border.

Change to the Selection tool by clicking on it in the Toolbox and move the selection arrow out onto the drawing surface. Hold down Option. Notice that a small + appears beneath the selection arrow. This tells you that you are using a variant of the standard Selection tool, called the *Object Selection tool*. At the same time, the name in the information bar changes to reflect the new tool name. This tool is also available from the Toolbox as an alternate when you click on the Selection tool. The Object Selection tool allows you to select an entire figure by clicking on any part of it. Move the Object Selection tool to the anchor point at the top of the diamond and click the mouse button. All the anchor points of the diamond should become black, as shown in Figure 3.6.

Moving and Duplicating Objects

You are going to move and duplicate this diamond, so you need to be able to move all the anchor points together. When you move objects, only selected anchor points move, allowing you to reshape an object if you desire. If you want to keep the same shape, though, you need to select all the anchor points together. Using the Object Selection tool—either directly from the Toolbox or by pressing Option—is the easiest way to do so.

Move the selection cursor to the bottom anchor point of the diamond—the point (16, 22)—and hold down the mouse button. The cursor changes to an arrowhead. While you continue to hold down the mouse button, drag the arrowhead and the diamond to the point (36, 29). Hold down Option and release the mouse button. This creates a copy of the diamond. If you had just

Figure 3.6

When you select the first diamond, all of its anchor points will turn black.

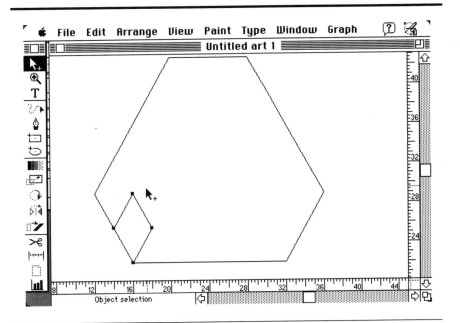

released the mouse button, you would have moved the original diamond to the new position instead of making a copy. If you did this accidently, press ⌘-Z or select Edit ➤ Undo to start the process again.

Notice, as you do this, that the cursor and information bar change to describe what is happening. For example, the cursor changes to a double arrowhead and the information bar says *Copy* when you press Option after moving the diamond. By checking these two items, you can always tell what Illustrator thinks you want to do. This provides valuable feedback and allows you to double-check your work as you proceed. In the exercises in this book, I will describe actions using the same words that appear in the information bar, so you can check your actions as you go along.

You could have simply redrawn the diamond at the new location. Since the diamond is quite a simple object, that might have been just as fast as moving it; however, I want to show you how to duplicate and adjust *any* object. You will often create complex graphic elements in Illustrator, thus it's very useful to know how to reposition or copy them without having to recreate them every time. Here, we chose the bottom anchor point as the point to move because it can be precisely positioned.

Rotating Objects

Now you need to rotate the diamond back inside the border to create the next graphic element in this design. Select the Rotate tool from the toolbox. The cursor changes to a +. Move the cursor to the bottom of the second diamond. Place the cursor on the bottom anchor point and click. The cursor changes to a filled arrowhead. Move the cursor to the top of the diamond, click and hold on the top anchor point, and rotate the diamond to the left until it is in the position shown in Figure 3.7. Make sure you align one side of the diamond along the border as shown, and then release the mouse button.

As you have just seen, using the Rotate tool requires two steps. First, you select the point that will be the center of the rotation; in this case, the bottom anchor point. Then you grab any part of the selected object and rotate it into the desired position; here, that part was the top anchor point.

Figure 3.7

The second diamond being rotated

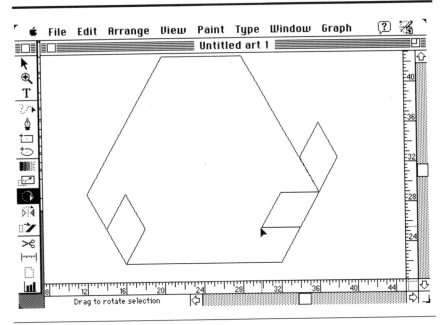

Notice that, after you have completed the rotation, the cursor returns to +, so you can choose a new center of rotation. The point chosen as the center of rotation need not be on the figure selected; any point can be set as the center of rotation. Usually, however, the center of rotation is either on the figure or near it; otherwise it is difficult to visualize the result of the rotation. If you had wanted to copy the diamond after rotating it, you would have used Option as you did during the original move. Moving and transforming an object is similar to copying an object instead of moving the original.

You see that the diamond is still selected, because all of its anchor points are black. Now you want to move a copy of this diamond to the top of the border and reposition it.

Since you will have to use the rotate tool again once the diamond is copied and moved, it would be inefficient to change tools. Illustrator has an easy way to avoid the problem. Press and hold the ⌘ key, and the cursor will change to the selection arrow. If you release the ⌘ key, the cursor will change back to the rotate cursor. This is one way to change from any tool to the Selection tool and back again, without going to the Toolbox. Let's use this technique to move and rotate a third diamond into position.

Press and hold the ⌘ key to change to the selection cursor, and use the mouse to move the selection cursor to the anchor point at (36, 29). Click the mouse button and drag the diamond to the position (20, 42p8). Hold down the Option key—while you continue to hold down the ⌘ key—and release the mouse button to create a copy of the diamond, as shown in Figure 3.8.

Release the ⌘ key and the cursor will change back to the rotate cursor, so you don't have to reselect the Rotate tool. Position the rotate cursor on the anchor point at (20, 42p8) and click to set the center of rotation. Then move the arrowhead cursor to the top of the diamond and rotate it to align the side of the diamond with the top of the border.

Because you copied the second and third diamonds from the first, they all share the same paint attributes; when you copy an object, all its qualities,

Figure 3.8

*Move and copy to obtain
a third diamond.*

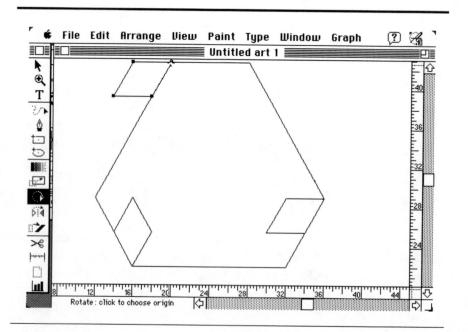

such as its paint attributes come with it. You could change these once you make a copy if you wanted to by selecting the Paint Style dialog box and making the desired change. In this case, though, you want to keep them the same. Now let's connect the diamonds to create a pattern in the interior.

Select the Pen tool again and click on the anchor point on the top of the first diamond that you drew, at (16, 29). Draw a straight line from that point to the point on the edge of the top diamond that is closest to (22, 39). The point coordinates will be exact if your diamonds were exact; if not, it isn't important. In each case just select the anchor point that is closest to the given coordinate.

The pen cursor is still a +, indicating that the next point will continue the existing path. In this case, you don't want to continue this line; you want to start a new line. To do so, you must reset the pen cursor to an × by clicking on the Pen tool in the Toolbox. The figure should now look like Figure 3.9.

Complete this part of the interior pattern by adding two more lines, connecting the interior point of each diamond with the side of the following diamond in clockwise progression. Reset the pen cursor between each line

Figure 3.9

Position the first connecting line.

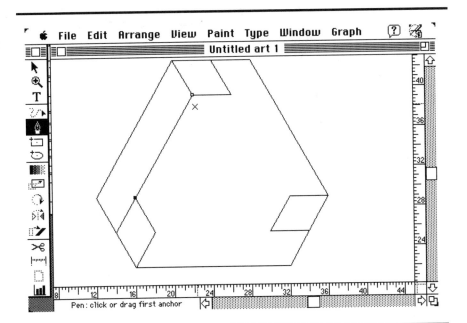

so that they are not connected. This will give you lines from the (approximate) points (26, 39) on the top diamond to (32, 29) on the second diamond; and from (30, 25.5) on the second diamond to (18, 25.5) on the first diamond. The resulting figure should look like Figure 3.10.

This completes the first part of the interior of the figure. This is already an interesting design, but you still have more to add.

Next, you will add a series of three interlocked bars to complete the interior design. There are several ways to do this, but, for the sake of simplicity, you will just draw a line of the correct length to a predetermined point. In most exercises, I will give you a way to calculate these coordinates rather than simply tell you what they are; for now, however, the most straightforward method is best.

Draw another straight line from the top diamond at its interior tip, from about (26, 39) to (20, 27).

Figure 3.10

Add two more connecting lines.

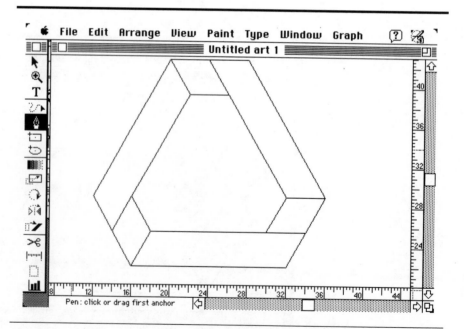

Reset the pen cursor by moving it to the Pen tool and clicking. Then make two more lines, as follows. First, from the top of the second diamond, point (30, 25p4), draw a line to meet the line you just drew at the point 35p8 on the y-axis. Second, from the top of the first diamond, point (16, 29), draw a line straight across to meet the line you just drew at 29 on the y-axis. This completes the figure, and the final result is shown in Figure 3.11.

Previewing Your Work

This is all very nice, but the graphic doesn't yet really look on the screen the way it will when you print. Illustrator provides an excellent method for seeing artwork before you print, called Preview mode. Let's now look at the figure as it will appear when printed. Select View ➤ Preview Illustration or press ⌘-Y. This shows you the final figure, with all its changes and settings, as shown in Figure 3.12.

Figure 3.11

The completed figure

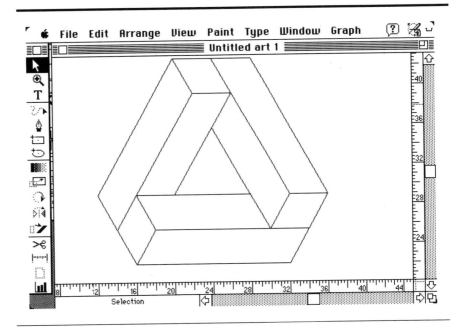

Figure 3.12

*You can see how your
printed output will look
in Preview mode.*

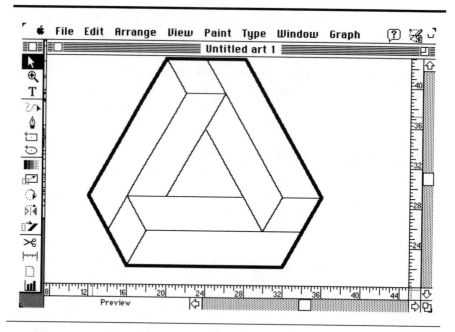

Figure 3.12

*You can see how your
printed output will look
in Preview mode.*

Saving Your Work

After doing all this work, you don't want to lose this artwork, so let's save it under the name EXERCISE 3-1. You can do that with the following final steps to this exercise. Select File ➤ Save.

Since the current artwork is unnamed, you will see the Save dialog box, shown in Figure 3.13.

If the file already had a name, the dialog box would not appear and the Save command would simply update the existing file on disk. You can also execute the Save command from the keyboard by pressing ⌘-S. If the file already has a name and you wish to save it without replacing the existing file, you must use the File ➤ Save As command. In this case, enter the name **EXERCISE 3-1** in the box labeled Save illustration as and click on the Save button.

For now, you can leave the other selections on this dialog box as the default values. Illustrator allows you three choices of file format and five choices of

Figure 3.13

The Save dialog box

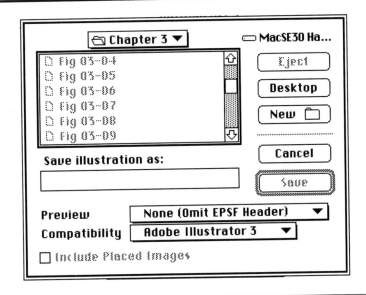

how to save the preview with your file. The Preview selections are

▶ with no preview and no PostScript header.

▶ without a preview but with the Encapsulated PostScript (EPS) header.

▶ with a Black & White preview for the Macintosh.

▶ with a Color preview for the Macintosh.

▶ with a preview for use on an IBM PC.

All of the formats that include a preview also include the EPS header, which is an integral part of these formats. Because Illustrator 3 has many new features that don't work in earlier versions, you can also save your file in a format that is compatible with Illustrator 1.1 and Illustrator 88.

Each of these choices is available in the pop-up menus next to the Preview or Compatibility items in the dialog box. Most of the time, you will want to save your file with no preview and in the Illustrator 3 format, as you will do here. The other options allow you to place Illustrator artwork into other applications, on both Macintosh and IBM systems, using the EPS format; and they allow you to make the file available to earlier versions of Illustrator—at some loss of features—by using appropriate compatible file formats. You will learn more about these other choices later in the book.

Notice that the name in the title bar changes to the name that you have given the artwork, EXERCISE 3-1. This name will always reflect the document that you are working on. Later, when you are using artwork and templates, you will see the names of both files in the title bar.

Exercise Summary

Now you have completed your first project. In some ways, this figure is very easy: it uses only straight lines, for example. I think you will agree, however, as you look at the final Preview output, that this is a very elegant result that would be much more difficult and time-consuming to do on paper.

EXERCISE 3.2: SQUARE AND CIRCLE FAN

Next you will do an exercise that uses the Rectangle and Oval tools to draw an interesting fan pattern. Like the previous exercise, this one does not use any prepared template as a guide but, unlike the last exercise, it does not re-quire precise placement of elements. In addition, this exercise requires that the elements be fixed in relation to one another. You will use the Rotation tool to ensure that the elements are in the desired relationships, regardless of where you begin or how you size them.

Normally, as you work through an exercise, you will be given a series of steps to follow. Here, however, I would like to go a little more slowly and explain a few things.

Start with an empty drawing surface. To do this, choose File ➤ New. You will see the Template dialog box, as shown in Figure 3.14.

Since you want to start a new piece of artwork, select None. Then choose View ➤ Show Rulers (⌘-R) if the rulers are hidden.

Figure 3.14

The Template dialog box allows you to use a template with your Illustrator artwork

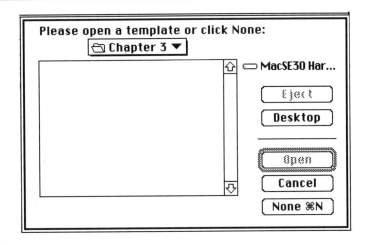

Drawing with the Rectangle and Oval Tools

Select the Rectangle tool. The cursor changes to a +. Position the rectangle cursor at about (24, 40). Note that accuracy isn't too important here. Click the mouse button and hold down Shift while you drag the cursor to about point (38, 26). The result should look something like Figure 3.15.

You have just created a square box on the page, with the upper-left corner at the point where you started (24, 40) and the lower-right corner at about the point (38, 26). You may notice your arrowhead cursor move away from the edge of the square; this happens because you are constraining the shape to a square. By careful motion, you will see that the cursor can be moved back to the corner of the square without changing the shape at all. If your box is not quite how you want it, just delete it—select Edit ➤ Undo (⌘-Z) or press Delete—and start again, moving the cursor more slowly to keep it positioned on the edge of the square. Remember, though, that precision isn't necessary for this exercise.

Choose Paint ➤ Paint Style (⌘-I) and set the attributes of this square as follows: Fill White; Stroke Black 100%; Weight 1; all other values to their default settings.

Figure 3.15

Use the Shift key to constrain your first rectangle to a symmetrical square.

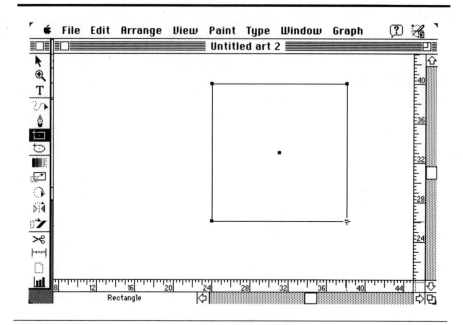

It might seem that there is no difference in filling a figure with white and having no fill at all, at least if you are outputting to a white surface, such as paper. That is not correct, though, because Illustrator places graphic objects in *layers*. If an object in an upper layer has no fill, the objects below it show through; if it has white fill, they do not. In this exercise, you are going to have a series of overlapping objects and you want each subsequent one to mask the ones beneath. To get that effect, you need to fill the objects with white. This is a good example of when an object is both stroked, to show its outline, and filled.

Now you need to place a small circle in the interior of the square. You want to place it off-center, but along the imaginary diagonal line that connects the bottom-left and top-right corners of the square. You could, of course, calculate the coordinates of the desired position, but that would be long and tedious and (for those of us without a great memory of high-school algebra) perhaps difficult. Alternatively, you can place the circle by eye, but estimating the location of the diagonal is a bit tricky. Fortunately, there is an easier way.

Select the Pen tool from the Toolbox and draw a straight line from the bottom-left corner of the square to the top-right point. The result is shown in Figure 3.16.

With the line selected, choose Arrange ➤ Make Guide (⌘-5). This turns the line that you have just drawn into a *guide*, which is indicated by a dotted line on the screen. Guides are special lines or shapes that can help you place or design artwork, but that are not part of the final artwork itself. A guide does not appear on the final output and cannot be selected or moved by ordinary Illustrator operations, so it won't get in your way as you work. In addition to drawing your own guide, as you have done here, you can also click on either the horizontal or vertical ruler bar and drag guides out onto the artwork.

Now select the Oval tool from the Toolbox. Move the + cursor to a point along the diagonal line above and to the right of the center. Press the Option key so that you can draw the oval from the center instead of the edge. Click the mouse button and hold down Shift to draw a small circle that looks like Figure 3.17.

Figure 3.16

Draw a diagonal line to assist in placing the circle.

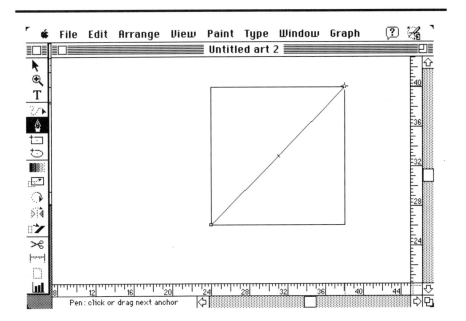

Figure 3.17

*Hold down both
Shift and Option to
draw the interior circle*

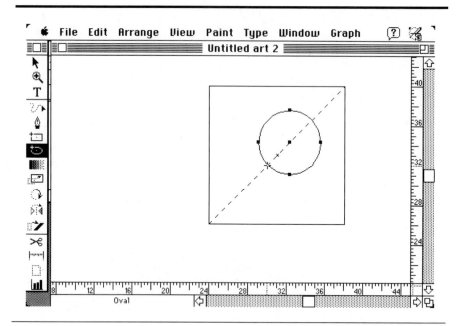

Because the Paint Style attributes for the circle have the same settings as were used for the square: Fill White; Stroke %Black 100; Weight 1, you don't need to reset them. Illustrator remembers the last used settings for the Paint and Type selections, and will associate them by default with any new artwork. Keep this in mind, so you can group your work to create common elements at the same time and minimize Style changes.

Creating the Other Graphic Elements

To do this, you will rotate this element around its lower-left corner to create a series of overlapping squares, somewhat like a hand of cards fanned out around a common point. You are already familiar with the Rotate tool from the previous exercise; now you need to know how to move these shapes as a group. Switch to the Selection tool. Place the selection cursor (the arrow) somewhere above the top left of the figure and click and drag the cursor to a point below the bottom right of the figure, as shown in Figure 3.18. You will see a dotted rectangle appear on the screen as you drag; be sure that the

Figure 3.18

*Drag the cursor to make
a selection marquee that
surrounds the entire figure.*

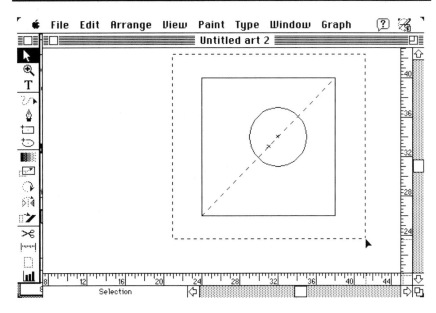

rectangle covers the entire figure and then release the mouse button. All anchor points in the figure should become black, showing that they have all been selected.

Grouping Objects

The dotted rectangle is called the *selection marquee*. All anchor points within a marquee are selected at one time. This is a great help when you are working with a large area or number of objects or when you have overlapping anchor points and objects, as you will see later. Here you want to collect all of these anchor points into one unit; you do that by making them part of a *group*. To do so, choose Arrange ➤ Group.

This makes all of the selected anchor points and their associated objects into a group. You can tell when things have been grouped by a simple test. Use the Selection tool and click anywhere away from the objects. All the anchor points disappear since none of them are selected. Now click anywhere on the object. If all the anchor points are selected—that is, they all become small black squares, the object is grouped; but if the anchor points appear as hollow squares, the object is not grouped. The composite shape of the square and circle is a group since all anchor points are selected if you click on any part of the shape. You can take grouped objects and make them part of a larger group.

Rotating the Grouped Objects

Now that you have made the elements of this figure into a group, you can perform any movement or transformation on the group as if it were a single object; in this case, you want to rotate it to a new position. Be sure that the figure is selected. Then select the Rotate tool from the Toolbox and place the rotate cursor on the lower-left corner of the square. You want to rotate the square around this corner point seven times, so that you have a total of eight overlapping squares. To do this and arrive at a perfectly symmetrical shape, each copy must be rotated exactly 45° from its predecessor. You could do this by eyeballing, but the odds are that you would be off a little. Since these are squares, any deviation will be obvious by the end of the rotation. Illustrator provides an excellent method for handling such situations. Hold down Option as you place the rotate cursor over the bottom-left corner of the square. Notice that the right arm of the cursor extends somewhat, and the information box changes from *Rotate* to *Rotate dialog*. Now click on the lower-left corner point. You will see the dialog box shown in Figure 3.19.

This dialog box (which you can also access by selecting the Rotate dialog tool from the Toolbox) allows you to specify precisely the angle that you want to move the selected object. It also allows you to make the rotation to the selected object itself or to create a copy and rotate that. Enter **45** in the Angle box and click Copy. This makes a copy of the selected artwork, rotated

Figure 3.19

The Rotate dialog box allows you to specify precise rotations.

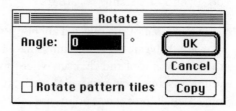

through exactly 45°. Notice that the resulting copy is automatically selected, as shown in Figure 3.20.

Now you want to make several more copies, rotating each through 45° from the preceding, until you have a full circle. You could, of course, do the rotate again (and again, and again...) until you had all the desired copies. However, Illustrator provides an easier and faster method. Choose Arrange ➤ Transform Again (⌘-D). This is the fastest and easiest way to make several successive changes to artwork. Press ⌘-D five more times to complete the circle of squares.

This looks pretty much like what you set out to produce, so let's preview the artwork to see how it looks. Select View ➤ Preview (⌘-Y). The resulting screen is shown in Figure 3.21.

Figure 3.20

A rotated copy of the artwork

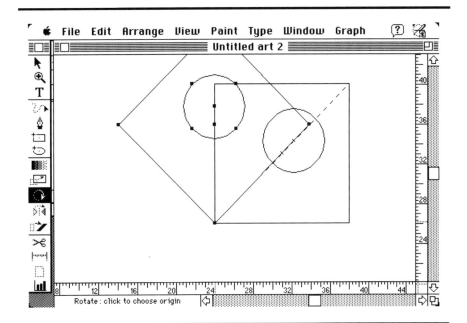

Figure 3.21

*Select View ➤ Preview
to preview the squares.*

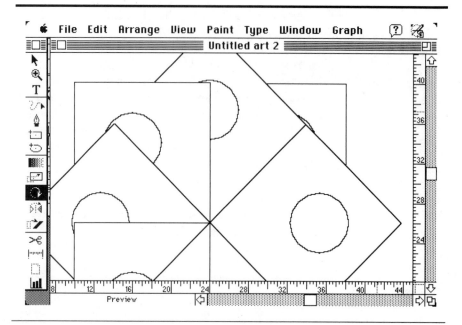

Editing Your Graphic

While most of the figure looks fine, the last square overlaps the first in an unsatisfactory way. What you want here is for the last square to appear to fold under the first, like the flaps of a box. This, however, is easier said than done. Illustrator has made every square paint over the previous squares. Since you chose to fill each square with white, the other, earlier squares do not show through—and you don't want them to. So how can you make the last figure slip under the first? Unfortunately, you cannot.

The appearance of these squares, and all Illustrator output, is determined by the order in which they are drawn. You can change and control that order; in later exercises you will see how to force a given paint order. But here you want an effect that cannot be achieved by control of paint order: you want all of the squares to paint exactly like they do, but the last should both paint over the previous square and under the first square. To do that, it would have to paint before the first square and after the last one, an obvious contradiction.

To get the desired effect, you need to erase the part of the last square that overlaps the first one. Notice that you don't have to do this for any of the squares but the last; the rest have conveniently fallen into place to create the desired effect. So using Illustrator is more convenient than doing this with ink and paper, but a bit more difficult than doing it with cardboard or paper cutouts, where you could slip part of the last figure under the first.

Ungrouping Objects

Select View ➤ Artwork Only. This takes you out of the preview and allows you to make changes to your artwork again. In *Chapter* 4 you will learn all about artwork and templates. For now, let's finish this design. Before starting, be sure that the last square is still selected, as it should be. If not, use the Selection tool to select the entire square and circle. Then choose Arrange ➤ Ungroup.

Before, you grouped the elements of each of these squares so that they could be rotated as a unit. Now, you need to *ungroup* them so that you can remove the portions of the figure that you want to erase. Let's begin by getting a closer look at the first spot that needs work. Select the Zoom in tool from the Toolbox and move the zoom cursor (a small magnifying glass with a + inside it) to the point where the sides of the first and last squares cross. Click once.

The Zoom in and Zoom out tools allow you to magnify or reduce the view of the desktop, with nine possible levels. Let's magnify the view by a factor of two—200% of the normal level—so that you can see more clearly how to adjust the figure. Notice that the zoom is centered around the point where the zoom cursor is located when you click: in this case, the point where the sides of the two squares intersect.

Cropping the Square

Now you need to cut away the part of the square that overlaps and obscures the first square. You do this as follows.

First, you must ungroup the square itself. The Split Path tool cannot make a cut at the end of an open path, and there are some restrictions on cutting grouped paths or objects. It's not likely that you will ever try to make a cut at the end of an open path deliberately; it is like trying to cut a piece of string at the end. You must ungroup the object after the cut and then perform the changes that you want. You may be surprised that the square is still a group, but remember, you grouped the square, line, and circle earlier. The Ungroup you performed above only returned you to the previous arrangement of individual objects. Since the square and the circle are created as groups, they remained as groups. Make sure that the last square is selected. Then select Arrange ➤ Ungroup (⌘-U) to ungroup it.

Select the Split Path tool from the Toolbox. Move the scissors cursor, which looks like a +, just below the point of intersection of the sides of the two squares and click once.

You will see a new anchor point appear under the scissors cursor, as shown in Figure 3.22.

The Split Path tool cuts the path at the point where the scissors cursor is placed, just as a real pair of scissors cuts a piece of string, so this new anchor point divides the line into two pieces. Next you need to make another cut to

Figure 3.22

Position the cursor and click, and a new anchor point will appear.

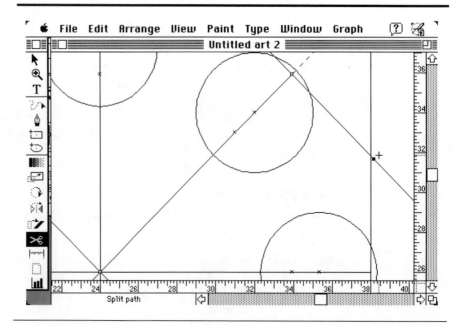

clear off the top section of the square that overlaps the first square. Move the scissors cursor to the center point (the point that you rotated all the squares around) and make another cut. You will see a new anchor point appear. You have now divided the top square into two pieces.

Use the Selection tool and the Option key to select the top half of the square as a unit and move it a small distance away from the rest of the figure, as shown in Figure 3.23. Then choose Edit ➤ Clear. The selected piece of the square disappears.

Although not strictly necessary, I always move any object that I am about to clear to ensure that only the object is selected and deleted. The Clear function can also be performed from the keyboard by using the Delete key; however, the menu selection seems to me to be surer and less prone to potential error. Remember that, if you do clear something by mistake, you can always choose Edit ➤ Undo to retrieve it.

Figure 3.23

Move the top half of the square away from the graphic.

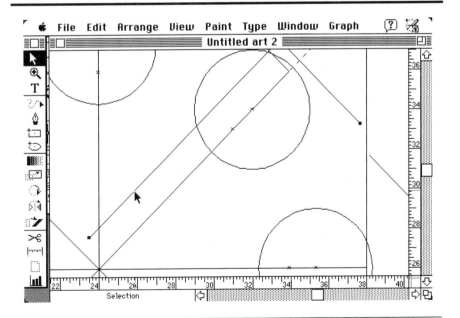

You may wonder how you could cut the top square at the center point, when all the figures overlap there. The answer is that the scissors work on the topmost object if there are several overlapping objects; since the square that you want to cut is on top, the scissors cut that path rather than any of the previous squares. Later, you will learn how to move objects so the one you want to work with is on the top of the drawing surface.

You still have to do some work here to make the figure appear correctly. If you simply left it like this, Illustrator would, in effect, draw a straight line between the two new endpoints of the top square and fill the resulting area with white when you tried to output the figure. Illustrator will always connect the endpoints of an open figure if you have selected any Fill option in the Paint dialog box; here, you have selected White as the fill. If you let that happen, although part of the first square would show through, the bottom part of it would be painted over. If you want to see how this would look, press ⌘-Y or select View ➤ Preview.

In any case, you need to correct this by drawing in lines to define the edge of the top square. Select the Pen tool and draw a line down the edge of the first square from the first point that you cut, to the point where the side of the first square turns in to the center. Finish the edge of the top square by connecting the point you just made with the center point.

You have now made the edge of the top square more or less match that of the bottom square. This ensures that the white fill in the top square won't cover any of the bottom square and will allow it to show through the way you want. Essentially, you have cut out and erased a piece of the top square so that it matches the edge of the first square. However, the point at the top of the square is not quite aligned with the edge of the first square. You can easily match these up as follows. Use the selection tool and select the top endpoint of the top square, where you made the first cut.

Using the Selection tool, move the anchor point slightly to the left, until the vertical edges of the top and the bottom square are aligned, as shown in Figure 3.24.

Figure 3.24

Move the top anchor point until the edges are aligned.

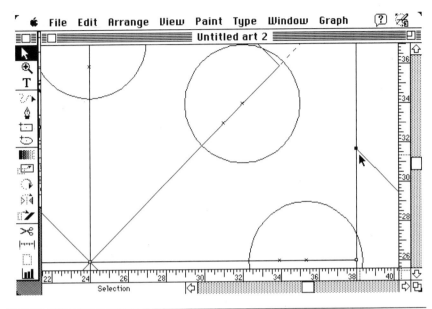

Cropping the Circle

This still leaves the circle painting over a part of the first square, so you have to follow the same steps you used to crop the rectangle to crop the circle. As you can see, the circle is already divided into quarters, but the anchor points are not where you can use them. You could simply use the scissors to cut the circle, ignoring the existing anchor points; however, this is not good practice, as it leaves you with two unnecessary anchor points. Every anchor point uses memory in your PostScript program and, ultimately, in the output device. The most efficient drawings are those that have the fewest number of anchor points. We will discuss issues of efficiency and performance later in the book.

For now, let's accept that you want to divide the circle at two of the existing anchor points and align it so that the remaining half-circle lies entirely below the edge of the first square. Use the Selection tool to select the circle in the top square. Select the Rotate tool from the Toolbox and position the rotate cursor over the center of the circle. Rotate the circle until two of the anchor points lie along the bottom of the first square, as shown in Figure 3.25.

Figure 3.25

Rotate the circle into
its new position.

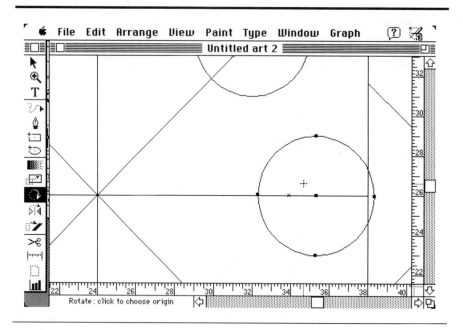

Choose Arrange ➤ Ungroup (⌘–U), to ungroup the circle. Remember that the circle, like the square, is a grouped figure. Do not ungroup the circle until you have rotated it, since you want it to rotate as a unit. As before, select the Split Path tool and cut the circle at each of the anchor points that lie along the base of the first square. These anchor points show additional lines and points connected with them when you make the cut. Don't be concerned; these are generated because the circle is made up of curved segments. You will learn about curved lines in *Chapter 4*.

Use the Selection tool and Option to select the top half of the circle. Choose Edit ➤ Clear to remove the selected segment.

Once again, you need to draw a line connecting the two anchor points that define the bottom half of the circle. If you don't, the white fill from the circle will cover half of the line that crosses along the top of the circle, making that line noticeably thinner than the parts on either side. If you want to see this in action, try selecting View ➤ Preview now.

Remember that each line has a weight, or line width, associated with it. When Illustrator draws a line, it places one half of the width on one side and one half on the other; so, if a line had a weight of two points, it would be drawn with one point on one side of the line on the screen and one point on the other. In this case, the final output line will draw one-half point on either side of the line on the screen. If you don't place a line for the edge of the circle, the white fill will cover the bottom half of this line, since the fill from the circle will go out to the exact location of the line on the screen.

Use the Pen tool to draw a line between the two anchor points, thus closing the half circle. If the endpoints are not quite aligned with the edge of the square, use the Selection tool to move them as you did earlier. The final result should look like Figure 3.26.

Now you have finished the alterations required to make the final figure. Let's move back to view the finished product. Select View ➤ Actual Size. This selection will always return you to the center of the page, with a magnification of 100%. Since you started this artwork there, this will return you to the

Figure 3.26

Align the half circle with edge of square.

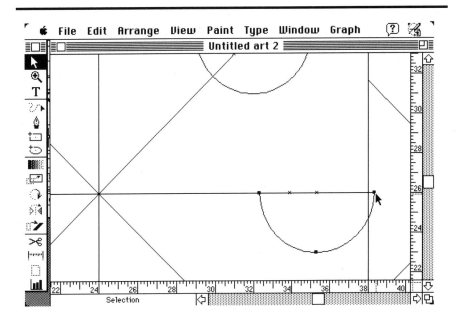

original view. Now select View ➤ Preview (⌘–Y) to see the final output version onscreen, as shown in Figure 3.27.

This preview still leaves a small part of the art below the bottom of the screen. If you want to see that, you can select the Zoom in tool from the Toolbox. Place the magnifying glass in the center of the screen and hold down Option. The + will turn into a –, indicating that you will be reducing the view of the artwork rather than magnifying it. This is the Zoom out tool, it is also available as an alternate in the Toolbox. Click once to reduce the view by 50%, which will allow you to see the entire graphic.

Printing Your Artwork

Now that you have seen your results onscreen, let's print the artwork. I will assume here that you have correctly chosen your Illustrator printer and that no further setup is required. Choose File ➤ Print. You will see a dialog box that looks something like Figure 3.28. It may be slightly different, depending on the version of the system that you are using.

Figure 3.27

A preview of the finished art

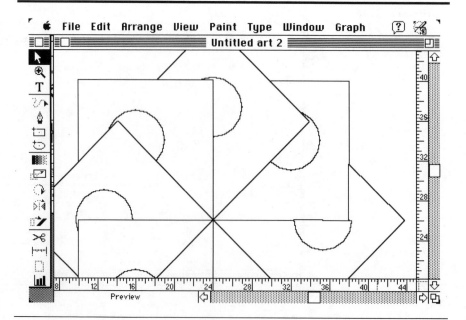

Accept the default page range of All and set the number of copies desired. Then click OK. This will print your artwork and produce a result similar to Figure 3.29. If you have trouble printing, choose File ➤ Page Setup to see your page setup settings; this is the major source of printing problems in Illustrator. You will learn more about the options in this dialog box in *Chapter 7*.

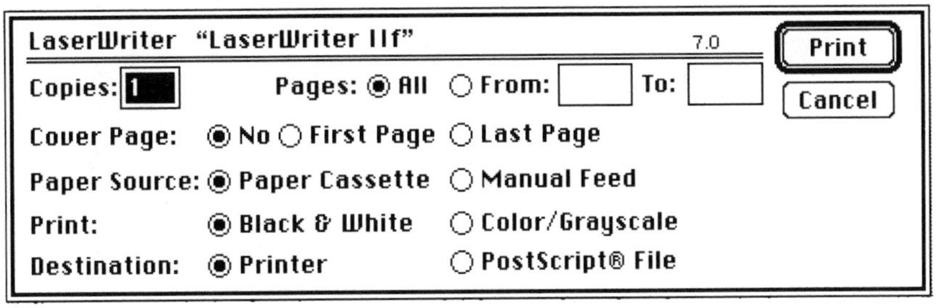

Figure 3.28

The Print dialog box (yours may differ slightly)

LaserWriter "LaserWriter IIf"		7.0	Print
Copies: **1**	Pages: ◉ All ○ From: [ ] To: [ ]		Cancel
Cover Page: ◉ No ○ First Page ○ Last Page			
Paper Source: ◉ Paper Cassette ○ Manual Feed			
Print: ◉ Black & White ○ Color/Grayscale			
Destination: ◉ Printer ○ PostScript® File			

Figure 3.29

The final printout of your artwork

When you are finished with the artwork, choose File ➤ Save and save it as
EXERCISE 3-2.

Exercise Summary

This completes the second exercise. Again, just using simple tools and
techniques, you've seen how Illustrator's powerful graphic capabilities can
make an interesting and unusual graphic.

SUMMARY

Now you have finished your introduction to Illustrator. Illustrator's many features allow you to make short work of tasks you formerly found tedious. As
you proceed through this book, you will learn more about Illustrator and see
how its features can be used to generate graphic images that were previously
very difficult and time-consuming. In *Chapter 4*, you will learn how to make
more complex figures, including curves and corners.

CHAPTER FOUR

Drawing Basic Lines and Curves

FEATURING

Finding templates

Associating artwork and templates

Using the Zoom in and Zoom out tools

Drawing curved lines

Modifying curves

Using the Pen tool

Using the Selection tool

Curve concepts

The examples in *Chapter* 3 used lines, pre-defined rectangles, and ovals to create images. Most graphics, however, are composed of curved lines or of a combination of curved and straight lines. You may have noticed that Illustrator is different from most other drawing programs in how it handles line creation. The major difference is that, in Illustrator, you select two points and create a line joining them. In most other programs, you "draw" the line by clicking and moving the mouse. The line is formed as you move the mouse and is always visible as a connection between the initial point and the current mouse position. Illustrator does not show you the line as you move the mouse; the line appears only when you have selected the second point.

This difference extends to drawing curves. Illustrator creates a curved line segment, as you will see, by selecting two end points, called *anchor points* and establishing two related control points, called *direction points*. These points, taken together, define the curved line segment.

Basically, all line segments in Illustrator are formed in the same way. Each has a beginning and an ending point, which are the *anchor* points, and each end of the segment has a controlling *direction* point. This is true for both straight-line and curved-line segments. In the case of straight lines, the direction points are identical to the anchor points, so you don't see or use them. Figure 4.1 shows you four curved lines and one straight line, showing both the anchor points for each segment and the direction points.

All the lines have the same distance between the beginning and ending points; the only difference is in the direction points. Lines 1 and 2 have direction points that move away from the anchor points at the same angle, but line 2's direction points are twice as far from the anchor points as line 1's. As you can see, this results in more of a bow in line 2 than in line 1.

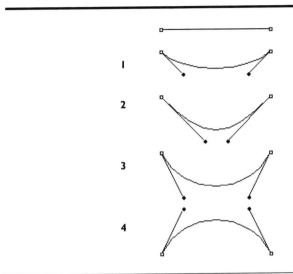

Figure 4.1

This set of lines shows
how direction points
influence simple curves.

Line 3 has direction points that move away from the anchor points at twice the angle of those in line 2. Notice how the line curves more sharply toward the anchor points. Technically, the line segment that connects the two anchor points will always be tangent to the line from the anchor point to the direction point. Since the line from the anchor points to the direction points in line 3 is steeper than line 2, the segment that is generated curves more sharply at the ends. In both cases the line is smooth, and rises to the same height— measured from a straight line connecting the two anchor points—but line 3 curves sharply at first and then flattens out, while line 2 rises more gradually. This is entirely due to the placement of the direction points.

Line 4 curves in the opposite direction from the other lines to demonstrate that the position of the direction points governs the direction of the curve as it moves away from the anchor point. The direction points are at the same angle as in line 3, but are twice as far away. You can see how the curve bends out to match the increased distance. In all the lines, notice that there is a direct relationship between the bell of the curve and the distance that the direction points are from the anchor point.

Figure 4.2 presents four additional examples of the interaction of direction points and curves.

Figure 4.2

Figure 4.2

This set of curved lines shows how compound curves are formed.

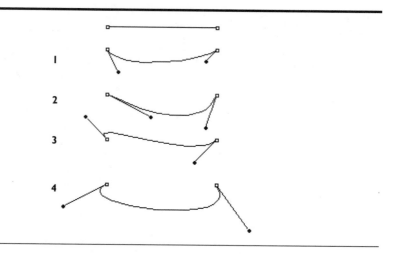

Once again, these lines are all the same length and are shown with a straight line for comparison purposes. This set of lines, however, has asymmetrical direction points to give you a sense of what you can do with these points. Line 1 is a simple example, where the direction point on the right is twice the size and at twice the angle of the one on the left. The curve starts slowly on the left, and then curves farther up and bends more steeply as it approaches the right anchor point. Note that the height of the curve is still governed by the direction points. The curve always adjusts to match the imbalance between the asymmetrical points. It is a kind of compromise between the two.

Line 2 shows the effect of different angles on each end of the curve. Again, the curve follows the same rules we observed earlier: the curved line segment is always tangent to the line formed by the anchor point and the direction point at the anchor point. Like line 1, the curve forms a kind of compromise between the two angles, becoming flatter as it moves toward the right anchor point to match the flatness of the line between the direction point and the anchor point.

Line 3 shows how a curve changes when one direction point is pulling in the opposite way from the direction at which the curve is approaching the anchor point. In such cases, the two direction points are on opposite sides of the curve. Here, the left anchor point has a direction point that is at exactly the opposite angle to the right anchor point and direction point. The curve flows smoothly toward the second anchor point, but then curves past it and then sharply reverses direction. Since a curved line segment must approach the anchor point on the same side as the direction point, it must go *past* the anchor point and then turn back. This leaves a small *s*-bend in the curve near the left anchor point.

Line 4 shows the effect of having both direction points on the same side of the curve but headed away from the opposite anchor point. As you would expect, the curve starts to follow the direction point away from the anchor point, as always, making a tangent to the line connecting the direction point and the anchor point. But the line starts to curve very quickly back toward the second anchor point and then passes over it to approach the anchor point from the correct angle—as defined by the tangent line. This gives a kind of egg-shape to the final curve.

These examples should give you some feeling for the interaction of anchor points and direction points. Illustrator does not have tools for drawing that mimic the natural action of a pen or pencil and paper. Nevertheless, after a little practice, I think you will become quite at ease with the Illustrator tools. You might even discover that you can use them quite intuitively to create figures of varying complexity. I strongly recommend that you open a new Illustrator file and play with the line segments as shown above. Try out various combinations of anchor and direction points to see the results, and note those that you think may provide interesting effects. As you explore, you will develop a sense of where the line segment is going to go when you have placed the anchor point and the direction point in a certain relationship.

One small point that you should note. If you want to play with line segments, be sure that each segment starts fresh, meaning that the pen cursor must be an ×, not a cross, when you start. Since these are not closed figures, Illustrator will not change back to the × cursor automatically when you finish a line. To force a new line segment, click on the Pen tool before you start each new segment. You can always remove all of the current lines by pressing the Delete or Backspace key twice.

ILLUSTRATOR'S THREE MODES

Illustrator has three ways of presenting images to you: templates, artwork, and previews. These three modes form a natural progression as you work with an image. A *template* is a bitmapped image brought into Illustrator as a guide for producing artwork. *Artwork* is the collection of line art and type that you generate using Illustrator's tools. The object of all of this work is the final image, which may be printed onto a page using any PostScript-equipped printer, and may be viewed as the *preview* image on your screen. You've already seen the artwork and preview modes in Chapter 3. There, you worked in artwork mode to create the image in Illustrator and then used preview mode to see what the output would look like before you printed it.

Now let's examine the third mode, the *template*, and discuss in detail how the modes interact. The interaction of template and artwork is probably the most important in Illustrator. There is nothing more difficult here than what you've already learned and used, though.

Templates and Artwork

Templates will be your normal starting point for creating artwork. A template is like a picture that you might place under a piece of tracing paper in order to create a drawing; in a similar way, the template lies under the Illustrator drawing area, showing through as a slightly dimmed sketch. You may wonder why you would want a template at all. As you saw in the last chapter, you can create Illustrator drawings with no preliminary sketches or drawings.

There are two reasons to use a template. First, if you are not—as, for example, I am not—endowed with much artistic talent or vision, you probably require some help in creating any drawings that go beyond simple lines and planes. Even if you are a talented artist, you may not be familiar with computer generation of drawings. Second, even talented artists will find that the tools and techniques of Illustrator do not lend themselves to the creation of original art in a natural way. Though very powerful and relatively easy to use, Illustrator does not provide the natural flow from mind to hand that is endemic to most sketching and drawing. Generally, you will find it most convenient to prepare drafts of graphic material in whatever manner you are accustomed to and then scan the image into Illustrator for final processing; this is a very natural way to prepare computer images.

Sources of Templates

Since templates are so fundamental to Illustrator, you might be wondering what they look like and where they come from. Templates come in two basic formats and may be generated from several sources. The formats are the Mac-Paint format and the MacDraw (PICT) format. You might be familiar with these formats from your previous work on the Macintosh.

These programs are certainly two good sources of templates. Generally, scanners produce MacPaint format output; therefore, any scanned image can generally be used as a starting point. Screen dumps and other types of graphic output, such as spreadsheet graphs, are also scanned in MacPaint format, and thus can also be used as sources. Frankly, I have never seen a Macintosh graphics program that didn't produce images in one of these two standard formats.

There is one additional source of template material to keep in mind: the large and varied selection of clip-art that can be purchased separately or that comes with many graphics programs. The Adobe Tutorial disk that comes with Illustrator is a fine source of template material. Note that the Gallery disks that come with Illustrator unfortunately do not contain templates for the elaborate images that they contain; only the artwork is provided.

Associating Templates and Artwork

There are two methods for associating a template with a piece of artwork. Choose File ➤ New, and you will be presented with the dialog box shown in Figure 4.3, which allows you to select a specific template to begin with.

If you choose a template, that template will remain associated with the artwork you create and will be included automatically with the artwork display whenever you work with the file.

Select File ➤ Open, and you'll be presented with another dialog box, as shown in Figure 4.4.

Figure 4.3

This dialog box allows you to start new artwork with an associated template.

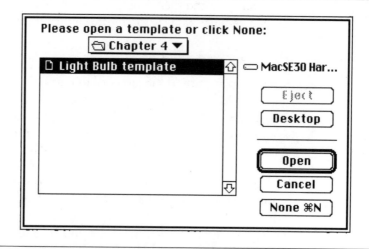

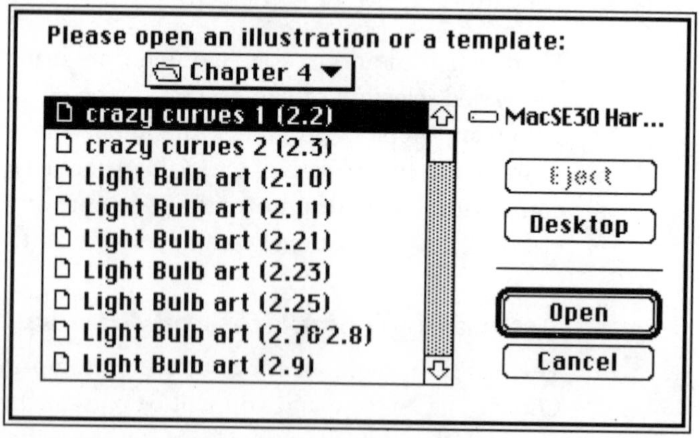

Figure 4.4

This dialog box allows you to open either existing artwork or a template.

This allows you either to open existing artwork or to open a template. If you open work on existing artwork, the template associated with it will automatically be included if available. "Available" in this context means that the template is in the same folder it was in when you originally created the artwork, and has the same name. If you open a template, you get a fresh drawing surface, labeled *Untitled Art*, followed by a sequence number, showing the selected template beneath; this is identical in effect to choosing File ➤ New and selecting the template.

If the correct template is not available when you open an existing artwork document, Illustrator will present you with a dialog box similar to Figure 4.3, which will allow you to associate a new template with the artwork. The only way to change the association of artwork with a template is to move or rename the template, re-open the artwork, and associate a new template.

Working with Templates and Artwork

Because of the close association of template and artwork, you need some way to distinguish them from one another. To some extent, you can distinguish the template from the artwork by its dimmed or grayed-out appearance; however, as you complete more of the artwork and match the template detail for detail, it can be difficult to determine where the artwork leaves off and the template begins. Illustrator provides several viewing options to help you cope with these difficulties. These options are found on the View menu, which offers three viewing methods.

The default mode is Artwork & Template. This option shows both the artwork and the underlying template, superimposing one on the other. This mode is the one you will normally be working in, since it allows you to see both what you want to do and what you have done.

The two other options—Artwork Only and Template Only—each allow you to view one of the graphic modes on the screen without seeing the other. The alternate graphic is hidden from view but not otherwise affected. Artwork Only is quite useful when you are working on complex graphics where the shading or other features of the template might hinder your seeing the exact placement or structure of the artwork.

Template Only is primarily useful for seeing exactly what is in the template after you have accumulated a substantial amount of artwork, which might obscure the original lines of the template. You cannot modify the template in any way; the template is a bitmap of a graphic image and Illustrator cannot handle bitmapped images. If you need to edit or modify the template, you will need to use a graphic program, such as MacPaint, that is designed to alter bitmaps.

I recommend that you follow some naming convention that allows you to easily distinguish templates from artwork on your disk; I also recommend that you adopt some filing standards to store your artwork and templates in a way that's convenient and easy to remember. Adobe suggests that you use the words *art* and *template* as the last words in the file names to designate the nature of the file. That is an excellent scheme, but any simple scheme will do, as long as you stick to it. As for folder organization, you might want to keep related art and templates in their own folder or perhaps make separate folders: one for artwork and one for templates. Again, the exact method is unimportant; create some reasonable structure and follow it.

Preview Mode

The View ➤ Preview Illustration command provides an additional viewing mode. This mode displays what your graphic will look like when it prints, right onscreen.

The preview mode supersedes all other modes, hiding them from view. You cannot change or edit the preview image; you must return to the artwork to make changes. You can move the preview image around on the screen by using the Scroll tool. To some extent, you can also reorient the output image on the paper.

Now that you have been exposed to Illustrator's modes for displaying images, we are ready to use these modes and some new techniques to create more artwork.

EXERCISE 4.1: CREATING SIMPLE CURVES

The first exercise in this chapter will take a simple template and convert it into Illustrator artwork. The template is a drawing of a light bulb that was prepared and saved in MacPaint. The drawing is quite simple, and you may wish to use some other template for your work (for example, the dog template that comes with Illustrator). The only requirement at this point is that the template consist of curved line segments.

The conversion of such a basic image into Illustrator may seem a bit over-simplified, but I believe that the first exercises need to be quite clear and precise, so you can understand the concepts behind the work before you begin your own more complex and more difficult graphics.

The Light Bulb Template

This light bulb template was prepared as a freehand drawing in MacPaint. The output, as produced by MacPaint, is shown in Figure 4.5.

Since I cannot reproduce the template on your computer, I ask you to copy it, or make something like it, using whatever drawing software you have available.

Figure 4.5

The light bulb template

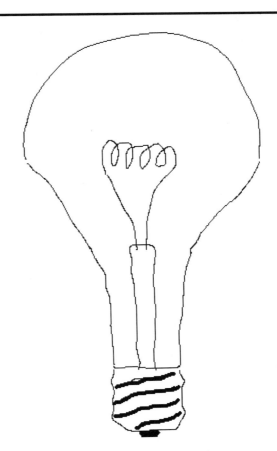

Remember that it isn't important that your image look like this one; the important thing is that it be suitable for learning purposes.

The template is quite simple in concept, but even so we are not going to do all of it at once. To begin with, you will just trace the outline of the bulb and the screw base. This will get you started in using several of the tools in Illustrator as well as introducing you to the creation of curved line segments.

Importing the Template

As we discussed earlier in the chapter, you relate a template to a piece of artwork first thing. Select File ➤ Open or File ➤ New and open your template. Either way you will get a screen that associates a new Illustrator graphic called *Untitled art* with the chosen template. The screen will look like that shown in Figure 4.6.

Observe two things about this screen. First, the title bar. It shows two names separated by a colon: *Untitled art 2:Light Bulb template*. The template used to open the file is *Light Bulb template* and Illustrator has associated this template with the

Figure 4.6

When you associate the light bulb template, a new clean drawing surface will appear.

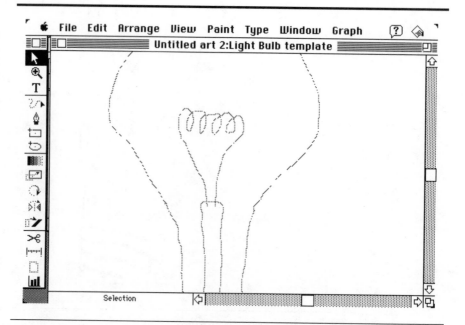

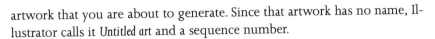

artwork that you are about to generate. Since that artwork has no name, Illustrator calls it *Untitled art* and a sequence number.

Also notice that the light bulb template has been positioned on the Illustrator page as a full-page image. If you look at the full-page view (choose View ➤ Fit in Window) you will see that the light bulb is the same size on Illustrator's page as it is on the sample page output shown in Figure 4.5, above. When you associate the template, the window opens on the center of the page in Actual Size mode, so you can see only a portion of the template.

The Zoom and Scroll Functions

You could use the Scroll tool or the scroll bars to move the template down or up so that you could begin tracing it. Sometimes, however, rather than rushing around the page, it's better to get farther away from it. Or you may want to get closer to match certain fine details of the template. Illustrator's Zoom in and Zoom out tools satisfy these requirements. The Zoom in tool is represented by the magnifying glass icon in the Toolbox; the Zoom out tool is an alternate to the Zoom in tool.

When you click on the magnifying glass and move the cursor out onto the drawing table, the cursor changes to a magnifying glass with a + in the middle. This indicates that the glass is in magnification mode. When you click the mouse, the image will be magnified to the next level of detail, centered on the point where the cursor is.

You can zoom out from the image either by selecting the Zoom out tool or by holding down Option while you are using the Zoom in tool. In either case, the magnifying glass has a − in it to indicate that you have selected the Zoom out tool. The next change will be reduction rather than magnification. Please try it now.

Select the Zoom in tool, move the cursor to just under the filament on the light bulb, and click once. This will magnify the filament to almost fill the screen. Now hold down Option and click again. This will take you back to the view you started from. You can effectively move the image around on the drawing table by careful selection of the points for a zoom, since the effect is centered on the position of the cursor.

Now use the Zoom out tool to step one click backward. Position the magnifying glass under the filament, hold down Option, and click once. Note that you can always select View ➤ Actual Size (⌘–H) to get back to the same view you started with: actual size magnification, centered on the page.

Tracing the Template

You are going to start by tracing the right side of the light bulb. Select the Pen tool and move the cursor to the top of the light-bulb template. Now click the mouse button and drag the cursor to the right. The cursor will turn into an arrowhead and remain that shape as long as you hold down the mouse button, and two points will extend from the center point. This process is demonstrated in Figure 4.7.

The center point is the anchor point (the small square). As you learned in Chapter 3, the anchor points for both straight and curved line segments are small squares.

The two points at the end of the line that extends out from the anchor point are direction points. They indicate the direction that the curve will take from the anchor point. Each direction point affects the side of the anchor point that it is on. Illustrator assumes that the curve you want to draw will be symmetric around the anchor point, so both direction points move simultaneously

Figure 4.7

Drawing the first point along the light-bulb template.

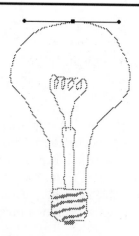

in opposite directions. Generally, this is a correct assumption; you will see later how you can change this default if necessary.

Pull the direction point to the right about two-thirds of the way to the right edge of the light bulb and release the mouse button. The cursor now changes to the familiar cross to show you that you are continuing an existing line. Position the cross about halfway around the globe of the light bulb and click and hold the mouse button. A curve will spring up between the first anchor point and this new anchor point. Drag the direction point under the arrowhead cursor downwards until the shape of the curve between the two anchor points matches the curve on the template. This is shown in Figure 4.8.

This is the basic technique for tracing curves. You click the mouse on the point you want to be an anchor point and then drag the direction point in the direction you want the curve to go. In *Chapter 5* we will discuss some rules-of-thumb for estimating where to place anchor points and how far to drag direction points to get a good fit. Remember that you can undo the entire current line by pressing the Delete key twice, and you can undo the last segment of a line by selecting Edit ➤ Undo (⌘–Z).

The important concept here, however, is that you can simply maneuver a direction point to get a curve to match your template. The position of the anchor point makes a significant difference in how much the curve bends.

Figure 4.8

Drag the direction point downwards until the shape of the curve matches the template.

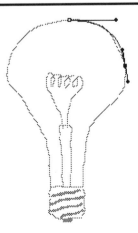

But since it is easy to undo line segments, feel free to experiment with placement of anchor points to see how easy or difficult it becomes to match the curve on the template.

Now move the cursor down to just above the point where the bulb curves down sharply toward the base of the light bulb. Place your cursor—which should still be a cross—here, and click and drag the direction point down towards the inside of the curve. Don't worry if the curve doesn't match exactly. Figure 4.9 illustrates this technique.

This time you really can't get the curve to match the template very well, because the line between the two anchor points is too straight, especially up towards the top point—the second point that you drew. This is caused by the fact the curve on top of the second anchor point moves toward the point at a different angle from the point. This causes the symmetry of the direction points to give you an unsatisfactory match on one side or the other. In this case, you matched the curve above the second anchor point fairly closely, but now you can't match the curve below very well.

There is an easy way to correct this discrepancy. Move the cursor back to the direction point that extends from the second anchor point toward the third. It is still a black ball, showing that it is selected for modification. What you need to do is to pull this direction point farther down without modifying the

Figure 4.9

The initial placement of the third anchor point will not match the outline exactly.

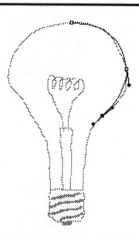

upper direction point. This will change the shape of the curve in an asymmetrical fashion, to match the template. To do so, press the ⌘ key. The cursor will change to the selection arrow. Holding down the ⌘ key, move the cursor to the direction point below the second anchor point and click and drag the direction point farther down the template until the curve matches the template. The end result is shown in Figure 4.10.

Notice, as you do this, that both the old line and the new line remain visible in the artwork. As soon as you release the mouse button, the old line will disappear and only the new one will remain. Also notice that this modification affected only one side of the anchor point, because the top direction point is tied down. When you're finished, the two direction points at the second anchor point are no longer symmetrical; later we will display them and you can see how they have been changed. You don't want to display them now because you're in the middle of constructing a complete figure. If you were to select the second anchor point for display, you would lose the continuity of the figure—that is, the cursor would change back to an ×.

Let's place two more anchor points. Place the next anchor point about the same distance *down* the stem of the light bulb as the third anchor point is *above* the stem. Click and drag to match the curve. This time, the curve is moving in the opposite direction from the earlier points, but the technique doesn't

Figure 4.10

Modifying the second anchor point allows you to match the template outline more exactly.

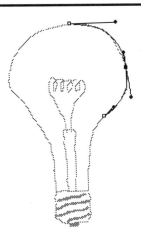

change. The next point should go just at the junction of the base of the light bulb and the bulb itself. The position of both points is shown in Figure 4.11, which shows the figure just after placement of the fifth point.

Now select the Zoom in tool and position the magnifying glass at the bottom of the light-bulb template. Click twice to magnify the image so you can see the fine detail necessary to match the smaller curves that make up the screw base of the bulb.

Notice that the template bits have become more pronounced and that you still can see the last anchor point quite clearly, along with its active direction points. Now you can use the techniques that you learned above to make curves match the template all along the base. Place the next anchor point a short distance up the first screw ring; the next on the other side of the curve that marks the ring; the next near the bottom ring; and then one on the other side of the ring. You can see how I placed these in Figure 4.12.

Use the same process to create the remainder of the base. Figure 4.13 shows the placement of the anchor points around the base to match the template curves.

Now use the Zoom out tool (and possibly the Scroll tool) to get back to the view you started with. Since light bulbs are symmetrical, you can pretty much pick points on the opposite side of the bulb that correspond to the

Figure 4.11

When you have finished the right side of the light bulb your Artwork & Template view should look something like this.

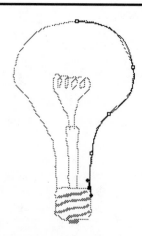

original points to trace the figure. In this case, don't be too concerned about matching the template closely. This template was drawn freehand, and thus may not have been very symmetrical to begin with. You may now wish to drop out the template and view the artwork only.

Figure 4.12

Trace the base of the light bulb by following the template along the right side of the base.

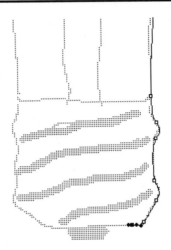

Figure 4.13

Complete the base of the light bulb by following the small curves that make up the left side.

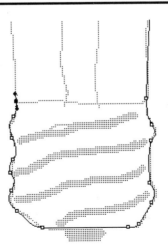

Finish up the light bulb. Remember to close the figure by placing the last point on top of the first one. When you have done that successfully, the cursor will change to an × again. You can see the anchor points that I used in Figure 4.14.

To add the finishing touches to this artwork, select Style ➤ Paint and set the painting parameters that you want. If you can't recall how to use this dialog box, review *Chapter 3*. Remember that all figures default to being filled with black; here, you want a simple outline, so click Fill to None and Stroke to 100% Black. Leave the line Weight at 1 point. Select View ➤ Preview Illustration to preview your image, as shown in Figure 4.15.

Let's finish this portion of the exercise by selecting File ➤ Save. This will present you with the dialog box that allows you to name the figure. I used *Light Bulb art* and saved the artwork in the same folder that the template is stored in. Then Illustrator will be able to match the two when we start again. In this case, both File ➤ Save and File ➤ Save As perform the same function.

Figure 4.14

The completed light bulb outline shows you all the anchor points that you use to make your artwork match the template.

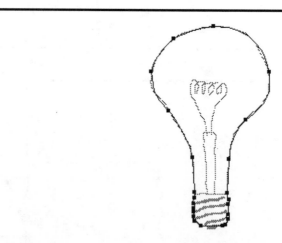

Figure 4.15

When you choose View ➤ *Preview Illustration, you see the outline of the light-bulb art as it will print.*

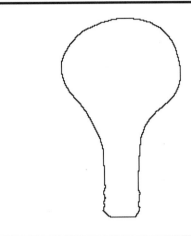

Exercise Summary

Now you have traced a complete, if basic, curved figure. You are now familiar with how to place and maneuver anchor and direction points and how they look both on the screen and on the final output. With these tools and techniques under your belt, you can now move on to modifying existing artwork by refining the light bulb art.

SUMMARY

There are many ways to select points within an artwork object in Illustrator. Remember that you can only modify points in artwork that have been selected. As we work along through more complex art, you will see that each of these methods of selection has a place where it is the preferred (and sometimes the only) method that will select the points that you want and no others.

Always save your modified artwork for future use. You can do this quite easily by simply selecting File ➤ Save (⌘–S). Do so now. There is no dialog box this time because the file already has a name; the new version simply replaces the old.

CHAPTER FIVE

Basic Drawing Rules

FEATURING

Useful drawing rules

Options for tool access

Shortcuts while
working on drawings

Modifying your artwork

DRAWING RULES

In the next exercise, tracing an outline drawing of an apple, you will practice the techniques that you learned in the last exercise. The exercise demonstrates some general guidelines for placing anchor points and direction points. It gives you practice matching curved lines to templates and provides a basis for further elaboration in later exercises.

The main focus of the discussion here will be on the placement of anchor and direction points. We won't discuss adjustment of the curved line segments, but if you have any problems with matching the curve or moving or altering a curve once you've created it on the artwork, re-read the sections in *Chapter 4* on placing and moving anchor points and direction points.

Exercise 5.1: The Apple Template

The apple template that we will use as an example is shown in Figure 5.1.

Figure 5.1

This simple apple template allows you to practice making curves to follow a template.

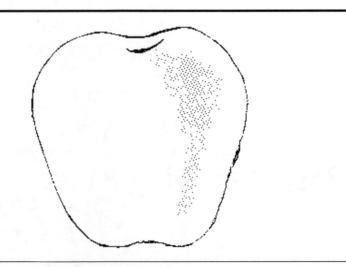

This is another MacPaint format template and is a simple outline of an apple with some shading. For now we will work on only the outline.

If you have a drawing program available, follow this sketch and create your own template. If you don't have a drawing program, follow the placement of the anchor points to create the artwork without a template. In this case you don't have to worry about matching the template. If you do create the artwork without using a template, please look carefully at the artwork:template figures to see how the two match. At some point you will have a template to match, so you need to observe the necessary techniques.

Tracing the Template

While you can start your artwork at any point on the template, the best places to start are those points that will have an anchor point on them no matter how you trace the image. Such points are usually the outside points of a smooth curve on the template. They are sometimes at the top or bottom of a figure when the curve there is smooth. Keep in mind that the curve will move smoothly to and from the point you select. It is most important to put the first point on a smooth, even curve, since you will return to this point in order to close the figure. If you place the first anchor point on a portion of the curve that will be difficult to match, you may not be able to make the artwork match the template when you close the figure. This can be extremely frustrating, particularly when you have already traced the entire figure.

The Bump Rule

The first rule about placement of anchor points is the *bump rule*. It tells you to place them on either side of a "bump" rather than on the top or bottom. If you think of a curved line as a series of hills and valleys, this rule says that the anchor points should go on the sides of the hills, not on the peak, and not at the bottom of the valley.

The exercises you did with simple curved line segments in *Chapter 4* demonstrate why this rule works so well. Illustrator always tries to make a smooth curve going to and from an anchor point, but you can easily make the segment between the points curve as radically as you like. So placing the anchor points on the side of the hill gives you a lot more flexibility to match the arc of the hill than working from the peak or the valley would give. The top line segment in Figure 5.2 gives you a graphic example of this rule.

Here the anchor points have been placed on each side of the peaks and valleys of the line. If you try to place them on the tops and bottoms, you will find that the curve cannot be as smooth and regular as you can get it when the anchor points are on the sides. The bottom line segment in Figure 5.2 shows the disadvantages of using anchor points at the tops and bottoms of the curve and clearly demonstrates why you want to follow the bump rule.

The bump rule can be applied to closed figures as well as wavy lines, to give you some idea of where to place anchor points along the figure. Of course, in a figure like the apple template, it may not be so obvious where the "bumps" are. There are clearly two bumps on both the top and bottom of the figure, but the long sides make it difficult to determine where you need to place another point. The slight but noticeable indentation along the right side of the apple template calls for an additional anchor point; it is a very gentle "bump", but I think it contributes to the overall shape. The placement of the anchor points for this exercise is shown in Figure 5.3.

In this figure, you can see how the bump rule influenced the placement of each point. The bumps are more or less pronounced along the template, so the placement of the anchor points varies to match the curves of the

Figure 5.2

The bump rule tells you to place anchor points on the sides of bumps rather than at the tops or bottoms.

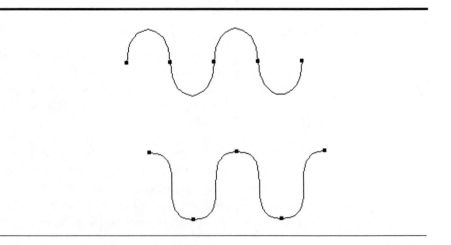

Figure 5.3

This shows you the correct placement of the anchor points for the apple template according to the bump rule.

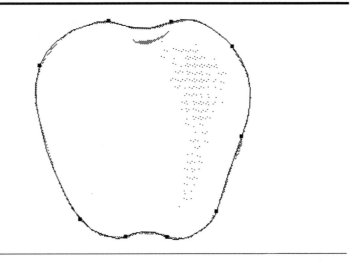

template. Nevertheless, two anchor points define each bump and are placed on each side of it to create the desired shape.

The Stride Rule

Figure 5.3 also illustrates the other good rule for selection and placement of anchor points: the *stride rule*. This rule says that you should trace a template using the largest strides possible that will still match the template: in other words, you should use the fewest number of line segments that will accurately render the template into artwork.

You can get some idea of how many strides to take to finish a drawing by combining this rule with the bump rule. We identified two bumps on the top of the apple, two on the bottom, and one shallow one on the right side—a total of five bumps. Two points are required to determine each bump—a total of ten points. Since this is a closed figure, however, two of those points will become one as you put the end of the last bump on the beginning of the first. So you need nine points to define your artwork, and you should try to make the apple artwork consist of no more than nine strides or segments (and no fewer—remember the bumps). Precisely nine points are used to define the artwork in Figure 5.3.

Following the stride rule is both efficient and accurate. First, you will find it much easier to match a template accurately when you use large segments. It is harder to manipulate smaller segments and more difficult to generate a smooth curve with them. Since Illustrator creates such smooth curves, you really want to let it do as much of the curve matching as possible. Every anchor point constrains the curve to attach exactly to that point, so the more anchor points you place, the more work you are doing that Illustrator could do for you. When there is a bump in the curve, guide the curve to match it by placing an anchor point; where there are no bumps, let Illustrator do the work.

You can visualize this most easily by thinking of straight line segments. For straight lines, corners are the equivalent of bumps for the curves. You need to place an anchor point at every corner because the line changes direction. But there's no point in placing anchor points between corners, since there is no change in direction: the line will run straight on anyway. The same logic applies to curved line segments. When there is a change in direction—at the beginning or end of a bump—you need to put in an anchor point; when there is no change, you don't need to add an anchor point.

Efficiency is the second reason for the stride rule. Illustrator generates code to match the curve at each anchor point that you create. Each point represents information that has to be generated, transmitted, and interpreted within the output device to draw the line that you have specified. So fewer points require less information, less storage, and less transmission time. This means faster output for your artwork. So keep the anchor points down to the minimum necessary to accurately match the template.

The One-Third Rule

The *one-third rule* governs creation of direction points. This rule says that you should make the line connecting the anchor point and the direction point about one-third of the total distance between the anchor point and the next anchor point. This rule is most useful on the first anchor point; after that, you will just position the direction points to match the template. Figure 5.4, a view of the artwork only for our apple, illustrates the one-third rule from the starting anchor point.

Figure 5.4

The length of this direction point from the anchor points illustrates the one-third rule.

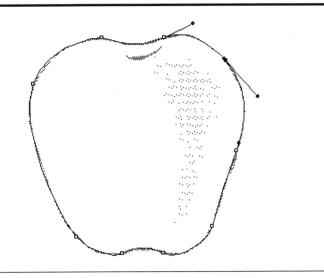

In this figure, the point on the upper-right shoulder of the apple was chosen as the starting anchor point for the figure. Notice how the direction point extends out about one-third of the distance of the first segment. The direction of the line is tangent to the curve of the template. These two features together give you a pretty good idea of how the first anchor point should look.

But the second and third anchor points illustrate clearly how the one-third rule does not apply once you begin to trace. The curve takes such a slight bend here that the direction points are only a short distance from their respective anchor points, while the distance between the anchor points is much greater than the lines from the direction points and the anchor points. But since these are continuations of the existing curve, there is no real difficulty in making the curve match the template and ignoring the one-third rule.

Completing the Apple

When you are done with the apple, preview it to see the final artwork in action. I recommend that you change the default 100% Black fill in the Paint Style dialog box to something a little more attractive. I used 50% Black with a stroke of 100% Black and a line Weight of 0.1.

Save this artwork since we are going to reuse it in later chapters when you work on new techniques to add more complexity to existing artwork. I saved it as *Simple Apple art* and stored it in the same folder as the template it was drawn from.

OPTIONS AND SHORTCUTS

This section covers ways to alter your artwork and discusses some shortcuts for making your work faster and easier. Up to now we have stuck, generally, to the most basic methods of doing things and accessing tools in order to ensure that you were able to easily follow what was done. All the techniques that you have learned are effective and straightforward, but you have probably wondered whether there were some shortcuts. Here they are.

Exercise 5.2: Refining the Light Bulb Art

First, let's add some features to the light bulb you worked on earlier. You saved the result as *Light Bulb art*, as shown in Figure 4.15 in *Chapter 4*. Load this artwork back into Illustrator. You should also have the template associated with the artwork loaded automatically with it. If the template isn't loaded, locate it and associate it with the artwork as described earlier in the chapter so that both artwork and template are visible. Remember that this is the modified version of the artwork, so it no longer conforms very closely to the template.

You are now going to add the filament in the center of the template to the artwork that you prepared earlier.

In the center you see a wire filament sticking up out of a glass supporting rod. You now want to add this to the artwork you have already prepared.

The filament and the rod are really two distinct objects. It will be best to draw each of them separately and then combine them in the form you want the final drawing to take. This kind of overlay is a common technique in Illustrator and one which you will find most useful.

Adding the Filament

First we will draw the filament in the center of the screen. This image is still rather small for the fine work that you want to do, so you need to zoom in on it. You could select the Zoom in tool from the Toolbox, position it over the filament, and click—but there is a faster way. As you will be magnifying around the center of the screen, you can dispense with the selection of a zoom point by using the magnification cursor. Just double-click on the Zoom in tool to make Illustrator magnify the image around the center of the screen.

Illustrator contains many such shortcuts to speed up your handling of images. To reduce the image instead of magnifying it, you could double-click the Zoom in tool while holding down the Option key.

The filament should now be in the center of your screen, showing from the top of the wire down to the top of the rod. If it is not quite centered, use the Scroll tool to move the image until it looks like Figure 5.5.

Figure 5.5

You magnify the center of the screen to show you the filament section of the template.

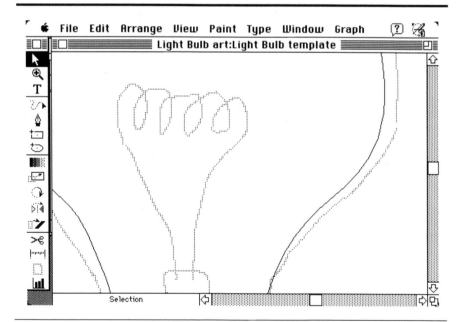

Unlike the previous portions of the artwork, the filament is not a closed fig-ure. It begins and ends in the top of the rod. Select the Pen tool. Beginning at the left-hand side of the filament at the top of the rod, place and adjust the first anchor points. Remember the bump rule and the one-third rule. Place three points: one at the start of the filament; the second around the first curve, about half-way up the side; and the third at the edge of the spiral band. These first three anchor points are shown in Figure 5.6, along with the positioning of the cursor for the next anchor point.

Notice how the next anchor point is positioned. As you may have realized, the spiral curve that forms the center of the filament is remarkably similar to the wave form that you saw in Figure 5.2 as an illustration of the bump rule. Here, the bumps overlap, but the principle for placement of the anchor points is the same. Go ahead and finish the spiral curve. Don't worry too much about the template, but use your eye instead to get a pleasing image. Notice that Illustrator is much easier to control in these circumstances than a drawing program would be, since you don't have to keep your hand steady while drawing the loops. In fact, the irregularity of the template loops is mostly due to my inability to trace a smooth curve. Finish the rest of the fila-ment by adding a point along the right side to bring the wire down. Then

Figure 5.6

Here is how you place the first four anchor points on the filament section of the template.

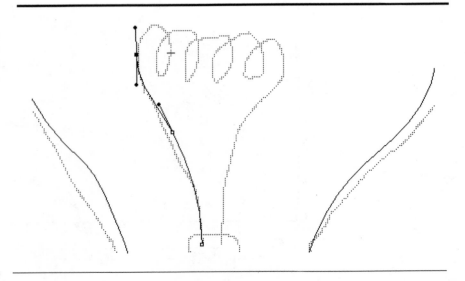

add the last point at the bottom right, opposite the starting anchor point, on top of the rod.

You may find that you begin to go off the screen as you pull the direction point down from the final anchor point. This results in very rapid scrolling of the image in the direction that you're pulling, and usually you will lose sight of the anchor point. Don't worry. Just release the mouse button and change to the Selection tool. Then move the offending direction point back up toward the anchor point where you want it. If necessary, use the Scroll tool to adjust the image so you can correctly complete the figure. Then get a wider view by double-clicking the Zoom in tool while holding the Option key down. The final result should look something like Figure 5.7.

To properly finish this part of the exercise, let's set up the filament artwork to appear correctly on the output. Remember that the default setup is to fill the artwork with black. You want the filament to paint as a thin wire, not a solid figure. Select the filament artwork by using the Option key and selecting any portion of the filament artwork. All the anchor points should appear as black squares. Now select Paint ➤ Style. Change the Fill option to None and the Stroke option to 100% Black. I used a line Weight of 0.5 points, but try various weights to see what you think is best. To see the result, exit the Paint

Figure 5.7

When you finish the filament section of the artwork it should look something like this.

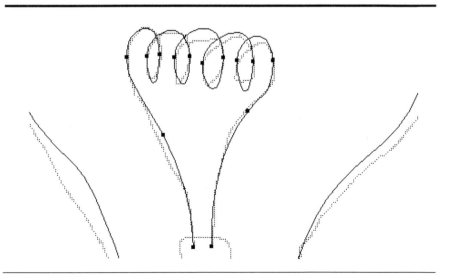

Style dialog box and choose View ➤ Preview. When you're satisfied, save the artwork so you have a backup point to return to. It's always a good idea to periodically save your work, especially when you come to a natural break point like this.

You may wonder why the filament artwork would paint as solid black when the figure isn't closed; after all, the two end points, although close together, are quite distinct. Actually, if the Fill option is chosen in the Paint Style dialog box, Illustrator closes any figure by drawing an implicit line joining the two endpoints of the figure to be filled. The result can be surprising if you didn't expect to fill the artwork.

No doubt you've noticed how often you want to use these zoom tools while you're drawing a figure to see more detail or more of the figure. You used the quick technique above to zoom in and out from the center of the screen, but you still had to move the cursor over to the Toolbox to access the Zoom in tool. Similarly, you had to readjust the figure several times to get the portion of the image that you wanted to work on in the center of the screen. This problem becomes more pronounced the more that you have magnified the image, since you need to move more to place the anchor points.

The two zoom tools are probably the tools most often used in conjunction with the various drawing tools. Because of the need to jump back and forth so often between these tools and a basic tool, like the Pen tool, Illustrator has some shortcuts for access that do not require moving back to the Toolbox.

Summary

This chapter introduced the bump rule and the stride rule for placing anchor points and direction points, and the one-third rule for placing direction points. Later you learned a variety of shortcuts for accessing tools and features quickly. Here is a summary of these shortcuts for reference and review.

Function	Access
To access the Scroll tool (hand)	Press and hold down the spacebar

Function	Access
To access the Selection tool (arrow)	Press and hold down the ⌘ key
To access the Zoom in tool (magnifying glass with +)	Press and hold down the spacebar and the ⌘ key
To access the Zoom out tool (magnifying glass with −)	Press and hold down the spacebar, ⌘ key, and Option key
To zoom in on the center of the screen	Double-click on the Zoom in tool icon in the Toolbox or double-click on the Zoom out tool while holding down the Option key
To zoom out on the center of the screen	Double-click on the Zoom in tool icon in the Toolbox while holding down the Option key; or double-click on the Zoom out tool icon
To select all points on a given figure	Press the Option key while selecting any part of the figure with the Selection tool

CHAPTER

SIX

SIX

Drawing Basic
Paths and Layers

ILLUSTRATOR'S PATHS

Illustrator creates artwork by linking line segments to form complete objects. The line segments that make up a graphic object are called a *path*. Because all Illustrator artwork is made up of paths, it is important that you understand how Illustrator displays and uses paths.

A path consists of a series of points. In Illustrator, the points that make up a path are connected by line segments. The points have a definite order, beginning with the first one that you place on the page and continuing to the last one in the path. The line segments may be straight or curved. A path may be *closed*, which means that the last point on the path is connected to the first point by a line segment, or it may be *open*, which means that the last point on the path is not connected to the first point. The points that define the line segments that make up the path are the anchor points.

How Paths Display

Illustrator displays paths on the screen in a variety of ways. The differences depend on what type of path is being displayed, and whether all or part of the path is selected. Let's look at the variety of path displays that you may see. Figure 6.1 shows a variety of paths, both straight and curved, with segments selected and not selected.

First, let's look at how Illustrator displays points in your artwork. Line 1 shows you two single points—since a path can consist of only one point. The point on the left is not selected and thus looks like a small ×. This is the display for a path that consists of a single point when the point is not selected. The point on the right also makes a path, but it has been selected. As a result, it has the standard appearance of a selected point, a black square.

Lines 2 to 4 show you three paths that each consist of two straight line segments. The first path, line 2, is unselected; as you can see, it is impossible

Figure 6.1

These examples show you how Illustrator displays paths under different conditions.

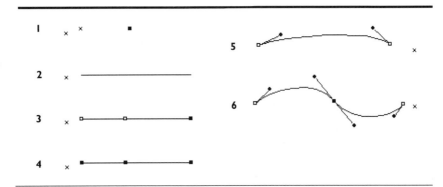

to tell how many segments are in the path. The second path, line 3, has the point at the right end of the path selected (the black square). Notice that all the anchor points that make up the path are visible. The anchor points that are not selected appear as small hollow squares. Selected anchor points always appear as solid black squares. In Line 4, all the points are selected. This selects the entire path and allows you to move it as a unit. These visual clues are important when you are working with complex artwork.

The other two paths on the page, lines 5 and 6, show you some things about curved segments as well as displaying some more types of points. The first segment, line 5, is selected; but none of the anchor points on the path are themselves selected. Since the segment that is selected in line 5 is curved, the two direction points are selected, one at each anchor point, that determine the actual placement of the curve between the anchor points. This happens when you click with the Selection tool on a single segment but not on an anchor point. Since you cannot see the anchor points when the path is not selected, as illustrated in line 2, you must sometimes select some part of the path to see where the anchor points are. In any case, if no points have been selected, then you have selected the path but not the anchor points. This is important, for example, if you want to move a path. Line 4, which is completely selected, can be moved as a unit. If you try to move line 3, where only a single point is selected, only the selected point will move. If you try to move line 5, where the path is selected but no points, the path itself will move, but the anchor points will not; in effect, you will move the direction points but not the anchor points.

Line 6 shows you a path consisting of two curved segments. The anchor point in the middle of the path is selected. This also selects the segment or segments connected with that anchor point; in this case, both the segment leading up to the point and the one leading away from it. The direction points that govern each of these segments are also visible. Don't be fooled here; even though only one direction point is shown at the end of each segment, the anchor points *do* have another direction point facing away from the ones shown. The other direction points are not visible because they are not part of the selected segments.

All of these paths are open. The beginning and ending points of an open path are called *endpoints*. Endpoints are important because they are where you can add additional segments if you want to extend the path. They also have some special properties that we will cover as we work through the exercises in this and later chapters. For example, you already know that you cannot cut a path at an endpoint.

Exercise 6.1: Joining Paths

There are two ways to extend an open path. One is to select the Pen tool, click on an endpoint of the path, and then continue drawing normally. This works quite well, and you will use this method in several of the exercises as we proceed. If you are drawing curves, you can use the Freehand tool instead. The second way to extend a path is to join it to another open path that you have already drawn. Here is an example that shows how this works. Figure 6.2 shows two open paths.

Figure 6.2

*Two open paths
that you can join to
make a single path*

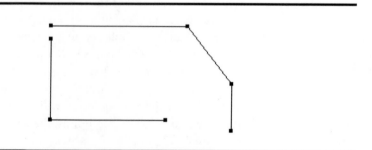

In this figure, each path is selected to show the anchor points. Each of these paths is painted as a line, with Fill set to None, Stroke at 100% Black, and a line Weight of 10. (You'll see why the lines are so heavy presently.) Let's suppose that you want to join these two paths at the top-left corner, where each has an endpoint. Your first thought might be to select one of the paths as a unit—so all the anchor points are selected—and drag it onto the endpoint of the other path, as shown in Figure 6.3.

Only the lower path is selected since it was the one that moved. If you click away from these two paths, the result will look like a single path—but it's not. How can you tell? When you select either of the paths you will see only the anchor points for that path. In Figure 6.3, notice that only the anchor points for the lower path are visible. This alerts you that the upper part of the figure is in fact a separate path.

Ah, you say, but why should I care? Figure 6.4 shows why you should care.

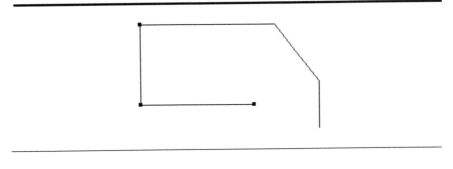

Figure 6.3

Two open paths after the endpoints at the top-left corner have been moved onto one another.

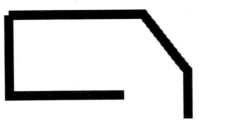

Figure 6.4

Here's how two open paths that overlap at an endpoint will appear when they print.

This is the Preview Illustration view (choose View ➤ Preview Illustration) of these two paths. There is a small notch in the upper-left corner where the endpoints of the two paths lie on top of one another. Because the two paths are still separate, Illustrator paints each one as if the other path weren't there. Because of that, the ends of the paths are squared off, and the top corner doesn't get filled in. The effect would be the same, although not so visible, even if the lines were very thin. Usually, this is not what you want when you join two paths.

Joining Overlapping Endpoints

There is a simple solution to this problem. Once you have moved the two endpoints on top of one another, choose Arrange ➤ Join. This brings up the dialog box shown in Figure 6.5.

In this case, leave the setting at Corner point, which is the default, and click OK. Now select View ➤ Preview Illustration and the notch will be replaced with a single corner. Notice that when you click anywhere on the figure, all the anchor points show. This tells you that this is now one path.

Although you have joined two of the endpoints on this figure, the figure itself is still an open path, since the other two endpoints are distinct and visible. You'll use this for some additional work in a moment, but for now, let's use it to illustrate another interesting property of open paths. So far, this path has only been stroked. However, it is possible to fill an open path, too; the question is, what happens when you do that? Select Paint ➤ Style and set the Fill to 30% Black in the Paint Style dialog box. Then return to the art-work and select View ➤ Preview Illustration. The result looks like Figure 6.6.

Figure 6.5

The Join dialog box allows you to link together any two endpoints.

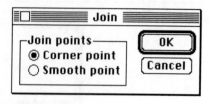

Figure 6.6

An example of how an open path will paint if you select Fill in the Paint Style dialog box

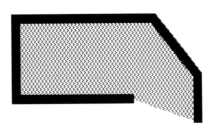

The fill color is placed inside the path exactly as if the two endpoints were joined by a straight line. When you set a Fill option for an open path, Illustrator implicitly closes the path when it fills it with the selected color. Since the default settings in the Paint Style dialog box are Fill with 100% Black and no Stroke, it's easy to accidentally forget and draw an open path that is filled. Figure 6.7 shows you two paths and Figure 6.8 shows you the results when you preview these paths.

The path on the right consists of three straight line segments in a z pattern; but the path has been painted as a pair of triangles. Since the path is filled and not stroked, Illustrator has connected the first and last points of the path to make a kind of Art Deco lightning bolt. If you ever see such strange patterns in your artwork unexpectedly, you should immediately suspect that you have filled something that you meant to stroke.

The pattern on the left is a simple, straight line and seems to display as one. This is a most insidious error, since the appearance of the line onscreen is almost normal. However, the line is not normal. In fact, it is exactly one pixel wide, since that is the smallest area that Illustrator can paint. Effectively what Illustrator has done is take the beginning and ending points of the line and close them to make a very thin rectangle. This is fairly visible onscreen, and will be visible (as a very thin hairline) on a LaserWriter. However, if you were to print to a high-resolution imagesetter, the line would disappear. To avoid this, set the paint values for your artwork as you go and be suspicious of lines that are very thin, unless you have explicitly made them thin.

Figure 6.7

Two open paths that have been filled with 100% Black instead of being stroked

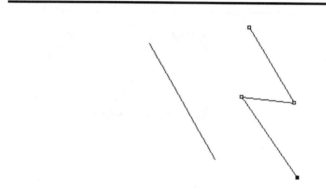

Figure 6.8

How the same two paths look when previewed

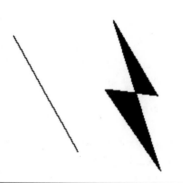

Joining Distant Endpoints

Besides connecting two overlapping endpoints, the Arrange ➤ Join command can also be used to connect two distant endpoints. Go back to the artwork in Figure 6.6. This is still an open path, since the other two endpoints are not connected.

To close these endpoints, select them using a selection marquee. Your screen should now look like Figure 6.9.

Once again select Arrange ➤ Join (⌘-J). This time, no dialog box appears. A straight line will connect the two endpoints, closing the figure. When you select two endpoints that are not on top of one another and choose Arrange ➤ Join, Illustrator simply joins them with a straight line.

Figure 6.9

*Select the two endpoints
for the Arrange ➤ Join
command.*

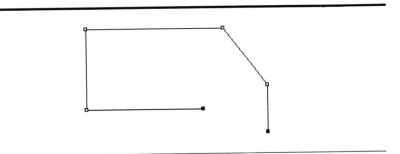

In this case, the two lines have the same paint settings, so the line joining them takes on those characteristics: Stroke 100% Black with a line Weight of 10 Points. The Fill settings also remain in effect for the newly closed path. If you join two endpoints that have different paint characteristics, the combined path will have the paint characteristics of the path that is in front; normally the last path that you drew. This can have some surprising results, so always check the paint characteristics of any paths you join.

Connecting Curved and Straight Line Segments

The methods that you have learned for joining paths allow you to connect any two open paths, no matter what type of line segments are used in them. However, you also need to understand how to connect straight line segments to curved ones while you are drawing a continuous path. So far, you have drawn paths with either all straight line segments or all curved line segments. This section shows you how to draw a path that contains both straight and curved segments.

The basic problem here is that, under most circumstances, you want Illustrator to continue making the type of line that you are already drawing. So if the line segment coming into the anchor point is straight, then Illustrator expects the one going out to be straight. Conversely, if it is curved, then the following segment is expected to be curved. If you want to follow a straight segment with a curved one, or vice versa, you must let Illustrator know that. This technique is quite simple. Here is a short, easy exercise that shows you how to do it.

Open a new Illustrator document with no template. If you want to match the figures here, show the rulers as well (⌘-R). Now select the Pen tool and draw a straight line segment from (16, 36) to (32, 36), using the Shift key to constrain the segment.

Now you want to add a curved segment to this line. If you simply move the cursor and click again, the resulting segment will be straight. To make a curved segment, you need to convert the right-hand endpoint into a curved anchor point. To do that, move the cursor to the endpoint and click. Continue holding down the mouse button and drag the resulting direction point down and to the right, to (36, 35). The result should look like Figure 6.10.

Now move the Pen cursor to (32, 28) and click and drag the direction point to (28, 27). This gives you a nice, rounded end to the figure. However, if you don't change it, the next line segment will again be curved. To add a straight line segment, go back to the anchor point at (32, 28) and click on it again. Now move the cursor to (16, 28), hold down the Option key (to force the line segment to be precisely horizontal), and click once. This adds a

Figure 6.10

You can convert the endpoint of a straight line segment into a curved line anchor point by clicking again on the anchor point and dragging the direction point.

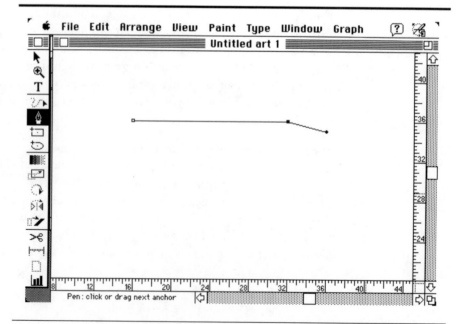

straight line segment from the last anchor point to the current one, as shown in Figure 6.11.

Now you can add another curved segment to complete the figure. Once again, click on the anchor point you just created at (16, 28) and drag the resulting direction point to (12, 29). Now move the cursor back up to the starting point at (16, 36) and click and drag the cursor out to (20, 37). Notice as you do this that there is no direction point underneath your cursor. The direction point is on the curved side only, away from your cursor. This happens because the starting anchor point is already set to a straight line and so does not have a visible direction point. This looks a little strange, I know, but it's quite consistent and understandable, once you're used to it. The completed figure, displaying all its anchor and direction points, is shown in Figure 6.12.

Note that the direction points extend from the anchor points only on the side with the curved segments. There are no visible direction points on the straight sides.

Figure 6.11

You add a straight line segment to a curved one by clicking once on the endpoint of the curved segment before drawing the straight line.

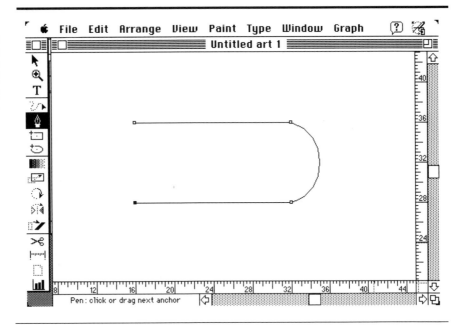

Figure 6.12

A complete figure with a combination of curved and straight line segments

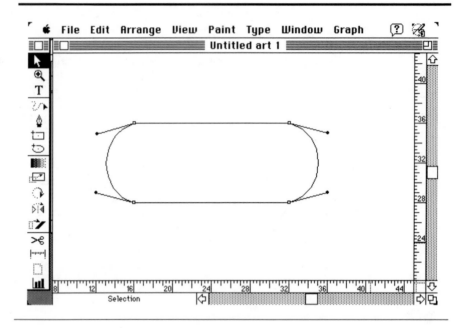

There are two points to learn here. First, every anchor point has two sides, which have different characteristics depending on whether the segment extending from that side is straight or curved. Second, you can convert an anchor point from a straight to a curved segment by clicking again on the anchor point and continuing the path. Later in the book you will learn about the special Convert Direction Point tool (an alternate to the Split Path tool), which will change any existing anchor point from straight to curved segments or vice versa.

CORNERS

One very important skill you have yet to learn is that of making corners on curves. You have already made corners when you joined straight lines together, as in Exercise 6.1, but let's discuss the issue of corners in more detail.

Corner Anchor Points

The basic structure of Illustrator curves is that the curve moves smoothly toward and away from each anchor point. The default direction points, therefore, lie along a straight line and are equidistant from the anchor point. You learned earlier how to control the curve shape by changing the distance of one direction point from the anchor point. But in all these exercises, both direction points and the anchor point between them lay on a single, straight line. If you want the curve to bend in a different direction, to form a pointed corner like a pointed arch, you need to alter that relationship so that the two direction points no longer lie on a single straight line. Instead each direction point lies on its own line. Then there is one line from one direction point to the anchor point on one side and a separate, diverging line from the anchor point to the direction point on the other side. Such points are called *corner points* in Illustrator.

Creating a Corner

At a corner point, the two diverging lines are still tangent to the curve at the anchor point. But since the lines diverge, the curve no longer moves in a continuous arc toward and away from the anchor point. Instead, it has become a corner. Figure 6.13 shows two similar curves. Curve A should look quite familiar, because it is the type of curve that you have created up to now. Curve B, however, has a corner point in the center of the arc, which changes the direction of the curve at that point.

Figure 6.13

Curve A is a continuous curve. Curve B however has a corner point in the middle of the curve.

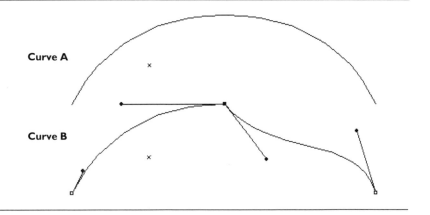

Curve A

Curve B

Notice that the left side of both curves is identical. In Curve A the direction points for the center anchor point are in a straight line, while in Curve B the direction points form two diverging lines with the anchor point. This arrangement of the direction points is the fundamental technique that you use to create curved corners.

To create this new line from the anchor point, move the pen cursor back to the anchor point, press Option, and click and drag the direction point to where you want it. The real trick to this is to have a good idea of where to place the direction point to generate the desired curve. Use the rule of one-third, which you learned in *Chapter 5*, as a guide: make the distance from an anchor point to the direction point about one-third of the total distance to the next anchor point. But the best way to learn proper placement is by practice. Therefore we will do an example to help you get a feel for the creating and placing of corner points.

Exercise 6.2: Revising the Apple Artwork

For this exercise, you can either use a new apple template and start your artwork anew, or you can work without a template, building from the artwork you created in *Chapter 5*. If you want to use a template, use MacPaint to modify your previous template to add a leaf and stem so it looks something like Figure 6.14. Save this file as *Revised Apple template*.

This is just the previous template with the addition of a stem and leaf. Now suppose you want to copy your previous artwork onto this template and then add the leaf and stem to create a new piece of artwork. (Copying the artwork would save you from having to retrace the apple.) You know, from the discussion regarding artwork and templates in *Chapter 4*, that you cannot simply associate a new template with an existing piece of artwork. You could delete the previous template and rename this template, but then you wouldn't be able to return to the old artwork and template combination. The trick to associating a new template with existing artwork without changing the old template is copying the artwork to a new document.

Start by calling up the previous artwork. Then select the entire artwork, using one of the methods you have learned: the selection marquee or the Edit ➤ Select All command (⌘-A). When the entire artwork is selected, all the

Figure 6.14

If you wish to use a template, revise your apple template to add a leaf and stem.

anchor points appear as black squares. Now choose Edit ➤ Copy. Close the old artwork and select File ➤ New. When the dialog box asks you for the template, select the Revised Apple template.

Finally, select Edit ➤ Paste. This will place the artwork from the Clipboard onto the current drawing surface in the center of the screen. The artwork may not be exactly where you want it, but you can just reposition it. The entire artwork that you just pasted onto the drawing surface is already selected, so you can use the selection pointer to move the artwork into the desired position. You may want to magnify or reduce the page to get the correct placement. When you're done, you should have the old artwork placed over the parts of the new template that it matches. This will look like Figure 6.15.

Figure 6.15

You can use cut and paste to match the existing artwork to a portion of the revised template.

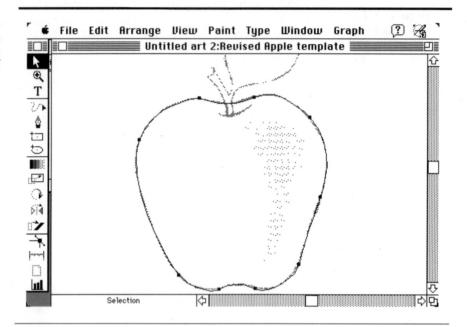

Adding the Leaf and Stem

You are now ready to begin tracing the leaf and stem for the apple. In order to accurately follow the new parts of this template and keep the current work in focus, you will need to magnify the view of the template and move around some. Start by magnifying the base of the stem to 200%.

Select the Pen tool and, beginning at the right-hand base of the stem, trace the stem and leaf until you reach the first serration on the leaf. Remember the bump rule and notice that there are just two bumps between the base of the stem and the beginning of the serration. At this point, your artwork should look something like Figure 6.16.

I have moved the artwork so that you can see all the anchor points that have been placed so far. In practice, the direction points on the top of the screen would have to be on the screen.

Now magnify the serrated part of the leaf. The first serrations on this side of the leaf are best represented as a series of straight lines.

Figure 6.16

As you begin the stem and leaf artwork, your screen will look like this.

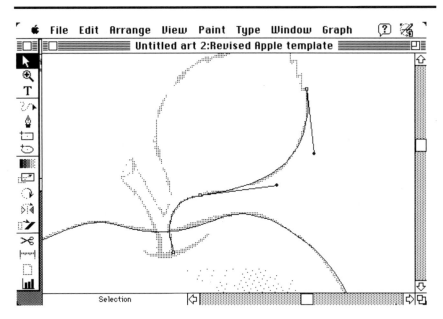

Remember that you change from an arc to a straight line by clicking once on the anchor point where the change occurs. This will eliminate the direction point on the side you are working on and make the next segment a straight line from the chosen anchor point. Figure 6.19 has an arrow pointing to the anchor point where the leaf artwork changes from a curve to a straight line.

Now you want to continue the end of the leaf with a curve. This will lead to the tip of the leaf, which will be a corner anchor point. Position the cursor on the tip and drag the direction point up and out to make the edge of the leaf curve *inward*. Then return the cursor to the anchor point at the tip and click on it while holding down the Option key; then continue to drag the direction point from the anchor point down toward the leaf. The final position as you do this should look something like Figure 6.17.

The delta cursor shows about how far to pull down the new direction point. You could move it anywhere, but since the leaf is fairly symmetrical at the tip, make the new direction point similar to the first direction point in length and angle from the anchor point. Now move down to the next serration on the top of the leaf and click and drag in the ordinary fashion to finish creating the curved corner point at the tip of the leaf. The final drawing should look like Figure 6.18.

You still have the full range of edit and movement controls as before. For example, if you wanted to move the corner anchor point in toward the leaf, you could just press ⌘ to activate the Selection tool and then move this

Figure 6.17

When you get to the leaf tip, you must add a corner anchor point.

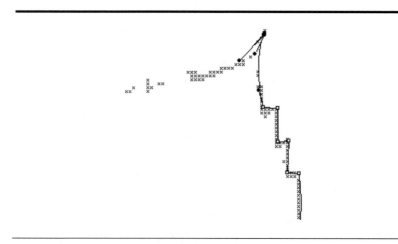

Figure 6.18

When you have finished the leaf tip art, your screen should look like this.

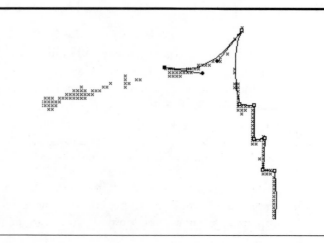

anchor point as you would any other. Similarly, you could move the direction points as you normally would if you wanted to alter the shape of the curve. Note that any movement of the direction point on one side of the corner anchor point will not affect the other side as it did in preceding exercises. You have effectively uncoupled the two sides.

Continue tracing the leaf edge, making the serrations with straight lines. To transition from a curve, such as the leaf tip, to a straight line, just return to the anchor point and click once on it. Then move the cursor to where you want the next anchor point for the straight segment and click again. Use this technique to create a finished leaf tip on both sides.

When you come to the last serration, change from a straight line segment to a curve. Go back to the anchor point, click once and drag the direction point the way you want it to go. You may find it helpful at this point to reduce the magnification of the leaf in order to finish the rest of the curve. Change magnification and then finish the leaf to the point where it joins the stem again. When you're done, the artwork should look like Figure 6.19.

This point is another corner anchor point. You want to turn the curve back up toward the top of the stem, so you need to change directions. As before, move the cursor to the anchor point, hold down Option, and click and drag

Figure 6.19

To complete the leaf, return to its junction with the stem.

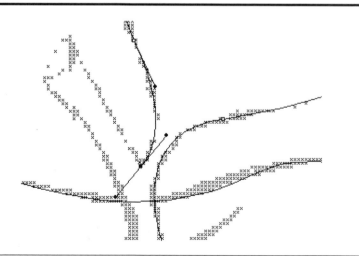

the direction point. Make sure the segment remains tangent to the curve shown on the template. Figure 6.20 shows the result, magnified.

Now move to the top of the stem, to the point of the oval that forms the cut end. Click and drag to create a curve that matches the template for the top of the stem. This point is also a corner point, so you have to use the Option-click-drag technique once again to move the direction point toward the other corner of the oval. Complete the top of the stem by creating another anchor point at the opposite end of the oval. This will leave you positioned to finish the stem. Don't worry for now about the rest of the oval that forms the cut end of the stem. Continue down toward the base of the stem in one arc and then close the figure with a straight line across to the starting anchor point. The result will look something like Figure 6.21.

Let's preview the artwork now. Choose View ➤ Preview Illustration. The new artwork is filled in with black, while the old artwork is still in the gray shade that you set for it earlier. Return to the artwork and template view of the drawing surface (choose View ➤ Artwork & Template) and select the new

Figure 6.20

To begin the stem, you must insert another corner anchor point.

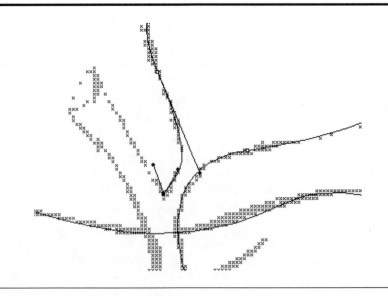

Figure 6.21

*When you have
completed the basic leaf
and stem outline, your
screen should look like
this.*

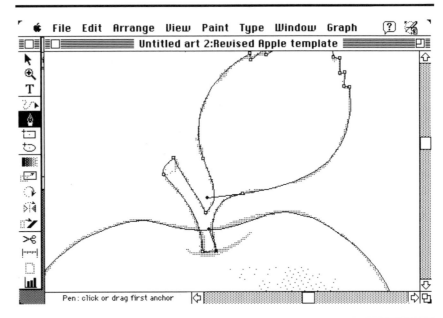

artwork. Choose Paint ➤ Style and set the Fill option to White and set Stroke
to 100% Black with a line Weight of 1. You need to set Fill to White instead
of to None to overlay the colored-in portion of the apple that lies behind the
stem outline. If you use None, the stem and leaf will be transparent and the
apple will show through even though the stem is painted in front of it; with
White, the stem will be painted, covering the apple.

Now zoom in on the oval at the top of the stem. You need to add the bottom of the oval to complete the stem. Select the Pen tool again and position
it on top of the first anchor point at the top of the oval. Click and drag a
direction point tangent to the bottom curve of the oval. Move down to the
anchor point at the bottom of the oval and complete the bottom of the curve
by clicking there. Draw the direction point out to match the bottom of the
oval. Figure 6.22 gives you a good look at this bottom arc using the Artwork
Only view (View ➤ Artwork Only).

Figure 6.22

Add the bottom arc to complete the top of the stem.

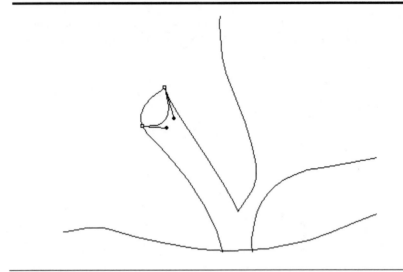

Summary

So now you have traced two complete, if basic, curved figures. You are familiar with how to place and maneuver anchor and direction points and you know how they look both onscreen and in the final output. You have also seen how the paint order or layers of your Illustrator artwork affects the final output. This still leaves a lot of ground for discussion and exploration, but at this point you have mastered the basic features of Illustrator. In Chapter 7, you will learn more about using graphics that have already been created, whether by you or someone else, as a basis for further modifications.

CHAPTER SEVEN

SEVEN

Reshaping Paths

ALTERING EXISTING GRAPHICS

In *Chapter 6*, you learned how to add details to an existing piece of artwork. In this chapter, you will learn techniques for inserting new art into an existing graphic or modifying an existing piece of artwork. You do this by changing or reshaping existing elements. Eventually, you may want to create a library of Illustrator images that you can call up and use as a basis for your work. Freedom and flexibility are some of the most impressive and desirable features of Illustrator artwork.

All of these techniques require you to select a portion of an existing artwork and cut out space for the new material. You will use the Split Path tool to cut into the existing artwork. This process can save you time and effort that you would spend on redrawing existing artwork.

The concept of the split path is suggested by the tool's icon: a scissors. Recall that you can cut an Illustrator graphic at any point of a figure, except at an endpoint. This would be like trying to cut a piece of string at the end.

If you cut in the middle of a line, you end up with two new endpoints at the point of the cut. If the segment is a curve, then each endpoint will have direction points suitable to the arc of the curve at that point. If the line is straight, of course, the endpoints will have no visible direction points. If you cut on an anchor point, you end up with two overlapping endpoints. The upshot is that you can cut off a line segment in its entirety and delete or move it without affecting the rest of the figure.

Exercise 7.1: Simple Modifications

Let's use the Split Path tool to modify an existing piece of artwork. Bring up the apple artwork that you used in *Chapter 6*, where you added a stem and leaf to the basic apple outline. You will modify the apple to add a second leaf.

Begin by scrolling up until the leaf and stem are in the center of the screen. Then use the Zoom in tool to magnify the junction of the stem and leaf. You are going to cut the entire leaf off the stem and copy it to make a second leaf. Get close to the stem and leaf junction so you can see what's happening as you make the cuts. Later, you can move back from the artwork to position the new leaf where you want it.

Select the Split Path tool and move the scissors cursor onto the drawing surface. Click once exactly on top of the anchor point at the top of the leaf and stem junction. You may find that this is easier to do if you use the Artwork Only view, since you are not following a template for this exercise.

After the cut, the previous anchor point will be selected, along with both segments. Move down to the curve below the stem and leaf junction and click again. This makes a second cut and divides the leaf image from the stem. Figure 7.1 shows the two cuts, with the first cut showing as a standard anchor point and the second showing as a selected anchor point. Notice that they still look like anchor points, since you have selected both sides of the cuts.

Now you are ready to duplicate the leaf. Zoom out so you can see the entire leaf and stem. Use the Selection tool and the Option key (or the Object Selection tool, if you prefer) to select the entire leaf. All the anchor points

Figure 7.1

Make a second cut to divide the leaf from the stem.

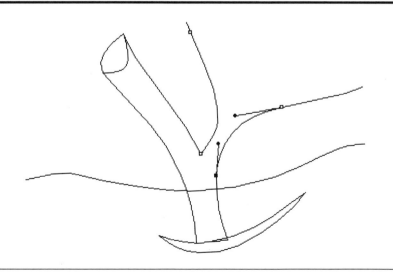

around the leaf should be selected, but none of the stem points will be selected.

Position the selection pointer anywhere on the leaf and click and drag to move the leaf image away from the apple artwork. Hold down the Option key before you release the mouse button so that you generate a copy of the leaf artwork rather than just moving the original image. Notice that the copy is automatically selected.

Now select the Rotate tool from the Toolbox, because you want to rotate the leaf copy to a new position before you reattach it to the stem. The Rotate tool cursor looks like a cross (+) to start with. This sets the center of rotation for the selected graphic. Double-check to be sure the copy is selected. The rotation won't work if nothing is selected. Even worse, if the *wrong* artwork is selected, you'll have a real surprise on your hands. So be attentive when you use these techniques.

Click the rotation cursor on the anchor point at the base of the leaf copy. This sets the center of rotation at the base of the leaf. The rotation cursor now changes into a delta cursor. Position this at the topmost point of the leaf and move it counterclockwise. Notice that the old image of the leaf copy remains visible. This is very helpful, since the leaf copy is in the same orientation as the original. Therefore, you can use the copy as a guideline for how much rotation looks appropriate and realistic. Figure 7.2 shows the copy of the leaf at about a 30° rotation as well as the starting position of the copy. Rotate the copy as much or as little as you think provides the best effect. Seeing both versions together helps you make an aesthetic judgement of how the finished leaves will look together.

When you release the mouse button, the copy of the leaf will move from its original position to the rotated position.

Now use the Selection tool to move the rotated copy over to the stem. Position the second leaf so that the connection to the stem fits correctly. It should overlay the original junction of the leaf and stem. Notice that the two leaves have the same relationship you saw during the rotation.

Figure 7.2

Rotate the leaf copy to make the second leaf.

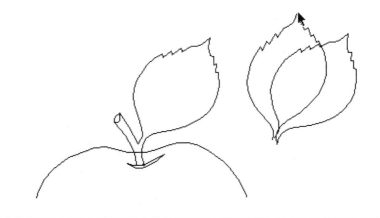

But there is one problem: The second leaf will paint in front of all the other objects in the artwork. This will not provide a nice image. Ideally, you want the second leaf in the background. To do this, select Edit ➤ Cut. Remember that the leaf has to be selected before you can cut and paste it (normally, the leaf will be selected after you move it, but, if it isn't, select it yourself). Now choose Edit ➤ Paste in Back. This moves the second leaf to the rear plane of the graphic, so that the stem and the first leaf paint over it. Figure 7.3 shows how the result looks in Preview mode.

Observe again how important it was to select White as the Fill attribute for the stem and leaf artwork. If you had chosen None, the second leaf would show through the first—a most unrealistic effect.

Adding Anchor Points

You can also use the Add Anchor Point tool, which is an alternate to the Split Path tool, to add an anchor point to a line segment without cutting the segment. This technique is quite useful for additional control of a line segment. Let's do an example so you can see how the process works and what it does. You can also access this tool by selecting the Split Path tool and holding down the Option key while you click.

Figure 7.3

When you have correctly cut and placed your second leaf, your apple looks like this.

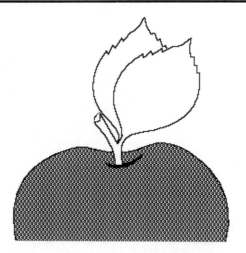

Since the two leaves that you added to the apple are identical, you can use this technique to make them slightly different. Use the Zoom in tool to magnify the top of the second leaf.

Let's modify the serrations on the second leaf to distinguish it from the first. Select the Add Anchor Point tool and move the cursor to the top-left side of the second leaf. Position the cursor along the curved segment that arcs down from the tip of the leaf and click slightly above the anchor point. Figure 7.4 shows you the results of this action.

Notice that the new anchor point has the correct direction points to define the existing curve between the two previous anchor points. The curve is unchanged by the addition of a new anchor point. But this new point allows you to maneuver the leaf edge in several new ways. You can now move any of the points that define the serration to provide a slightly different leaf edge appearance. To begin with, move the anchor point that is just below the new anchor point up to create another serration on the edge. Notice that the direction points stay usually just as they were, even while you move the anchor point. Sometimes the anchor point and direction points are very close together and it is difficult to make the adjustment smoothly. If this becomes a problem, you will have to perform the process in two steps: first move the anchor point and then adjust the direction point. The exact modifications you make here are not important; the important thing is to become familiar with this ability for adding an anchor point to a line segment and then adjusting the shape of the segment. Once you have the new anchor point, you use the same tools and techniques that you have used before. Try a variety of changes, changing whatever you want. Figure 7.5 shows you the changes that I made to make the edge of the second leaf a bit different from that of the first.

Figure 7.4

The Add Anchor Point tool allows you to add an anchor point anywhere along a line without cutting it.

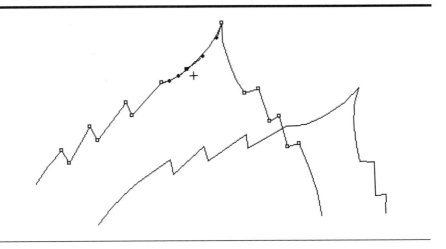

Figure 7.5

Make some small changes to make the second leaf different from the first.

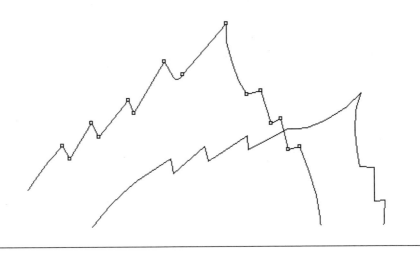

Exercise Summary

After completing these exercises, you should have a good grasp of the use of the Split Path tool. The basic use is to cut a line segment into two pieces. Optionally, you can simply insert an anchor point into the line without actually cutting it, by using the Add Anchor Point tool. Then you can manipulate existing line segments.

Exercise 7.2: Duplication and Centering of Groups

Another simple example may help reinforce the use of ungrouping to create new artwork. This exercise will also demonstrate some of the techniques for duplication of groups—in this case, of circles. We will create a graphic of a target seen through a gunsight. All the elements of this exercise are circles, squares, and rectangles.

Start again on an empty drawing surface. Set the rulers on for measurement and control. Start by selecting the Rectangle tool and creating a rectangle from (16, 24) at the upper-left corner to (30, 36) at the lower-right corner. Next, using the technique you used above on the circle, ungroup the rectangle. Then use the Split Path tool (the scissors icon) to cut off the top line of the rectangle and remove it. All of this follows the same pattern that you used in *Chapter* 3 to change the circle into a half-circle. The result should be an object that looks like Figure 7.6.

Now continue by connecting each of the upper corner points to the center point with straight lines. This creates a notched figure that will represent the

Figure 7.6

This is the simple beginning for our target graphic.

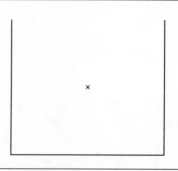

rear gunsight. Next select the Oval tool and position a small circle in the center of the notch. Remember that you can force a circle by holding down the Shift key while dragging the cursor. You can also use the Option key to access the Centered Oval tool, which draws the circle from the center outward rather than the more usual way, from one edge to the other. Since you want the center of the circle precisely placed over the center of the notch, the Centered Oval tool seems a better method. Of course, if you don't get the position quite right the first time, you can always relocate the circle, using the centerpoint and the ruler coordinates to ensure that the positioning is just the way you want it.

Once you have the circle positioned, draw a rectangle that is the width of the circle and that extends from the bottom half of the circle to the base of the notch. At this stage, the artwork should look like Figure 7.7.

If you use your art preview now, you will see the entire artwork painted black. Also, the ball on the front of the gunsight will be partially obscured by the rectangle. You want to select the circle, cut it out and paste it in front of the other objects. Use the Selection tool and choose Edit ➤ Cut and then Edit ➤ Paste in Front to do this. In the Paint Style dialog box, select the Paint attributes of 10% Black fill and Stroke.

Before you go on to create the target artwork, think about the final effect you're after. Obviously, the target will be behind the gunsight and must, therefore, paint after it. Here is where grouping can be a real asset. You will ultimately have to cut this artwork as a unit and paste it in front of the target.

Figure 7.7

Once you position the square and circle, your screen should look like this.

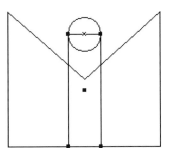

Therefore you should group this artwork now for later use as a unit. This illustrates the general issue of when to group objects: whenever you think that you will need the artwork as a unit. Choose Edit ➤ Select All and then Arrange ➤ Group.

Now you can create the target. The target will take the traditional form of concentric circles, with varying shades of gray. Create the circles off to one side of the existing artwork to help you select the target as a unit when it is done. This will also allow you to position it as a unit (remember that phrase?) over the gunsight. This saves a lot of redundant effort. Remember to use Shift to constrain the circle to be exactly round—you don't want to generate a lopsided target. Because you will be copying this object, any inaccuracy will be compounded as you proceed.

Start by creating a large circle, about 24 units in diameter. When you make the circle, be sure that the center of the circle is well outside the edge of the previous artwork; the reason for this will become obvious in a moment. In the Paint ➤ Style dialog box, set the attributes to a Fill of 70% Black with Stroke set to None. Next select the Scale tool and position the cursor over the centerpoint. Hold down the Option key and the cursor will change from a short cross (+) to an elongated cross, with the horizontal bar stretched out to the right of the cursor. This indicates that you are using the Scale dialog tool. When you click on the center point, the dialog box shown in Figure 7.8 will appear.

For now, set the value for Uniform Scale to 70% and click to activate Preserve line weights, if it's not already selected. Then click the Copy button. This will create a copy of the existing circle centered on the same point, reduced to 70% of its original size, and with the same line weight if you were stroking it (not relevant for this exercise, but you should keep it on as the default value). Next set the Paint Style attributes to 50% Black for this circle. Now select Arrange – Transform Again (⌘-D.) This produces another 70% scale copy of the circle with the same center and attributes. Fill this copy with White. Use the Arrange ➤ Transform Again (⌘-D) a third time to create yet another copy. Fill this with 100% Black. Make two more duplicates, and fill the inner one with 20% Black. You may have noticed that you didn't set a new fill value for

Figure 7.8

*Use the Scale dialog box
to set the options for the
target artwork.*

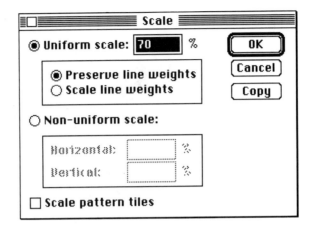

the ring just outside the center. By this point, the circles are beginning to appear too close together (a natural result of taking a continuous 70% reduction). As the circles become smaller, 70% of the figure becomes a smaller absolute number. For example, if you take 70% of 10 inches you get 7 inches; you have cut off 3 inches. But if you take 70% of the 7 inches, you only take off 2.1 inches, to go down to 4.9 inches, and so on. To compensate for this, you will delete the second ring. Select the second ring and choose Edit ➤ Clear to erase it. This leaves you with a target of five concentric circles, each with a different color value. The Preview image looks like Figure 7.9.

You proceeded from the outermost ring to the center for a very practical reason: namely, that each new object is painted after the preceding objects. If you worked from the center outward (as you certainly might think to do) each circle would overlay and thus hide all earlier circles. If you do it this way, the circles paint in the correct order.

Also, notice that the gunsight you drew earlier paints behind the target graphic. This is precisely why you grouped it; so that you could paste it in front once the target is correctly positioned.

Figure 7.9

This is a preview of target graphic by itself, before you combine it with the gunsight.

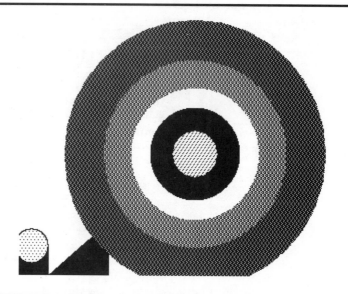

Now want to move the target into position over the gunsight, pasting the gunsight on top. To move the graphic, you want to group it. This can be done quite easily, using a simple trick. Click on the Selection tool and draw a small selection marquee around the common center point for all the circles. This selects all the circles at once, because, even though each circle has a distinct center point, all the center points lie on the same point. Even though the points overlap, Illustrator selects them all at once, in turn selecting all the anchor points of each circle.

Now choose Arrange ➤ Group (⌘-G) to group the circles. Move the target artwork over the gunsight until the second circle just rests on the edges of the notch. This should put the center of the target in line with the center of the circle and rectangle that form the front gunsight element. The result should look like Figure 7.10.

Now, select the gunsight, choose Edit ➤ Cut, and then choose Edit ➤ Paste in Front to move the gunsight in front of the target. The result will preview like Figure 7.11.

Figure 7.10

Place the target artwork over the gunsight.

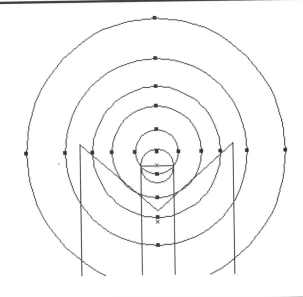

Figure 7.11

Here is the final preview of the target art with the gunsight correctly placed and painted.

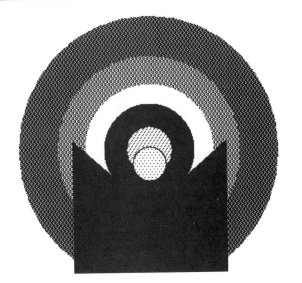

HANDLING GRAPHIC PAGES

Besides dealing with the individual elements in your artwork, it is possible to think of entire pages of graphics as single entities and to manipulate them together. There is no actual "grouping" that goes on. Instead, certain functions and processes in Illustrator use the entire page as a unit. For instance, Illustrator can present you with multiple windows or views on the same desktop. We will discuss all these issues in the remainder of this chapter.

Moving Graphics on a Page

There are several ways to move Illustrator artwork on a page. The most obvious is to select the entire artwork and simply move it. You would normally use the Fit In Window view when you're done to be sure that the artwork went where you wanted it to. This is both easy and effective.

There are, however, two problems with simply dragging objects around. First, when you have a very complex page, moving the artwork takes a long time because Illustrator has to redraw the image repeatedly on the screen. This can be quite annoying, sometimes making it difficult to place the artwork. The second problem arises when you're dealing with graphics larger than one output page. If your artwork requires more than one page to print, you will have to tile it on several pages.

Remember that the entire drawing surface is an 18"×18" area. For normal output, the page size you have selected is positioned in the center of this area, as shown in the Fit in Window display. You will learn shortly how to adjust the page size you are working on to match the paper in your printer. If you have a graphic that is larger than a single page of output, though, select Tile imageable areas in the Artwork board radio group in the Preferences dialog box (Edit ➤ Preferences). This automatically divides the drawing surface into a series of pages, as shown in Figure 7.12.

The center of the drawing surface is still your page, and there are partial pages surrounding it. Unfortunately, automatic tiling is seldom correct for large artwork. If you have a graphic that is larger than a single page, you probably will want specific portions of the artwork to display on single tiles.

Figure 7.12

When you tile the imageable area of your drawing surface, the Fit In Window view looks like this.

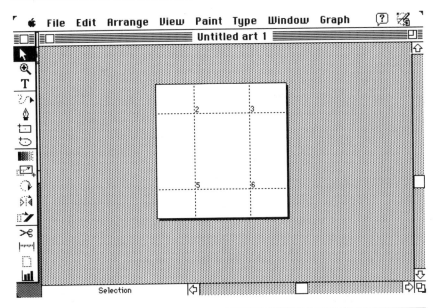

The Page tool allows you to adjust the tiling of the drawing surface so that you can have the artwork print across page junctions at any point that you want. This gives you complete control over the tiling process. You can also use these techniques to adjust the position of a smaller graphic. For example, if you have a complex graphic with a wide left margin and a narrow right margin, you can use this technique to center the output on the printed page. This is an alternative to selecting and moving the entire graphic.

The easiest way to see how this facility works is to watch it on the screen. To demonstrate this, start a new Illustrator drawing by choosing File ➤ New and selecting None for a template. Select Edit ➤ Preferences, click Tile imageable areas in the dialog box, and click OK. Now choose View ➤ Fit in Window. Next select the Page tool from the Toolbox. When you move the cursor out onto the drawing surface, you see that it is shaped like a cross (+). Click on the mouse button and the cross becomes the bottom, left corner of the primary output page. The entire page is shown as a dotted outline, and you can reposition this page anywhere on the surface

When you release the mouse button, the position of the primary output page is fixed, and the remainder of the drawing surface is tiled accordingly. In the same way, if you have only a single full page, that page will move to the new position without adding any tiling. Experiment with this mechanism on the blank surface to see how the process works.

The entire drawing surface can be tiled in as little as six letter-size tiles or as many as nine. (Obviously, if you are using larger page sizes, the tiles will be fewer.) Six-tile coverage happens when the primary output page is at one of the corners, while the nine-tile version happens when the primary output page is in the center of the drawing surface, the default positioning. Therefore, if you had a graphic that required the entire 18"×18" surface, you might well prefer to tile it into six pieces rather than nine. Since the actual output area on a standard letter-size page is about $7\frac{5}{8}$ ", ×$10\frac{1}{8}$", you can fit any artwork that is less than about 15"×20" onto only four tiles. In particular, an 11×17" (tabloid) page can be tiled into four letter-sized pages quite easily. Figure 7.13 shows you what the surface looks like if you tile it into six $8\frac{1}{2}$ ×11" pages with the primary page in the upper-left corner.

Figure 7.13

You can tile the drawing surface into as few as six pages by using the Page tool.

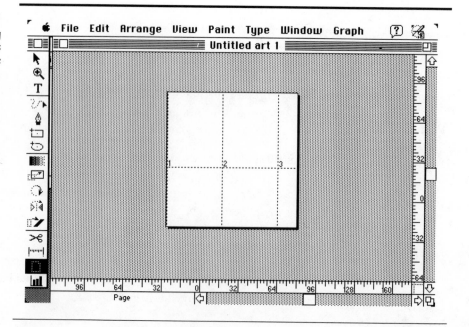

For most work, when fewer pages will suffice, you may well want to move the pages to other locations to match the artwork. Often, for artwork that extends slightly over the margins, the default tiling (with the major page in the center of the desktop) will be fine.

You may notice, if you have the rulers on as you move the primary page around, that the rulers do not move with the page. If you do not have the rulers on, put them on now (⌘-R) and move the page around to see this in action. The point (0, 0) remains in the same place even when you move the page tiles. This is necessary, when you think about it, because your graphic has been drawn with a given set of coordinates, and there is no requirement to change those; the only requirement is to change which coordinates match an output page.

It is possible to change the coordinate system on the page if you want to. This can be extremely useful in creating Illustrator artwork for editing or adding additional PostScript code. We will discuss PostScript issues in *Chapter 8*.

To move the coordinate system, you move the origin (0, 0) to the desired new location. When you do that, all the coordinates on your artwork will be changed to match, so don't be surprised to have some disk access occur when you use this technique with artwork already on the drawing surface.

You move the origin by using the *scale box* in the lower, right-hand corner of the rulers. This box provides the control for changing the origin. Click on the scale box and drag the resulting crosshairs to any position on the page. The center of the crosshairs represents the point that will become the new origin (0, 0) when you release the mouse button. This process does *not* move the page tiles. If you want to move both the origin and tiling, you must do each step separately. Having separate control over each one provides the flexibility to adjust them independently.

Exercise 7.3: Multiple Views

Another feature of Illustrator is its ability to open multiple views of the same page at the same time. This is most useful for those who have large screen displays, where large portions of different views can be seen at once. On a small display, space limitations make use of multiple views difficult.

Let's take a look at how this works in practice. Open up the *Revised Apple art* that you saved previously—or any other artwork that you prefer; we are not going to make any permanent changes to the artwork in this exercise. When you have it ready, move it to the left of the screen and select View ➤ Preview. This will result in a screen that looks something like Figure 7.14.

Now select Window ➤ New Window. A new image, identical to the previous one, will replace the first window. The only visible difference is that the title of the window now has :2 added to it. This indicates that you are looking at the second view of the artwork and template. Change the view back to Artwork & Template and then use the window size box and position controls to resize and move the second window to the upper right-hand corner of the desktop. At this point, you can see both windows at once (although only a portion of each), as shown in Figure 7.15.

Now change the Paint characteristics of the apple in the second window from 50% Black to 80% Black. As soon as you click on the change and return to the desktop, you will see the preview version in the first window change

Figure 7.14

Preview your drawing Revised Apple art.

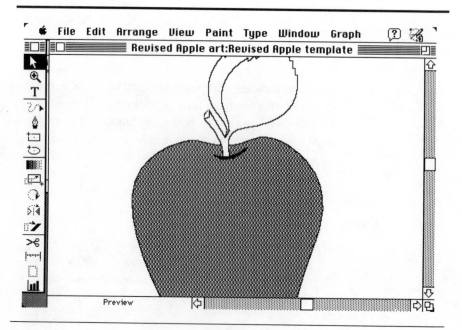

Figure 7.15

Reposition the second window so you can see both windows simultaneously.

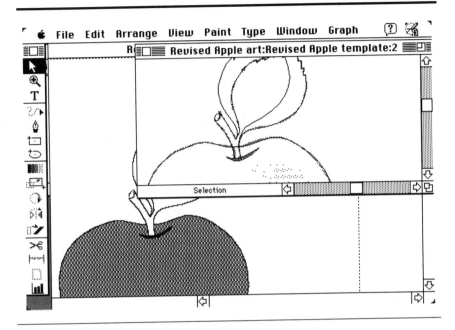

to reflect the new value. This is one valuable use for multiple views: they allow you to see the preview while you are changing the artwork.

Generally, Illustrator windows are managed in the same ways as other Macintosh windows. All the usual controls are available, such as those you just used to move and resize the second view window. In addition, Illustrator has two tricks that you can use to manage its windows. First, you can reposition an inactive window by holding down the ⌘ key and clicking on the title bar of the inactive window as you move it. This will move the window but leave it inactive. For example, you could use this technique to move the first window up behind the second (the active) window to see the title bar. This is shown in Figure 7.16.

As usual, if you click anywhere in an inactive window, it becomes active and moves to the front of the desktop. When it does, it may completely cover other windows. If that happens, you can send the current active window to the back by holding down ⌘ and clicking anywhere on the title bar. This

Figure 7.16

Hold down the ⌘ key to reposition an inactive window.

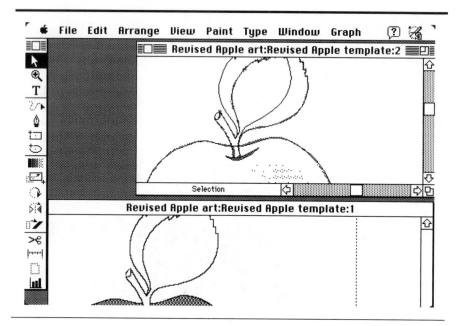

makes the current window inactive and sends it to the back of the set of windows; the next window in order becomes the active window.

All these windows or views reflect a single underlying artwork. Changes to any one of the windows will change all the other windows at the same time. Multiple views are just windows of the same object. Thus, if you save the document in any window, you save it for all the windows; and, if you close a window while there are still others open, you will not save any changes that you have made.

SUMMARY

This chapter has covered a variety of ways that you can modify your artwork. You have learned how to take existing elements in the artwork and reuse them to create new objects. You have also learned how to add features to your existing artwork. And, as a final touch, you have learned how to reset the page size and position on the desktop to help you place your graphics where you want them.

CHAPTER EIGHT

EIGHT

Text and Graphic Concepts

FEATURING

Type terminology

Using fonts

Postscript
language connections

FONTS

Up to now, you have been producing and outputting graphic images using the basic Illustrator tools and commands. This is entirely appropriate since Illustrator places primary emphasis on translation of images from bitmaps into high-quality, vector-based device-independent PostScript graphics.

Many graphics, however, require words as an integral part of the image. Illustrator enables you to place and edit type on a graphic image. In this area, Illustrator falls in between drawing programs, like MacPaint, that treat letters just like all other graphics and provide no facilities for editing or revising text once placed as bitmapped images; and complete word-processing programs, like Microsoft Word, that allow extensive edit and search capabilities on large text blocks. While Illustrator is not designed for heavy editing or text processing, I think you will find that it is capable of integrating text and graphics well.

Illustrator is very closely connected to the underlying PostScript language in the area of text generation and modification, so I have included a brief overview and discussion of PostScript and its ties to Illustrator in this chapter.

Type Definitions

Before you start to place text onto the page, let's define some important recurring concepts. These concepts are by no means unique to Illustrator or PostScript; they are the common language of printers and typographers. You need to know them to understand and express the requirements of your specific application.

A font is a set of type—a complete collection of characters and punctuation—in one style and size. Because the font gives a specific form and size to each letter or character that you type, your output device, whether a laser printer or a typesetter, can't create letter images without an active font.

This section and the next discuss general font issues. Many of these topics apply to all fonts, in any environment; some apply only to raster-output devices; none, however, are limited to PostScript and Illustrator alone. These general issues involve use of fonts; how fonts are constructed on raster devices, such as laser printers; families of fonts; and font names. Later in this chapter and the next we will discuss font issues that specifically relate to Post-Script and Illustrator. These include access to and scaling of fonts, types of PostScript fonts, and font operations like kerning and leading.

Type as Graphics

But before we get into all the technical aspects of fonts, let's consider type as a graphic object. The form of letters is one of the most ancient of graphic elements. As soon as humans began to write, they began to think about and modify the shapes that were used to convey language. Many languages, from ancient Egyptian to modern Chinese, use stylized pictures to represent words and concepts. The design of modern print typefaces grew out of the formal writing of medieval times: printing imitated calligraphy. Each letter in a quality typeface is a small work of art; each is an intricate graphic design.

The best type designs merge aesthetics and utility in perfect harmony. The beauty of a typeface is directly related to how well it performs its utilitarian functions of clarity, emphasis, and legibility. Each style of type is designed to enhance these qualities in various settings. Each style complements certain page environments or design requirements.

Fonts for Raster Output

As you know, typefaces were originally designed for printing applications. In these type consists of solid and continuous lines of ink. The task, then, is to translate these beautiful and essential objects from continuous lines into dots suitable for *raster-output devices* such as computer display screens and laser printers, which display images as collections of minute dots. This conversion is neither easy nor trivial, particularly for devices with low or medium resolution.

The problem is to carry over all the nuances of the typeface design into the series of dots that form an image on the raster output device. The process of matching the outline of a character in a font into pixels is a special case of *scan conversion*. In many cases, fonts are enhanced by adjustment of the pixels to create the most harmonious and attractive characters at a given font size. This is known as *font tuning*. The conversion to pixels is most noticeable with very small type sizes, where the features of individual letters may be only a few pixels in size. In this case, the characters may appear ragged or uneven; in extreme cases, on low resolution devices, certain characters may become indistinguishable.

Using Fonts

Fonts are changed within a document for many reasons. For fun, you could show off the variety of fonts available with a laser printer. Or you might need to make some point stand out, or to differentiate certain portions of the text—instructions from data on a form, or headings from body text, for example. In any case, choosing fonts generally involves considering three requirements.

The first thing to think about when evaluating fonts is legibility. This is obvious but often overlooked. The object of printing anything is to have it read, preferably with minimum strain and maximum ease. Many fonts have been designed specifically for clarity and readability, particularly in a limited space. Use of a crisp, clear font helps pack a maximum of information in a small space while keeping it legible.

Second, fonts are used to emphasize a point or make a statement. Sometimes this clashes with legibility, as in fonts that imitate handwritten script or gothic lettering. Generally, however, emphasis is provided either by using bold or italic fonts or by increasing the size of the font used—or both. This is useful for dividing one type of information from another; for example, instructions on a form are often printed in italic type to make them stand out from the information requested.

Third, fonts are used to enhance the quality of the finished output. A typeset page certainly has more impact and credibility than one that is merely typewritten. Typeset quality fonts provide quick and certain recognition for letter shapes to the eye. This clarity of shape is an essential element of a fine font.

Font Families and Font Names

The simplest way to group fonts is by design, or *typeface*. Most of these designs have names, which represent a complete range of fonts with a common design but in different sizes and styles. Such a set of fonts is called a *font family*. Remember that a font, properly speaking, is only one size in a particular style of typeface design. Earlier in this book I used the term "font" for what we have now defined as a font family; for convenience, I will continue to use "font" in this way whenever there will be no confusion.

These font families can be classified into three categories by certain distinctive design elements.

- *Serif* fonts have small lines finishing off the major strokes of each letter, similar to the effect left by a calligraphic pen on paper. The Times font family, which is widely used in newspapers, is a serif font family.

- *Sans-serif* fonts, as you might guess, are distinguished by the absence of these small lines. Helvetica is a sans-serif font family. Generally, serif fonts look more traditional, while sans-serif fonts have a more modern appearance.

- *Typewriter* fonts like Courier fall into neither of the above groups.

Font Sizes

Every character in a font has height and width. The width of a character within a font is called *pitch*. In *fixed pitch* or *monospaced* fonts—for example, typewriter fonts— all characters have the same width. Most fonts, however, are *variable pitch* or *proportional* fonts and have different widths depending on the shape of the individual character. So in a typewriter font like Courier an i takes up as much space as a w, while in a proportional font like Helvetica the w will be much wider than the i.

Font height is generally given in points, just like the spacing on the page. The size of a font is related to the size of the characters, but does not measure it precisely. Instead, the point size of a font measures the distance required to keep *ascenders* (for example, the top of an h) and *descenders* (for example, the bottom of a y) from touching each other in successive lines when the h is below the y. The usual size for reading type is 10 point. Smaller numbers in points indicate smaller type; 4 point is about the smallest readable type. As there are

72 points in an inch, 36 point type, for example, requires half an inch between successive lines of type, and the characters are proportionately wide. As with type styles, type size is varied to achieve an effect, to mark off special sections of text, and to aid understanding.

Font Access

You must make all fonts available to your output device before Illustrator can use them. To begin with, every PostScript output device comes with some built-in fonts—at a minimum the Times, Helvetica, and Courier families. All the fonts that you will use in this book are from this minimum set of built-in fonts.

There are two other methods of making fonts available. *Downloading* is sending a copy of the font from your computer to the printer to be stored in the printer's electronic memory. The other method is to create an entirely new font by using specialized applications or by making bitmapped images of the necessary characters.

So the fonts must be available to the printer. Each copy of a font requires memory within the printer controller, and each make and model of printer can hold a different number of fonts in its memory. Sometimes there is a trade off between the number and size of the fonts and the size and complexity of the pages that can be handled by the printer.

The fonts, or some approximation of them, must also be available for display on your screen. These *screen fonts* are important because Illustrator uses the same mechanism to generate the Preview image as the printer uses to generate the image on the output page. Illustrator ships with the Adobe Type Manager (ATM) software. ATM uses the PostScript font outlines stored in your System folder to generate screen fonts for display in Illustrator. This not only gives you the highest fidelity text display (since these are the identical fonts that you will use on your output) but also allows you to use character outlines as graphic elements. If you don't have the necessary PostScript fonts available for ATM to use, you will not get the same output as you see on the screen. Generally, Illustrator will allow you to access only those fonts that it knows are available for screen viewing, but in some systems you may know that certain fonts are available on the printer but not be able to access them from your Illustrator program. If this happens, make sure that the PostScript outlines for those fonts are installed and available to ATM. Then you will be able to use them.

Font Sources and Ownership

Not all fonts are public property. In fact, almost all the high-quality, elegant fonts are private property. These font designs are licensed to companies who want to incorporate the fonts into various devices. Adobe Systems, the developer of PostScript, has licensed a wide variety of classic and modern fonts—for example, Times-Roman and Helvetica—for use with PostScript devices. Many other vendors also sell high-quality fonts that can be used with your Illustrator package.

ILLUSTRATOR AND POSTSCRIPT

Since PostScript and Illustrator are intimately connected, some knowledge of PostScript is highly valuable for working with Illustrator output. PostScript is the output mechanism by which Illustrator communicates with the rest of the world. Illustrator generates PostScript application code tailored to the generation of images. Although a complete programming language, PostScript itself is oriented toward that end.

But don't worry—you don't need to become a PostScript programmer. Illustrator does such a good job of generating PostScript code that it is usually preferable to use it rather than to hand-code artwork. Nevertheless, there are times when you may wish to add your own PostScript code to Illustrator, or when you might modify Illustrator output. In addition, you will be able to understand Illustrator concepts and operations much better when you understand the mechanism used to implement them.

You need two types of information to make maximum use of Illustrator. First, you need some idea of what PostScript is, how it works, and how the power of Illustrator is really the power of PostScript harnessed in a more friendly and accessible way. Second, you need to understand how these PostScript concepts have influenced Illustrator in its operations. Both of these areas are covered in this section.

The influence of PostScript in Illustrator is shown in two ways. First, Illustrator has certain characteristics, such as device independence, which are based on characteristics of the PostScript language. Second, Illustrator has adopted a format and structure for its output and screen presentation that are influenced by PostScript language format and structure.

Special Strengths of Illustrator

Illustrator has four special strengths derived from its use of PostScript and its special approach to translating the graphics that you see on the screen into PostScript code:

- Resolution independence
- Screen presentation method
- Image manipulation facility
- Modular output code

Resolution Independence

Resolution independence is essential to what Illustrator can do for you. Since Illustrator generates PostScript output and PostScript is, by design, independent of device resolution, Illustrator output can be generated on any device equipped with a PostScript interpreter, from a 2500 dpi typesetter to a 300 dpi laser printer, and even on a 72 dpi screen. The PostScript language interpreter converts the graphics generated by Illustrator into the correct settings for the output device being used. So the output from Illustrator can be run, without any changes, on a wide variety of devices and will produce essentially the same output on all of them.

Screen Presentation Method

Illustrator uses PostScript output to create the images on your screen as well as on the page output. This gives you increased fidelity between the screen display and the page output and ensures that the graphics shown on the screen are correctly reflected in the PostScript output. This is why you need to use PostScript fonts for your output, for example.

Ability to Manipulate Images

Illustrator's powerful ability to manipulate images on the screen is not directly a result of PostScript, because the image is maneuvered on screen by Illustrator before the movement gets translated into PostScript code. Nevertheless, PostScript plays an important part in the handling of images. Illustrator's screen images have to be translated into output that will create that same effect on a page. All of the Illustrator screen tools and transformations are based directly on PostScript concepts, and many reflect specific PostScript operations.

Modular Output Code

Illustrator produces a special structure of PostScript output that can be used directly by other PostScript applications. This means that you can create a graphic in Illustrator, import it into other applications that generate PostScript, such as Microsoft Word, Aldus PageMaker, or QuarkXPress, and have the same high-quality output from your graphic that you will get for the text.

This special output is called *Encapsulated PostScript* and involves both programs understanding and using certain structuring conventions. We will discuss it in much more detail in *Chapter 15*.

PostScript Language Characteristics

The PostScript language's special characteristics derive from its being both a programming language and a page-description language. Let's look briefly at several important features. PostScript is

- Interpreted
- Device-Independent
- Graphically Powerful
- Page-Oriented

PostScript as an Interpreted Language

PostScript is an interpreted language, like BASIC or APL. PostScript operators are understood and acted upon by another program, the interpreter, which generally resides in the controller of the output device (e.g., the laser printer). Use of an interpreter allows definition of many program requirements as the commands are being executed, which provides flexibility and sensitivity to the current state of the output and the output device. It also allows for immediate feedback, error recognition, and command execution, which makes interpreted languages easier to debug and correct.

The main disadvantage is that, because the interpreter is itself a program, there is an additional layer of software being executed. This can slow things down. In PostScript's case, this loss is usually not great, since the interpreter is running by itself in the output device, so it doesn't take up the resources of your computer. Also, recent generations of PostScript output devices incorporate features to speed up and improve this output processing, such as RISC (reduced instruction set computer) processors and PostScript Level 2.

Interpreted languages do not, in themselves, impose any specific structure on a program. So PostScript does not place any required structure on a document description, the PostScript equivalent of a program.

Illustrator, being a product of Adobe Systems, the creator of PostScript, follows a well-defined, published standard approach. We will examine this more fully later in *Chapter 15*. You don't have to use these conventions to create successful PostScript page descriptions, but following them makes clear what each part of the program is doing, so you can easily compare and modify programs.

PostScript is dynamic in that it provides feedback to the programmer or the PostScript application. This is particularly valuable in determining the current state of the execution environment—for example, whether a certain font is currently loaded and available.

It is also dynamic in that PostScript page descriptions can be defined and modified as they are created by definition of new operations from the basic set of graphic and procedural operators. Thus programs like Illustrator can define a series of new operations that correspond to the actions that you take to draw on the screen and use these to create the desired graphic output. This dynamic process, which also is a function of the interpreter, makes PostScript significantly more powerful than alternative page description mechanisms.

Device Independence

PostScript's independence of any specific output device is a great strength. The interpreter adjusts and converts PostScript commands to each device's requirements. PostScript can provide specific, device-dependent information when necessary to construct a page or an image.

This independence provides two major benefits. First, you can generally remain unaware of the specific requirements of the output device. Second, a page described in PostScript can be proofed on one device and then produced on another with no modification of commands or operators. So you can proof, correct, and reset pages quickly using a laser printer, then generate them for final printing output on a typesetting machine. In this way, you gain the benefits of automated processing and quick turnaround while still having high-quality output. This benefit has created much of the excitement about "desktop publishing."

PostScript's Graphic Power

Since PostScript is especially designed for creating and manipulating graphic objects on a raster-output device, I believe that the best way to think of PostScript is as a method of drawing electronically. It is, in a sense, electronic calligraphy. Almost thirty percent of the operators deal with graphics. Many of these operators are intuitively similar to the actions of a calligrapher handling a pen—raising it, positioning it on the paper, inking it, and then stroking each character onto the page. PostScript's powerful primitive operators, such as scale and rotate, can be combined in many ways to produce dramatic and surprising output, as you have seen in the Illustrator exercises.

PostScript's flexibility makes it the language of choice for serious work, particularly work combining text and graphics. PostScript makes combining text and graphics easy and natural by treating individual characters as graphic objects that can be positioned, scaled, and rotated.

PostScript as a Page Description Language

Raster-output devices prepare a unit of output at a time by setting each pixel on the output to a precise value. Such a unit is conveniently referred to as a "page," even though it may consist of something other than an actual piece of paper. Because PostScript describes these units independently, it is called a "page description" language. For black-and-white output, these pixels are set to either zero or one, representing black or white. The description of a unit of output is therefore a complete map of these values for the entire surface to be output—often a full page, but sometimes less because of design or other considerations.

PostScript graphics, instead of being built up of individual pixels, like bitmaps, consist of lines, curves, and text characters as individual objects. The PostScript language does this by using powerful primitive operators that correspond to how you ordinarily handle graphics. These operators can be combined to produce a wide range of complex output.

POSTSCRIPT ERROR CORRECTION

Users who generate complex artwork or who move their artwork into other applications may find that they have trouble printing. This can be exasperating, since often only a short and cryptic error message is displayed, or perhaps no message at all. Short messages happen because the Apple Laser-Writer driver software (the file name LaserWriter in your System folder) screens out error messages and only relays a short and general message for all PostScript errors. This results in the famous "Your document is OK, but could not be printed" message—a frustrating message if you wanted to print.

Sometimes, when there is an error, you don't get any message at all: the output device simply stops processing your document and returns to ready status. This happens if the Macintosh system finishes sending the complete document to the printer before the PostScript interpreter in the device finds an error. Then the interpreter has no way of telling the Macintosh that the error occurred.

The solution to such problems is to purchase a commercial error reporting package, which will trap these errors and print a page that tells you what happened and how to fix it. In my biased opinion (since I wrote it) the best commercial error reporter is the PinPoint Error Reporter. This is available from the following company, along with other useful PostScript tools and information: Cheshire Group, 321 S. Main Street, Suite 36, Sebastopol, CA 95472; telephone (707) 887-7510.

SUMMARY

This chapter has given you a brief look at the general nature of fonts and appropriate font terminology. This will help you not only with Illustrator but also with other applications that use a variety of fonts. You also saw some of the reasons why Illustrator uses PostScript language for its output. Both of these discussions give you valuable insight into how Illustrator creates graphics. In the next chapter, you will use this information in a more concrete way as you use Illustrator to add text to graphics.

CHAPTER NINE

Adding Text to Graphics

FEATURING

Using the text tool

Creating a logo

Creating a letterhead

Selecting fonts

NOW THAT WE have established a common terminology for dealing with text, we can turn to using type and text in Illustrator images. This chapter will focus on inserting text into graphics, using images that you have already created as part of the previous exercises.

Note that the selection of type styles and sizes is quite arbitrary; as mentioned in *Chapter 8*, I will limit the type selection to those fonts built-in to every PostScript printer, so that every reader will be able to do the exercises. If you have more appealing fonts available that you want to use, please do so; they will not affect the exercises.

EXERCISE 9.1: ADDING TEXT TO A LOGO

In *Chapter 3*, you created a stylized triangular graphic. Now you will return to that image and add text to make a complete letterhead. Eventually, we'll develop a complete page, with this logo and letterhead at the top.

In order to make a letterhead out of the logo, you need to do two things: reduce the size of the artwork and add the company name and address. These steps can basically be done in two ways: you can do it by measure, or you can do it by eye. These two methods are not exclusive; you can use both in combination if that gives you the best results. For those readers who are graphic artists, or experienced in layout and design, doing it by eye will probably be the preferred method. For those not so gifted, the measurement approach would be preferred. We will use a combination of the two methods, so you can see how both are used.

You are going to be creating a new piece of artwork based on an old one. You could make changes to the old artwork and then save it under a new name. This is risky though, because if you accidentally saved the artwork under the old name, you'd lose the old artwork. Illustrator does not save a backup version of a changed document. Instead, I prefer to start work on a blank drawing

Plate 1

A letterhead, ad, and
business card for
a holistic health
business. Illustration
and typography by
Delia Brown.

Cowboy Buddha Botanicals

Suzanne Halston
142 Dirt Rd
Denver, Co
74201

Fall Sale!
50% off all products!

Sept 15th to Sept 18th
essential oils
natural soaps
herbal shampoos

Cowboy Buddha Botanicals
142 Dirt Road Denver Colorado 74201

Cowboy Buddha Botanicals

531-7642

Suzanne Halston
142 Dirt Rd
Denver, Co
74201

Plate 2

An illustration for a
book cover separated
into cyan, magenta,
yellow, and black.

Plate 3

The final image printed with all four colors. Illustration by Harumi Kubo.

Plate 4

*Using Overprint,
the bottom circles will
combine colors, while
the top ones won't.*

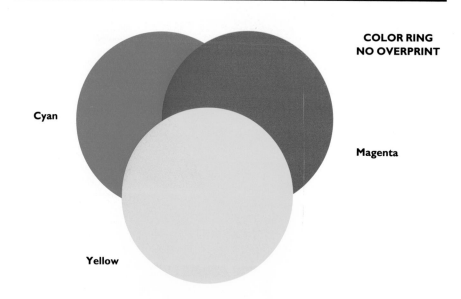

Cyan

Magenta

Yellow

**COLOR RING
NO OVERPRINT**

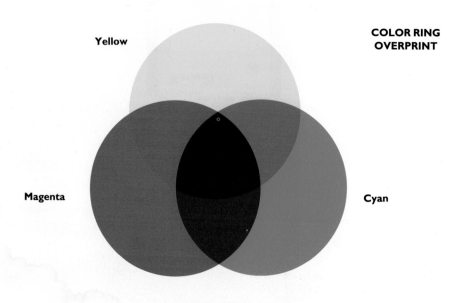

Yellow

Magenta

Cyan

**COLOR RING
OVERPRINT**

Plate 5

The cyan separation of the color circles shows how the two images differ

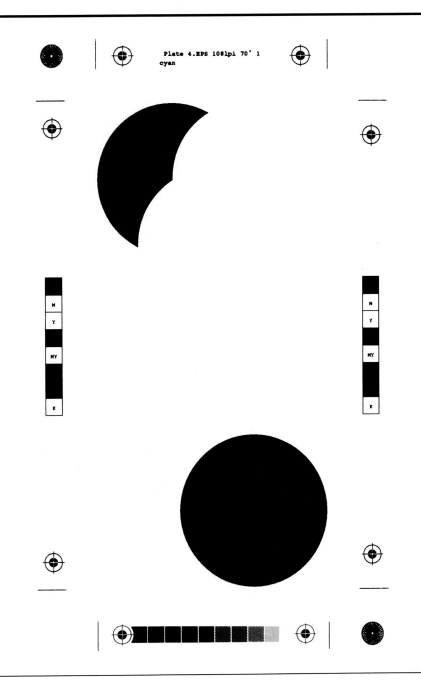

Plate 6

The menu for a
cafe. Illustration
and typography by
Delia Brown.

Le café dans le jardin

• Lunch • Menu •

Salad Niçoise	8.25
Crêpes avec les fruits	6.75
Le bagette avec fromage et fruit	5.50
Soupe d'ognion	5.25

Coffe drinks

Cafè latte	1.50
Café au lait	1.25
Espresso	1.00
Thé	1.00

Pastries and desserts

Croissant	1.75
Pain au chocolat	2.00
Crème caramel	2.50
Glaces	2.25

Plate 7

A children's book cover. Illustration and typography by Charlotte Carter

Plate 8

This selection of artwork shows some of the color options you can use in Illustrator.

surface and add elements from previous artwork as desired. This ensures that the old artwork cannot be lost or overwritten by the new.

Scaling the Logo

As a first step, open a new drawing surface in Illustrator (⌘-N). This will get you the familiar blank drawing surface labeled *Untitled art* 1. Use ⌘-R or select View ➤ Show Rulers to show the rulers, so that you can make exact placements. I will give coordinate values in the exercise so that you can follow exactly if you want. Now open the saved version of the artwork Exercise 3-1 (or whatever name you gave it). This completely obscures the first drawing surface.

The first step is to reduce the logo to an appropriate size. The original artwork fit into a frame 24 picas wide and about 21 picas high. You want to reduce this to a box approximately 7 picas wide and 6 picas high. When you created the logo, you sized each piece to match every other piece, so the logo should be reduced proportionately to maintain these relationships. Also, you would like to proportionally adjust the line width for the strokes. This is easy in Illustrator.

Using the Selection tool, select the entire figure. Since this artwork consists of several non-grouped objects, you cannot simply click on it with the Object Selection tool to select all of it. When you're done, every part of the graphic should be selected (all anchor points should be black squares). Next select Edit ➤ Copy (⌘-C). Now select File ➤ Close Window. This closes the top window and returns you to the first window that is still empty. Select Edit ➤ Paste (⌘-V) to paste the artwork to the new drawing surface. This gives you a fresh copy of the art to work on.

Now select Arrange ➤ Group (⌘-G). This makes all the artwork into one unit, so you can scale and move it more easily. Next select the Scale tool from the Toolbox. This tool reduces or enlarges objects. In this case, you want to shrink the logo artwork.

The scale operation is a two-step process. The first step is to determine the point about which the scaling operation will occur. This point is called the *scale origin*. Once this is set, you can scale the selected artwork by picking a point and dragging it to create the desired scaled shape. You could use any fixed point on the edge of the artwork as an origin; for convenience, in this case you will use the bottom-left corner point. This will result in the bottom-left anchor point remaining in the same position on the drawing surface, while the rest of the artwork shrinks down toward it.

You could do this scaling visually, but that might not give you quite the result you want. Instead, you will use the optional Scale dialog tool to make these adjustments, which offers several advantages over manual scaling.

For one thing, the scale will be much more precise. Also, the Scale dialog box allows you to select scaled line weights, independent of the Preferences setting.

There is just one difficultly to using the dialog box, and that is that you don't know exactly what the measurements are. In this case, it won't be difficult to determine the precise percentage reduction. It is just the ratio of the 7 point width you want to the existing 24 point width. Since you want uniform scaling, you can use this ratio (which is about 30%) for the entire figure. There is also a sneaky way to get Illustrator to do the work, which you'll learn about in *Chapter 11*.

The cursor should still be shaped like a cross and the Scale tool should be selected. Go to the bottom left-hand anchor point, and hold down the Option key before you set the scale origin. Notice, when you press the Option key, that the cursor changes shape from a cross to a sort of sideways t. Now click the mouse to set the scale origin. You will see the dialog box shown in Figure 9.1.

We will discuss this dialog box in more detail in *Chapter 11*. For now, there are several features to notice about this box.

You have a choice of either scaling the line weights or keeping them the same. Sometimes you will want to keep the lines the same width, regardless of the scaling. Generally, the default option, which is to scale the line weights, is correct. In this case, simply leave the default setting of Scale line weights on.

Illustrator also has a Preferences setting that will scale line widths as you scale an object manually. So if you halve the size of a figure, you will also halve the thickness of the lines in the figure. If you don't make this adjustment, the lines in your artwork look quite a bit darker and thicker in the reduced version

Figure 9.1

The Scale dialog tool presents you with this dialog box for precision control.

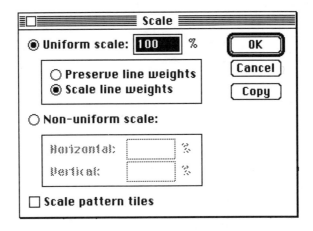

than in the original artwork. You could reset the line weights, but if you had to do many such operations it would be tedious, time-consuming, and perhaps even impossible if the artwork is very complex. This scaling feature is identical to the one in the Scale dialog box.

In addition, you have a choice between scaling the figure uniformly (the same in both the *x* and *y* directions) or nonuniformly (using different horizontal and vertical scaling factors). As we discussed earlier, you want to scale this figure uniformly along both axes. Therefore you want to enter the previously calculated value of 30% into the Uniform scale box. Now click OK to make the change. The result will look like Figure 9.2.

This is now an appropriate size for a logo in a letterhead. To ensure that you don't lose all your work, you may wish to save the artwork at this time (⌘–S).

Adding Text to the Logo

Now let's add text to the logo. You want to add the name of the company, Cheshire Group, and their address and telephone number. You will place these to the right of the logo, with the name of the company being larger than the other information. All of these should be approximately centered on the page, with the logo between the name and the left edge of the paper.

Figure 9.2

When you have reduced the artwork with the Scale dialog tool it will be suitable for a logo.

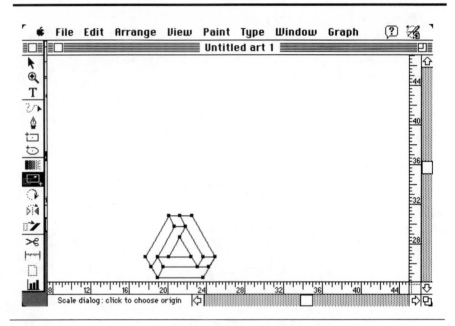

Before adding the text, however, you need to see more of the page for accurate placement. Select the Zoom out tool from the Toolbox and reduce the view of the drawing surface. Use the Scroll tool to position the drawing surface so that you can see the top of the page. You will begin by roughly placing the logo in the upper-left corner of the page. Use the Selection tool and grab the grouped artwork by the top-left corner. Move this to the position (8, 60). Later, you can make some small adjustments to get the best positioning relative to the name and address. Finally, use the Zoom in tool to get back to 100% magnification by clicking once on the middle of the page. This should allow you to see close to the right edge of the page as well as the left edge of the logo graphic. Now you are ready to place the text.

Next you want to add the company name, CHESHIRE GROUP. This name should be placed about halfway up the logo artwork and about halfway between the left and right margins. The logo artwork is approximately 6 picas high and 7 picas wide, as we calculated earlier. Since the upper-left corner of the logo is at (8, 60), the logo extends to approximately the 13 pica position on the x-axis and down to the 54 pica position on the y-axis. You can verify this by using the selection cursor to point to the anchor points on each side of the graphic and note the coordinate position on the crosshairs.

To position the text for the company name vertically, you want to be along the y-axis line at 57 picas. And you want to center the text along the x-axis at a point halfway between the edges of the page, which are at 0 and 51 picas. That would be at the point 25.5. For convenience, however, and to balance the logo graphic, place the text center point at 26.

Placing Text on the Letterhead

Select the Text tool in the Toolbox. The cursor changes to a special text cursor.

The form of this cursor may be familiar to you from other applications.

The small horizontal line in the center of the cursor represents the baseline of the type that you will place on the page. The outline around the basic cursor changes to tell you what type of text you will place. In this case, the rectangular outline behind the cursor tells you that this is the basic Text tool.

Wherever you place the cursor is the *anchor point* on which the text block that you create will be located. The anchor point is the fixed point around which text is arranged or shaped. In some ways, this functions just like the anchor points for lines that you have been working with earlier. In particular, the text anchor point changes color and shape to indicate whether the associated text block is selected.

Now position the text cursor on (26, 57) and click. This sets the text anchor point and begins the text entry process. You could now start entering text, but first you want to set the font and other characteristics for this block of text. To do this, select Type ➤ Style. You will get the Type Style dialog box, as shown in Figure 9.3.

There are quite a few options to examine in this box, and we will discuss them all in the next section. For now, you can just complete the letterhead by a few simple actions.

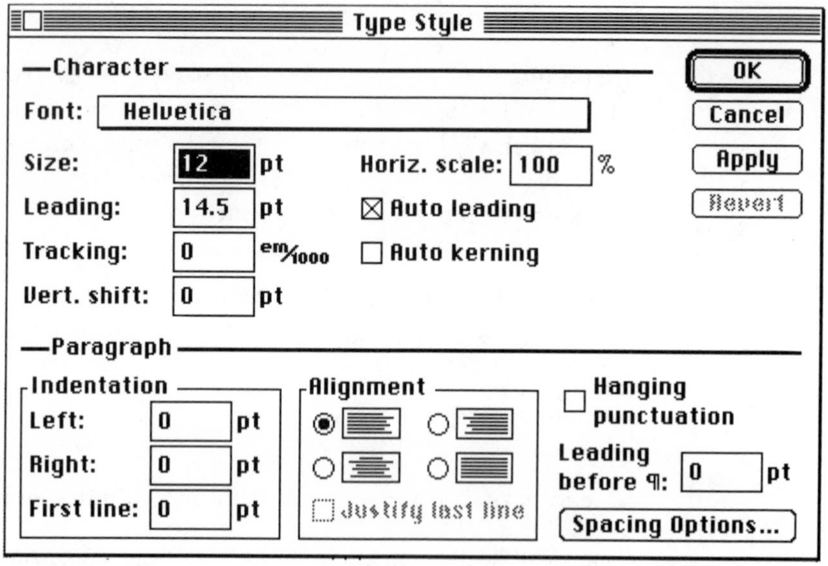

Figure 9.3

The Type Style *dialog box
allows you to set all the
controls for your type.*

Move the cursor (the arrow) up to Font block at the top of the box. This is
the Font submenu. When you click in this box, it displays a menu of recently
used fonts, with the selection Other as the first entry. Select Other to display
the Font dialog box, shown in Figure 9.4.

This dialog box is divided into two lists. On the left side is the list of fonts
installed in your system; on the right is a list of styles for the chosen font.
Each individual font will have at least one style, and may have many styles
associated with it. Since Helvetica is the default font, it is already chosen in
the font list. Go to the style list and click on Bold Oblique. This establishes
Helvetica-BoldOblique as the current font. This is basically a bold, italicized
version of Helvetica. Now click OK to return to the Type Style dialog box.

Notice that the name *Helvetica-BoldOblique* is now displayed in the Font submenu box. Now move the cursor to the Size box and change the size to 24.
Move down to Leading and change that to 24 also. Both size and leading are
measured in points, as is typical in typesetting and printing. Finally, move
over to the Alignment group and click on the lower-left icon, which represents

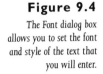

Figure 9.4

The Font dialog box allows you to set the font and style of the text that you will enter.

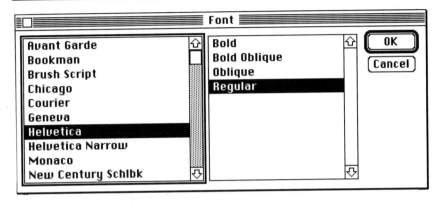

centered text. The rest of the settings in the box are fine for now. Click OK to return to the desktop.

Now type the words **CHESHIRE GROUP**. This will place the text string that you just entered, CHESHIRE GROUP, on the page, centered on the point you selected (24, 57), to be printed in 24 point Helvetica-BoldOblique, with 24 points between each line of text. The result should look like Figure 9.5.

Now let's add the address. Since you cannot set different leading or alignment values for a single block of type, you must make a new type block. To do this, return to the Toolbox and click again on the Text tool. Place the cursor at (26, 55) and click to set the anchor point; then select Type ➤ Style (⌘–T). You will again get the Type Style dialog box, which will still reflect the values you entered earlier.

You want to change these to enter the address and telephone numbers. Select Helvetica as the font, Size as 10 points and Leading as 14. Keep the centered alignment and click OK. Now enter the first address line as

6061 Van Ness, Suite 800 San Francisco, CA 94111

followed by a carriage return and then the second line

TEL: (415) 555-7205   FAX: (415) 555-1212

Figure 9.5

*You place the first
line of text here.*

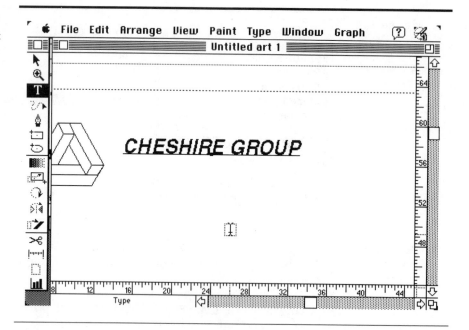

There is a single space before the beginning of the TEL and nine spaces between the two telephone numbers for alignment. It would be possible to
align these two lines separately, but it is quite time-consuming and no more
effective than the technique used here. You will see the address lines appear
on the screen, centered along the same vertical line as the company name, as
shown in Figure 9.6.

To see how the letterhead looks, first zoom out so you can see both edges
of the page and then select View ➤ Preview. This is a little small to see any
detail, but it gives you the placement of the letterhead on the page. To get a
full view, select File ➤ Print to print the page. The output should look like
Figure 9.7.

Finally, save your work as *Letterhead art* so you can continue to work on this
later in the chapter.

Figure 9.6

This shows you the completed name and address as a part of the letterhead artwork.

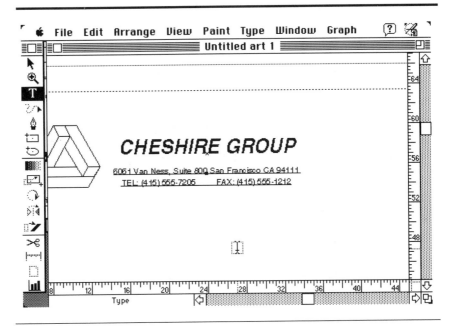

Figure 9.7

This shows you the finished letterhead artwork and its position on the output page.

ILLUSTRATOR'S OTHER TEXT OPERATIONS

Now that you have done some basic work combining text with graphics, you are ready to explore more of the options and operations of the Text tool. This section provides definitions and discussion to go along with the earlier examples, and includes another exercise where you'll develop a complete form using Illustrator. It also explains the limitations of text handling in Illustrator and gives you some warnings about appropriate and inappropriate use of text.

Text Tool Operations

The place to begin is back at the Type Style dialog box. Look again at Figure 9.3, which shows you the Type Style dialog box. This box can be accessed in two ways. The first you have already met: by selecting the Text tool and clicking on a specific point to start placing text. You can also get to the Type Style dialog box by selecting a block of existing text and choosing Type ➤ Style (⌘-T). This will show you the Type Style dialog box filled in with the parameters that were set for the selected block. You can modify any of these parameters at any time, unlike most painting programs.

The top portion of the dialog box shows the font that is currently in use, listing the fonts that you have used in your artwork. In addition, by selecting Other (⌘-Shift-F) you can see a list of all the fonts available on your system. This list can be scrolled by using the scroll bar. The names on the left are the names of the fonts, and the names on the right are the styles available for the selected font. You can also access this submenu and its associated dialog box directly by using Type ➤ Font.

You will occasionally see artwork that was originally prepared on a system with a font not installed on your system. For example, the company name, CHESHIRE GROUP, might be set in Palatino and generated on a system with the Palatino typeface. If the page were imported onto a system that contained only the basic fonts, though, the Palatino type family would become unavailable. You will also see a simple alert dialog, warning you that the font is not installed in your system and that it will not display properly. Illustrator will retain the name of the required font in the artwork, but will use Helvetica to display the text on the screen. This means that the screen display will no longer accurately reflect the final output.

The effects on the printers are somewhat different. Illustrator will always try to use the correct font; that is, the font that you requested from the list. Even if the font is not installed on your system, Illustrator assumes that the printer will have the correct font available. It will then be your responsibility to provide the font if it is not already resident in the printer. Illustrator will download fonts for you if they are available on your system but are not resident on the printer. In all cases, if a font isn't resident on the printer when your document prints, you will get a default font in its place (usually Courier).

You have already used the Size and Leading parameters. These two boxes specify, in points, the size of the requested type and the distance between two successive lines of type, respectively. The leading is used only on successive lines within the same text block.

Note that these, too, can be accessed directly from the Type menu as Type ➤ Size and Type ➤ Leading. If you select these from the Type menu, you will see a submenu of various point sizes, with an Other selection (⌘-Shift-S) at the top. Choosing Other takes you to the Type Size/Leading dialog box, which has the same settings as this section of the Type Style dialog box. Remember that the Leading values on the submenu are point sizes, not type sizes. If you want to match the leading value to your type size selection, choose Auto in the Leading submenu.

It is possible to use values for leading that result in various type effects. To begin with, leading the same as type size is the minimum necessary to avoid overlapping of letters on successive lines. At the extreme, if you enter a leading value of zero, the lines of type will overlap completely. It is also possible to use negative values for leading; in that case, the second line of type will appear above the first line by the leading amount.

The next box will be labeled Tracking or Kerning, depending on whether you have selected a block of text or have placed the insertion caret between two letters. If you are entering text, then the insertion caret is automatically placed between two letters and the box is labeled Kerning. If you have selected a block of text, either by highlighting the text or by selecting the text anchor point, the box is labeled Tracking.

The Tracking box, which you will have the opportunity to use soon, specifies the distance between letters in the text block, in points. A Tracking value of zero, which is the default value, means that the letters are spaced according to their usual width in the font. The tracking value is an amount of space added onto the usual font spacing. As was true for the leading, you can enter negative values for tracking. This will move the letters closer together and may result in overlapping of some or all the letters.

Tracking should not be confused with kerning, which is the adjustment of certain pairs of letters to make a more pleasing appearance. This form of positioning is available by placing the inserting caret between any two letters in a block of type. You can then adjust the distance between the letters on each side of the caret in increments of $\frac{1}{1000}$ of a point. If you are working with a 20 point font, 10 units of kerning would be 0.2 points. You can also let Illustrator do the kerning work for you by checking Auto Kerning in the Type Style dialog box. If this box is checked, Illustrator uses any kerning information built into the selected font to provide individual letter-pair kerning. Note, however, that using automatic kerning on any large block of type will slow down display and printing—perhaps considerably. If you need to kern a block of type, you should leave kerning off until you are ready to make the final adjustments to the type.

The Vert. shift box allows you to move a line of text above or below the baseline of the text by the amount of points set in this box. This can be used for setting subscripts or superscripts, for example. The Horizontal scale box allows you to compress or expand a line of text while keeping the vertical height of the text fixed. This can be very useful for squeezing a line of text into a small space. Note that this is different from changing the tracking, which compresses only the space between characters, not the characters themselves.

The bottom section of the dialog box provides controls that apply to blocks of text, rather than to individual characters. The first section allows you to set indentation for text blocks. This controls the distance of the text itself from the anchor point (on the left) and any enclosing path (on the right). In general, some indentation is quite useful, particularly if the enclosing path is stroked, since the stroke itself requires some space. In addition, you can specify special indentation that is only applied to the first line of text in the block.

The Alignment box offers four selections for aligning the text to the selected anchor point. The top-left icon provides left-justification. This is how you will position your text normally and it is the default selection. This alignment is directly available from the keyboard as ⌘-Shift-L. The bottom-left icon, which you used in the example above, provides centering of the text around the anchor point (⌘-Shift-C). The top-right icon provides right-justification with a ragged-left margin (⌘-Shift-R). Finally, the bottom-right icon provides full justification, with even margins on both edges of the text (⌘-Shift-J). If you select full justification, then you have the option to apply this to the last line of the text by turning on the radio button Justify last line.

Since the last line is usually not justified, this option is off by default. All the alignment options are also directly availble by choosing Type ➤ Alignment.

The Hanging punctuation checkbox and the Leading before ¶ box are specialized controls. If hanging punctuation is checked, any punctuation marks, such as quotes, commas, periods, and so on, at the ends of lines will be allowed to fall outside the text margins; if it is not checked, the punctuation will be kept inside the margins. The Leading before ¶ option allows you to set a special spacing between the last line of text in one paragraph and the first line of the next. The value you enter here is added to the normal line leading when you start a new paragraph. Note that this control only applies when you are using the Area Text tool.

The last button on the Type Style dialog box is labeled Spacing Options, which allows you to set spacing for your text. This is also available by selecting Type ➤ Spacing Options (⌘-Shift-O). These controls are primarily used for setting spacing for justified type. You can set both the amount of space that is placed between words and the amount that is placed between letters to achieve the justification.

All of these features, taken together, give you unrivalled control over your text in Illustrator graphics.

POSTSCRIPT AND TEXT OPERATIONS

This section discusses many aspects of font use and text and character construction from the viewpoint of the PostScript language that underlies Illustrator. Some of this may not be of interest to you just now; if you find any of it too complex, you can just skip to the examples later in the section. You will be able to complete all the work in this book without this information. However, as you use Illustrator in your daily work, I believe that you will eventually want to understand in more detail and depth how text placement and usage are affected by PostScript concepts and operations.

PostScript Fonts

PostScript treats text characters as general graphic objects subject to appropriate manipulation just like any other graphic; a box or a triangle is conceptually no different to the PostScript language than a *g* or an *R*. Thus PostScript has no problem combining text and graphics on a page. In a very real sense, all pages are graphic images to a PostScript output device.

PostScript Font Access

PostScript describes fonts through the use of special dictionaries, called *font dictionaries*. Each font dictionary is referenced by a PostScript font name, like Helvetica or Times-Roman, and provides information and procedures for building all the characters contained in that font. You have already seen the PostScript font mechanism at work in the exercises. When you select a font name and style from the Font dialog box, Illustrator translates that information into the correct PostScript font name, which is the name that you see in the Type Style dialog box. The name of the font is used by Illustrator as a link to the font dictionary. This font dictionary is then used by the PostScript interpreter to define the process for rendering characters in a text block onto the current page. Because of this dictionary lookup method, it is very important to have exactly the correct name for a font. If you don't get the name right, the interpreter will never find the font and will use the default font (usually Courier) instead.

There are two important points to remember here. First, that PostScript actually does draw each character, using appropriate graphic operations; and, second, that the PostScript interpreter creates characters through the use of a font dictionary that contains all the information required to produce a given font, including appropriate procedures for rendering each character.

Types of Fonts

Most PostScript fonts contain characters that are defined as outlines in the font dictionary and then processed by the interpreter, which fills them in to make the character. PostScript can thus render text at all sizes with a minimum of distortion, performing a wide variety of other graphic operations on the characters. Both Times and Helvetica are defined as outline fonts. Some PostScript fonts contain characters that are defined as lines to be stroked rather than outlines to be filled. Courier is such a font.

It is also possible to create PostScript fonts directly, as images that are rendered by the interpreter as a series of pixels. Such fonts are called *bitmapped* fonts. No PostScript built-in fonts are done this way, but it is possible for a PostScript user or application to create and work with bitmapped fonts.

Because the characters in PostScript fonts can be stroked or filled as required, they can also be modified by use of the Paint ➤ Style selection. All of the usual paint selections are equally available and applicable to type. For instance, you can make the type show on the page in the usual range from black to white, depending on the Fill setting. This provides an easy and effective way to show white lettering against a dark or patterned background, for example. You can also use the Stroke options to change the letters to outline form. For example, you can set Fill to White and Stroke to 100% Black with a thin line width to generate letter outlines. Of course, the appropriate line width will depend on the size and style of the type being used. Finally, you can also select Type ➤ Select Outlines to make your characters into graphic objects. This allows you to use the paths that make up the characters as part of your artwork, where you can not only color or stroke them, but you can also distort them in a variety of ways. This option, however, is only available if you have Adobe Type Manager (ATM) software installed on your system.

Advantages of PostScript Fonts

Characters in PostScript fonts are generally created by the equivalent of the path construction and painting operations. This is entirely consistent with the design of PostScript and the notion of type as a graphic object. There are several benefits to this approach that may not be obvious at first glance.

First, this approach to creating characters preserves the quality of the fonts. In very fine (and expensive!) typesetting, each letter of each font is handcrafted to give the look and feel that the type designer had in mind. This may mean, for example, that the stroke widths or relative sizes of letters within the same font group at different point sizes are subtly different. While most PostScript fonts can't go quite that far, they come closer to this careful craftsmanship than other alternatives. In particular, since PostScript effectively draws each character at the correct point size, it preserves the relative size and weight relationships down to the finest resolution available. In addition, PostScript fonts contain special coding to make the characters look correct at small point sizes by adjusting the actual lines that make up the characters. Many electronic fonts, on the other hand, are simply reductions or enlargements of a fixed size of characters; this means that the font becomes coarse and unappealing at sizes different from the design size. This doesn't happen as severely with PostScript fonts.

In addition, this process of drawing the characters forms an important part of the device independence of PostScript. Because PostScript is independent of device-specific qualities like resolution, it must have a way to represent characters that will be able to place the characters in precisely the same relative positions on different devices, while allowing the maximum resolution that the device is capable of producing.

Summary

There are a wide variety of effects that you can generate using type in Illustrator. Because type characters are just another graphic object from Illustrator's (and PostScript's) viewpoint, most of the other tools in the Toolbox can be applied to text blocks. Indeed, only the Pen, Oval, and Rectangle tools have no applicability to text manipulation. All the other tools, such as the Rotate and Shear tools, can be used with good effect on text. In addition, you should remember that text can be filled and painted like any other object. This combination provides some powerful graphic images for you to work with. *Chapters 10 and 11* discuss the use of these tools, and as you work the examples in them, you will see type used as a graphic object in a variety of ways. However, don't think that you are limited to the techniques demonstrated. Anything that you can do to a square or a circle, you can do to type.

CHAPTER TEN

Painting Graphics

FEATURING

Graphics review

Paint style features

Using character outlines

Color options

Using standard color

Using spot color

Printing color comps

A TERMINOLOGY REFRESHER

Before we begin, let's briefly review all the terminology that you have encountered in the preceding chapters. Illustrator artwork is composed of graphic objects which, as you have seen, may be grouped together to be used as a single entity or left separate for individual work. In either case, every Illustrator object consists of one or more *paths*, each of which has a beginning and ending point. If the beginning and ending points are identical, the path is said to be *closed*, and if they are distinct, the path is *open*. A path is composed of connected straight or curved *line segments*. The path itself has no visible shape; you can have a path that exists on the drawing surface but does not show on the final output.

For a path to be visible, it must be *painted*. There are two basic methods for painting paths. The path may be *stroked*; that is, each line that composes the path is drawn as if by a pen. Alternatively, it may be *filled*; in that case, the interior of the path is colored in as if with a brush. The interior of a closed path is determined by a simple mathematical rule, called the *non-zero winding number rule*. An open path is implicitly closed before being filled by drawing a straight line between its two end points. If you want, a path may be both stroked and filled, as you saw in Exercise 3.2, where the shapes were stroked in black and filled with white. Note that paths are never implicitly closed when they are stroked, even if you are filling them at the same time. If an open path is both filled and stroked, the stroke follows the exact path while the fill obeys the rule for implicit closure.

Fill Options

Illustrator provides several choices for filling a path. These are chosen from the Paint Style dialog box, accessed by selecting Paint ➤ Style. The Fill choices are a series of buttons and associated boxes where the values can be inserted, as shown in the box labeled Fill, part of the Paint dialog box.

If None is chosen, the path is not filled at all, whether it is stroked or not. Obviously, there is no value associated with None.

Older versions of Illustrator used lines or rules on a page for placement or measurement with both stroke and fill set to None. Such lines will not display in Preview mode or print on your drawing, but they can still be seen when you are working in the Artwork mode. In Illustrator 3.2, this is no longer necessary. As you saw in Exercise 3.2, you can now make a guide out of any artwork. Guides are preferable to this technique of uncolored lines because guides look quite distinctive on the desktop and they cannot be accidently selected or moved with your artwork.

The alternative to None is to fill the path with some color; either White, Black, Gray, a Pattern, or a color. Colors can be selected as either Process Color or Custom Colors. Process Colors are composed of the three primary colors used in printing—Cyan, Magenta, and Yellow—plus Black; when you select the Process Color radio button, a series of four boxes appears that allows you to set the individual components of the desired color. Custom Colors and Patterns must be defined, using Paint ➤ Pattern or Paint ➤ Custom Color before they can be used. We will discuss how to define both patterns and custom colors later in this chapter. When you select either Custom Color or Pattern, the Paint Style dialog displays a scrolling list of all the defined items in that category. You can select one from the list for your artwork.

White is given a special button of its own, as it is usually a conscious choice, but it is really just 0% Black. True black is generated by specifying 100% as the value of Black, while shades of gray are provided by using other percentage values, from 1% to 99%. Remember that Illustrator will always provide the best approximation of the shade of gray that you request, but the device on which your output will be generated usually has specific limitations on how many levels of gray it can produce. Because of that, shades of gray that are not very far apart (typically within 5% or so) may not be distinguishable on your output.

Illustrator will display colors appropriately on a color monitor. Although Illustrator cannot show you color output if you don't have a color monitor, you can still choose color values for the Fill options. If you use these settings, you can specify the percentage of Cyan, Magenta, and Yellow, as well as Black, to generate color output on a PostScript color printer or for color separations.

If you are using a Custom Color, you can also set a percentage Tint for that color. Correct setting and use of these color values is a complex subject and we will discuss it in more detail later in this chapter; however, with correct use, you can generate almost any printed color for your output. If you set colors in your artwork here and then produce your output on a black-and-white device, the color values will be changed into shades of gray automatically. You can also use output with color values as a source for utilities such as Adobe's Separator program, which will separate the colors into individual pages of output for use as color separations by your printer. The Overprint check box, which is at the bottom of the Fill section, is also used in color separations. In the *Appendix*, we will discuss setting up and using these features to generate color separations.

Stroke Options

As an alternative—or in addition—to filling a path, Illustrator provides for stroking the path. A path is stroked as though by a pen, with the color of the ink defined by the controls in the box labeled Stroke. These controls are exactly like the ones for the Fill box. Note that, if you select both stroke and fill, the colors used do not have to be the same. The stroke is applied after the fill, so that the figure will look correctly outlined in the color chosen for the stroke. The width of the line painted by Illustrator is given by the Weight parameter, which specifies the width in points (72 points = 1 inch). The painted area lies equally on either side of the path, so that a line with a weight of four points, for example, will extend two points on either side of the path. This was an issue when you constructed the figures in Exercise 3.2, where you had to allow for the width of the lines when you were both painting and stroking a path.

In addition to these controls, there are several others in the Paint Style dialog box. All of these apply to stroked lines only; only the Fill box applies to filled objects. First, at the bottom of the dialog box is a wide box marked Dash pattern. This allows you to set the path to be stroked in either a solid line, which is the normal default, or in a dashed pattern which you can specify. You specify the dash pattern by giving values, in points, for the length of the dash and the gap between dashes. You may specify up to three pairs of dash and gap widths; after the given pattern is used the first time, the pattern is repeated in cycles for the length of the path. You will use the dashed pattern commands later in the book.

The Note box allows you to set a note into the PostScript language output generated by Illustrator. The Flatness setting, which is normally 0, controls how curved paths are drawn on your output. Both of these features require a discussion of the PostScript language, so we will defer discussion of them to *Chapter 15.* In general, the default settings of these items can be left as they are.

If you create an object and check the Mask checkbox, that object is used as a *clipping path* for all other objects on the artwork. A clipping path works something like a stencil, allowing you to place other objects in front of the mask to hide portions of them.

The Reversed checkbox is a special effect that is only available when you are using compound paths. This allows you to paint part of the path in one color and part in another.

The Caps box shows the three varieties of line cap that are available. The *line cap* governs the method Illustrator uses to finish the open end of line segments. You may choose a line ending that is square and flush with the end of the line, called a *butt cap* (the default). You may also choose to end a line with a half-circle, called a *rounded cap*. Finally, there is a square end, like the butt cap, that extends out from the end of the line by one-half the line width, called a *projecting square cap*. Each of these is illustrated in the box labeled Caps; you select the desired line cap by clicking on the appropriate picture.

In the same way, you can control how Illustrator joins lines. Every time two stroked line segments are joined together to form a corner, Illustrator connects them with a special *line join*, which fills in the corner so that it paints correctly. The first is a *miter* join, where the edges of the two segments are extended until they meet, as is done in a picture frame. The miter join is the default, and when it is used, the Miter Limit box—described below— is also active. The second is a *rounded* join, where the two segments are connected with a circular arc. The diameter of the circle will be equal to the width of the line. The last join is the *bevel* join, where the two segments are finished with butt caps and then the notch, which would otherwise be left between them, is filled in by a small triangle. When you close a path, the ends of the two lines will also have a small notch or gap, depending on the choice made for the line cap. In this case, Illustrator also fills that gap according to the join pattern, to ensure that the final connection is smooth and has the same form as the other corners.

When you specify a miter join, there is the possibility that extending the edges of the lines out until they meet will form a rather long spike. This can happen if the lines are large and the angle that they meet at is small. For these cases, Illustrator will change from a miter, or pointed, join to a bevel join when the spike reaches a certain length. The Miter Limit box controls this. The miter limit is the ratio of the length of the spike to the width, or weight, of the line. It must always be one or greater, and the larger it is, the longer the spike will be before the join changes to a bevel. A miter limit of 1 is the same as setting a permanent bevel join, since the spike will always be at least equal to the width of the line.

Examples for Line Cap, Line Join, and Miter Limit

Let's look at an example that illustrates the various settings for the stroke. The important point here is not to actually accomplish the example, but rather to understand how the settings for line cap, line join, and miter limit work and how the results look onscreen and on your output.

Begin with the settings for line cap and line join. Start with a clean Illustrator desktop. The example will use ruler coordinates for placement, which you show by choosing View ➤ Show Rulers (⌘-R), but you can ignore them if you want.

This example generates nine triangles in a 3 × 3 array, so that every combination of line cap and line join can be shown. Triangles were used so that the corners would be sharp enough to show some difference with each of the options. The method here is to create one triangle and then duplicate it across to make a row of three, and then duplicate the row upwards to form the array. Use the pen tool to draw the first triangle. The base of the triangle is horizontal, from (12, 26) to (16, 26); and the triangle is equilateral, so that all sides are the same size and the angle joining the sides is exactly 60°.

Making a precise equilateral triangle isn't essential; whatever is easiest to make will work fine. Select Paint ➤ Style and set the Fill to None and the Stroke to 100% Black, with a line weight of 4. Leave the other settings at their default values. Now use the selection tool to select the entire triangle. Remember that all the anchor points must be black squares for the entire figure to be selected; you can select the entire figure by using the Object Selection tool, either directly from the Toolbox or by pressing Option with the Selection tool. Pick up the bottom-left corner of the triangle, drag it to (20, 26), and duplicate it there. Hold down the Option key when you release the mouse button to make a duplicate. Then duplicate the triangle again with the same corner moved to (28, 26). Remember that holding down the Shift key as you move will constrain movement to be exactly horizontal. Now you have a row of three triangles, as shown in Figure 10.1.

Now select all the triangles. You can do that with the selection marquee or by choosing Edit ➤ Select All. Grab the row of triangles by the corner at (12, 26), move it up to (12, 32), and duplicate the row of triangles there. Remember that you can force the motion to be exactly vertical by holding down the Shift key as you move. Now duplicate the row again with the left corner at (4, 38). This gives you the complete set of nine triangles, arranged in three rows and three columns, as shown in Figure 10.2.

Figure 10.1

This row of triangles forms the basis for this exercise.

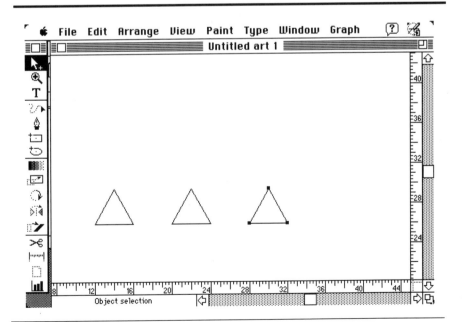

Figure 10.2

This array of nine triangles can be used to demonstrate a variety of line features.

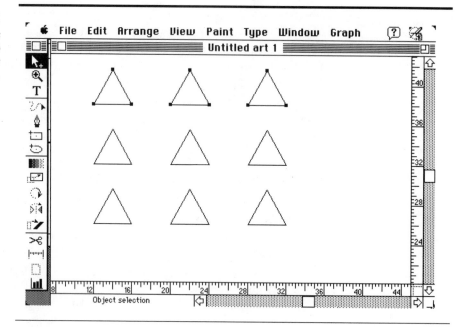

Ultimately, each one of these triangles will represent one of the possible combinations of line cap and line join. So that the settings being used for each triangle will be evident at a glance, let's add a set of angled lines along the side (to show the line join setting) and a set of straight lines across the bottom (to show the line caps). As before, the fastest way to do this is to make the line one time and duplicate it. You can begin by drawing a line from (36, 25p8) to (38, 29) to (40, 25p8). This gives a nice angled line that echoes the tops of the triangles across the rows.

Now duplicate that line two times upwards in line with the other rows of triangles. This takes care of the line joins. For the line caps, add a single, short line under each of the columns. The first line extends from (12, 23) to (16, 23). Then duplicate that line under each column of triangles. The final result should look something like Figure 10.3.

Now that you have all the elements in place, you need to set the various line cap and line join options. This can, of course, be done individually for each element; however, there is a faster and easier way. It is possible—indeed,

Figure 10.3

This completes the line cap and join demonstration array.

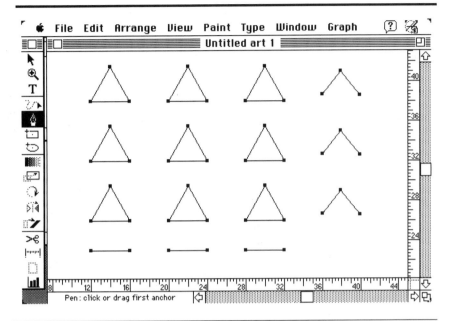

often desirable—to set certain characteristics for a group of graphic objects in common, and that's what you should do here. First, use the selection tool and the selection marquee to choose all of the elements in the first column: the three triangles and the line.

Now get the Paint Style dialog box by selecting Paint ➤ Style (⌘-I). Notice that the settings that you made previously still show, even though you have selected multiple objects. Since all these objects share identical settings, all the settings can be shown in one box. Now use the selection marquee to select the second column. Again open the Paint Style dialog box. This time, change the line cap in the Caps radio group from butt caps—the top entry—to rounded caps—the middle selection.

Finally, select the third column of triangles and the associated line and set the caps to square, extended—the bottom selection. This establishes the line caps for the figures.

Now you want to set the line joins. In this case, each row of figures, comprising three triangles and the angled line, will be set together in much the same fashion as the columns were set. Again use the selection marquee to select the top row of figures, including the angled line at the end of the row. Get the Paint Style dialog box. Notice this time that the Caps radio group shows no particular button chosen.

This shows an interesting fact about setting Paint attributes for a group of objects. The Caps values for these objects are all different, since you set each column to a different value. The fact that no value is highlighted in the Caps radio group warns you that the Caps setting for these objects are not all the same. You can still change the value to make them the same if you want; the lack of a selection is simply a warning. The Paint Style dialog box takes this approach whenever you have selected a series of objects that do not share one or more values. You should keep this in mind, as it occasionally happens that multiple objects are selected inadvertently, resulting in all or several choices in the dialog box that would normally be filled in remaining empty; under those circumstances, changing them to a single value may have unexpected results. Notice that when a choice is not applicable, such as a line cap or join for an object that is not stroked, the choice is dimmed and cannot be selected. Here, the choice is active but no value is shown; this is your warning that the selected objects have different values for this choice.

Use the selection marquee to select the middle row and set the Joins for that row to rounded joins. Then select the bottom row of triangles and set that for bevel joins. Now you have finished setting all the values in this array. Each of the triangles has a different combination of line cap and line join, as illustrated by the caps shown on the straight lines at the bottom of the column and by the join shown at the right of the row.

This is good, but it is quite difficult to see the difference between the normal square, or butt, caps and the extended square caps (columns one and three). It would be better if you could see the path as well as the stroked result. You can get that effect by painting the path with a thin, white line and placing that line over each thick line. You must set the thin line with butt caps, so that the stroked line doesn't extend past the end of the path. Then the thin white line will paint over the larger line, showing the effect of the type of line cap. Making such overlays is an essential part of using Illustrator to its fullest extent.

There is an easy way to do this overlay. Start by duplicating the first line some-what below itself. Use the Shift key as you move to ensure that the line only moves vertically. Then go to the Paint dialog box and set Fill to None, Stroke to White, and Weight to 0.3.

Since this is a copy of the first line, butt caps are already in use and don't need to be selected again. Now move this line back up and overlay the first line. Notice that there appears to be only one line, and that line is selected. Actually, there are two identical paths here, with the top one—the line you just created—still selected. If you want, preview this to see the effect.

When you are ready, copy the selected line to the right, using the Shift key again to insure that the movement is constrained, until the line lies directly over the second line. Press Option before releasing the mouse button to make a copy. Notice that the copy is now selected. Move this again to the right to exactly cover the third line and duplicate it. Now you have made thin, white lines placed over each of the first three thicker lines, as required. If you preview this, it is hard to see the exact placement of the thin line over the thicker; to help see the result select the Zoom in tool and magnify the center line. Then the final result looks like Figure 10.4.

Using this same approach extended to the angle lines, and adding some text, you can generate the printed output shown in Figure 10.5.

This tells you about line caps and line joins, but what about the miter limit? To avoid making this section too long and tedious, I will not give a full ex-ample here. Instead, let's just briefly look at how the miter limit parameter af-fects the result that you get in output. The miter limit, as you learned earlier, is the ratio of the line width to the length of the spike made when two lines join at an angle. If the lines are wide and the angle is relatively small, the spike can extend quite some distance from the join, possibly distorting the figure. To control this, you can set the miter limit, which is the maximum ratio that you will accept before the miter join is changed into a bevel join. The miter limit may be set to any number from 1 to 100, with 1 forcing bevel joins at all corners, and therefore being equivalent to setting the line join parameter to beveled joins. The default miter limit is 4, which provides that most corners will be mitered, but that sharp corners will be beveled. It is quite enough for most situations. Let's construct an array again to show the

Figure 10.4

This is a preview of the lines with a white overlay line in place.

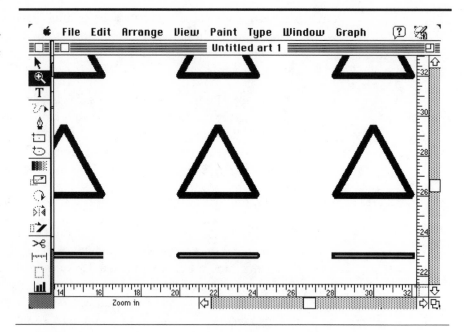

Figure 10.5

This is the printed output of line join and cap demonstration array.

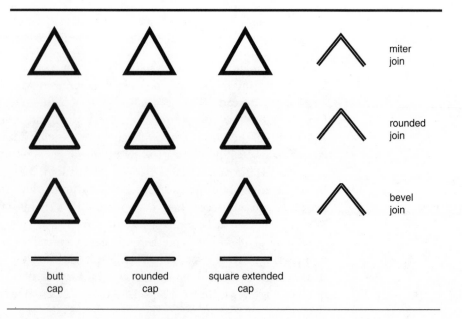

variations that can occur for different angles of join and different values of the miter limit parameter. This array is shown in Figure 10.6.

In this figure, the line weights are 5 points, and the angles are 10°, 20°, and 45°. As you see, the default miter limit provides mitered corners for joins over about 20°. The 45° join shows a clear instance of a miter join, while the 20° and 10° joins are beveled. Increase the miter limit to 6, however, and the 20° join remains mitered while the 10° join is beveled. As you see, the new value permits the spike at the corner to extend quite some distance from the actual corner point. Finally, setting the miter limit to 12, as shown in the top line, keeps even the 10° join as a miter join. Here the spike extends quite far from the corner. This gives you some idea of the variations possible between the miter limit and the angle of join.

You should also note that the width of the lines being joined has some effect here. The ratio of the miter to the line width will, of course, always be the same for any width of line; however, the line width determines whether you can see the spike. For normal line widths of 1 point or less, the effect of the miter limit is pretty much invisible. For lines with a greater width, as in the figure above, the effect can be quite dramatic. You might want to check the effect of

Figure 10.6

This shows you how the miter limit and the angle of join interact.

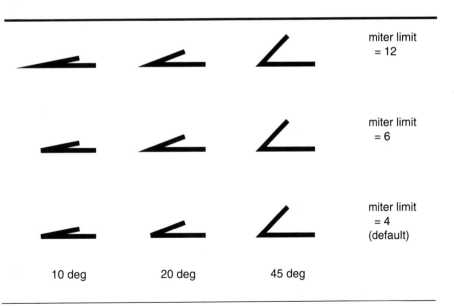

miter limit
= 12

miter limit
= 6

miter limit
= 4
(default)

10 deg   20 deg   45 deg

changing the array above from a 5 point line to 1 point. The change in joins still exists when you do, but it becomes almost unnoticeable.

TYPE AS A GRAPHIC OBJECT

In *Chapters* 8 and 9, you saw how to use text with your graphics. However, one of the most interesting and exciting features of Illustrator is that you can use character outlines as graphic elements as well as for text. This is possible for two reasons. First, the characters that you are using come from PostScript fonts, which are composed of character outlines. These outlines are the result of small PostScript programs that actually draw each character on the output. Second, you are using Adobe's Type Manager (ATM) software that is shipped with Illustrator. This means that you are seeing the same outlines on the screen that you will use when you print your output. Since ATM is already using the character outlines from your PostScript fonts to draw on the screen, it is a small step to converting those outlines into Illustrator paths and using them for graphics.

When you have ATM installed, you can convert any characters that you have selected that are from Type 1 fonts into outlines. Type 1 fonts are PostScript font outlines that you use both to print on your PostScript printer and, with ATM, to display characters onscreen. Note that you cannot create outlines for fonts that are not Type 1 fonts. For example, Macintosh system fonts like Geneva and Chicago are not Type 1 fonts. In addition, you cannot make out-lines from any Type 1 fonts that are not installed in your system. If you have imported a graphic from another system that uses a font that you do not have, then you will not be able to use that font to create character outlines.

Once you have turned any character or set of characters into outlines, they be-come just like any other Illustrator object. Well, almost any other object—ac-tually, the outlines are created as compound paths. Compound paths are a special form of Illustrator path and behave something like grouped objects. We will discuss compound paths in *Chapter* 12. As far as character outlines go, you can either use the outlines directly as compound paths or you can select Paint ➤ Release Compound (⌘–Option-U) to change the compound paths into ordinary Illustrator paths. You can select, distort, or otherwise transform these paths as you would any other Illustrator path.

Exercise 10.1: Using Character Outlines

Let's use outlines in a simple exercise so that you get some idea of how they work. This exercise will simply take the word *PARADE*, change it into outlines, and distort it. Then you will draw a simple background for the text to make a graphic element.

There are a few issues that you need to keep in mind as you work with text outlines. First, outlines can be very complex. For this reason, you might have trouble printing them. You should always keep the amount of text you are using to a minimum, particularly when the text is in a font whose outlines are quite complex—for example, Zapf Chancery. For this exercise, you will use only one word, *PARADE*, and you will use the regular Helvetica font, which has quite simple outlines. Second, the font that you use must have a Type 1 outline available on your system. The ATM software that comes with your copy of Illustrator includes outlines for the Helvetica, Times-Roman, Symbol, and Courier font families. However, most PostScript printers come with other font outlines, such as Bookman and Zapf Chancery, built in to them. You can use these fonts for printing, but you cannot use them as outlines unless you have the matching font outlines stored on your Macintosh. If you try to use one of these fonts for outlines, you will get an error alert box.

If you see this box, check the font selection for your text block. If the font is not installed in your system, either install it or use another font. If the font is installed, be sure that it is a Type 1 font and not a TrueType font. Also be sure that the font is installed correctly in the Extensions folder inside the System folder on your hard disk.

Move to the center of the desktop and type the word **PARADE**, using the Helvetica font, 72 point size, with Left alignment. Then click on the Selection tool in the Toolbox. This leaves the text block selected, as shown by the visible anchor point and the line underneath the text itself. At this point, you screen should look something like Figure 10.7.

Now choose Type ➤ Create Outlines. This changes each letter in the text block into simple lines, just as if you had drawn lines around each letter. This also removes the text anchor point and the text underline, since the letters are no longer part of a text block.

Figure 10.7

This is the basic text that you will use for this exercise.

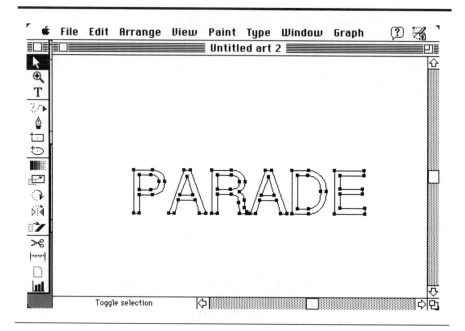

Remember that these outlines are compound paths, and so behave very much like grouped objects. For example, if you deselect the outlines and then take the Selection tool and click on one of the letters, you will see that the entire letter is selected as a unit, just as if it were a group. To change the letter outlines, you can do one of two things: Either use the Direct Selection tool to access individual anchor points in the path or remove the compound-path attribute. The latter is more sensible and easier. Therefore select all of the letter paths by using ⌘-A and then choose Paint ➤ Release Compound (⌘-Option-U) to remove the compound-path characteristic from your letterforms. This allows you to access the paths individually, just like any other Illustrator object.

You might notice here how Illustrator tries to help you remember the keyboard commands that correspond to various menu selections. The keyboard commands for Arrange ➤ Group and Arrange ➤ Ungroup are ⌘-G and ⌘-U, respectively. This seems fairly easy to remember, using G for Group and U for Ungroup. If you are working with text boxes, you can link these boxes so that the text flows from one to another. In a sense, this is again a form of grouping for these objects, and the corresponding keyboard commands for

Type ➤ Link and Type ➤ Unlink are ⌘-Shift-G and ⌘-Shift-U. As you just saw, compound paths are also similar to groups, and the keyboard commands for Paint ➤ Make Compound and Paint ➤ Release Compound are ⌘-Option-G and ⌘-Option-U. Even though these commands are on different menus and do different jobs, they are similar in some ways, so Illustrator uses the same basic keys, G and U, for all of them. This simple mnemonic scheme helps you associate all of these commands and even reminds you that the commands have some features in common.

Now use the Selection tool to distort the tops of the letters, bringing them each up and out. There are no specific directions for this, so just do it as the spirit moves you. My spirit ended up with the letters shown in Figure 10.8.

Use the Paint Style dialog box to set the attributes for these letters to Fill None, Stroke 100% Black with 2 point line Weight. As a final effect, draw a wavy line below the letters, using the Pen tool, that is somewhat longer than the letters themselves. Paint this with Fill None, Stroke 40% Black, and line Weight of 4. Then move the line slightly up and duplicate it by using the

Figure 10.8

You can distort letter-forms into any shape once you have made them into outlines.

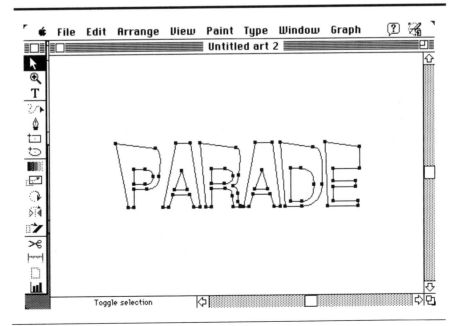

Option key. Continue the series of lines up the letters, using ⌘-D (Arrange ➤ Transform Again) until you have covered all the letters. Now choose Edit ➤ Send to Back to move the lines behind the letters to form a background for them. This makes an interesting effect and will preview something like Figure 10.9.

Figure 10.9

You can create some interesting effects when you distort letterforms to make them part of your artwork.

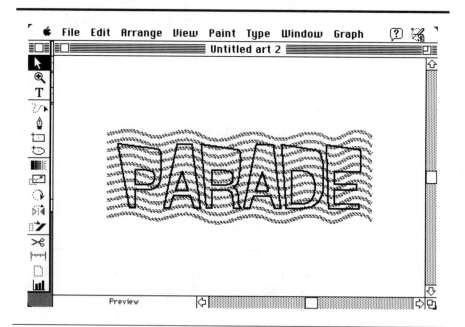

Coloring objects

Besides allowing you to paint objects in black, white, or shades of gray, Illustrator also allows you to paint in color. However, color brings with it a lot of complex issues. Without raising any aesthetic concerns, simply using color correctly is both complex and difficult. This section provides you with a brief overview of how you can set and use full color in Illustrator. It should be enough to help you use Illustrator for color output on PostScript color printers. This section, along with the *Appendix*, which covers use of the Adobe Separator program, should allow you to produce basic color separations. However, if you are going to do serious color work, on a professional and consistent basis, this is not a substitute for a thorough understanding of the color printing process and a close working relationship with your printing professional.

Let's begin with an introduction of color display and printing. All colors can be reduced into three components of light: red, green, and blue. These three colors, in appropriate combinations, make up all the colors, shades, and tints that you see around you. These colors are called the *additive primary colors*, and are generally abbreviated RGB. These are the colors that are used by your computer screen to display colors. The absence of any color, black, occurs when there is no amount of RGB set; that is, when no light is transmitted. White, on the other hand, occurs when all the three components are transmitted with equal intensity; full white light occurs when each component is at 100 percent.

When you deal with printed material, however, the physics of light and color demand that you work differently. To begin with, white is the *absence* of any color on the page. With printed materials, you use the *subtractive primary colors*. These are cyan, which is the absence of red; magenta, which is the absence of green; and yellow, which is the absence of blue. Conceptually, black is equal amounts of each of these colors, and full black occurs when you have 100 percent of each component. Since printing requires ink or some other opaque medium, though, using 100 percent of each color would require three heavy layers of ink on the page. This generally will not produce a satisfactory result, so printers add black to make printed colors accurate. Then shades of black ink can be substituted whenever there are equal components of the other three colors. These four colors are usually abbreviated CMYK, where K stands for black. These colors are *process* colors. You can use these four colors to print artwork in any color.

Illustrator, too, uses the CMYK color percentages for setting colors. These settings are translated into red, green, and blue for display on your Macintosh screen if you have a color monitor and have enabled color for your display. However, Illustrator can assign colors to artwork even if you don't have a color display. The colors that you assign to the artwork are used when Illustrator prints to your PostScript output device. If the PostScript output device has color printing capabilities, then the artwork will print in color; if it is a black and white device, the colors are automatically converted into shades of gray.

Onscreen Color

If you have a color monitor, then you can see the colors that you assign to your artwork on the screen. Understand, though, that the colors that you see onscreen are only approximations of the colors that you would see on printed output. This happens because your screen uses RGB values for color representation, while Illustrator uses CMYK. Although theoretically identical, in practice these do not translate quite perfectly from one to the other, due to the differences in the color phosphors that make up the screen display, color reproduction technology, inks for printing, and other factors. The colors displayed on your screen may also vary depending on the amount and type of light falling on the screen and for other, external reasons. So only use the color onscreen as a guide to what your final output will look like.

Also keep in mind that displaying colors does take time and processor cycles that you might prefer to spend on drawing or other work. This isn't simply limited to Illustrator; most applications work faster in black and white than in color. For simple document and color values there isn't a noticeable difference, and the color display is both attractive and useful. If you are working with complex, colored documents (combining tints and blends of color), though, you will probably find that turning off the color display makes your work go faster and easier. You can always turn the color back on when you are assigning color values or when you are near completion of the artwork to see the work as it will look on output.

Exercise 10.2: Process Colors

Now that you have the theory under your belt, let's do a simple example that will show you how to use Illustrator to set color values for your artwork. This exercise will draw a simple bunch of grapes for use as an icon on a map; we'll color the grapes purple. Start with a standard, empty Illustrator drawing surface. Use the Oval tool and the Shift key to draw a small circle near the center of the drawing surface. Now select Paint ➤ Style (⌘-I) to set the colors for this grape. Figure 10.10 shows you the settings that you should use.

Let's do the Fill first. To set these values, select the Process Color radio button. When you do that, the bottom section of the Fill box changes to show the four process colors: Cyan, Magenta, Yellow, and Black. Enter the desired percentages of each component into the associated box. In this case, you should

Figure 10.10

*Use these settings
to create a light
purple grape with
a darker outline.*

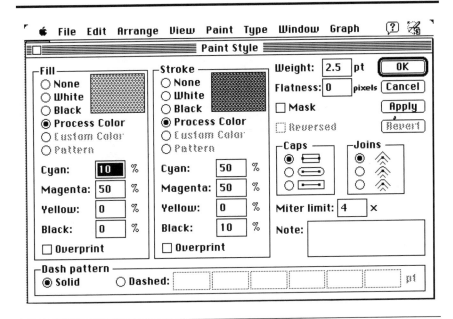

use Cyan 10%, Magenta 50%, Yellow 0%, and Black 0%. The color that you set here appears in the tint display at the top of the Fill section if you have a color monitor; if not, it is displayed as a shade of gray. Next set the Stroke for a darker shade of purple. Click on Process Color again, and set Cyan 50%, Magenta 50%, Yellow 0%, and Black 0%. Use a stroke Weight of 2.5 points. Because you are using shades of color here, the stroke outline needs to be wider than you would make it if you were using black. Click OK to return to the artwork.

If you want to see how this looks, you can preview the artwork now. If not, let's continue by adding more grapes to the bunch. You do that by simply moving and duplicating this grape over and over. Remember that grapes grow in a more or less triangular pattern and, since a bunch of grapes is round, some will be in front of others. The easiest way to create this illusion is to place some of the grapes at the top of the bunch after you have created ones lower down, to create the illusion of dimensionality. However you do it, the final artwork should look something like Figure 10.11.

On a color monitor, you can preview this in color; on a black and white monitor, it will preview like Figure 10.12.

Irrespective of your monitor, the artwork itself is in color. Plate 8 shows this bunch of grapes, along with some other artwork, printed on a color Post-Script device.

Figure 10.11

The bunch of grapes after you have used duplication to fill it out.

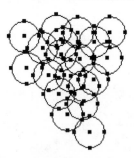

Figure 10.12

Colored objects are converted into shades of gray when you preview or print them on a black-and-white device.

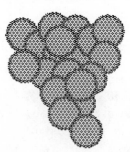

Custom colors

Beside the four process colors, you can also define and use custom colors. Very often, when you want only black and one other color on your artwork, it is preferable to use *spot color* or two-color processing when you are printing. Full-color output requires four inks and four passes through a printing press. If you are using only one color in addition to black, or if you need a special color, such as a metallic color ink, then your printer may recommend that you use only two inks: black and an ink that is mixed to be the exact color that you want.

Illustrator supports this type of printing by the use of custom colors. Custom colors are defined in Illustrator by selecting Paint ➤ Custom Color. This presents you with the dialog box shown in Figure 10.13.

Although custom colors are not normally printed using process colors, you define them in this dialog box as a combination of process colors. This provides two benefits. First, it allows you to see the colors onscreen if you have a color monitor. Second, it allows you to print color proofs, or *comps*, on any PostScript color printer. At the same time, Illustrator remembers your custom color name and assignments, so that you can create appropriate separation negatives using Adobe Separator.

Once you have defined a custom color, the name that you supply in the dialog box will be displayed in the Paint Style dialog box when you select the Custom Color radio button. To use the custom color for a Fill or Stroke

Figure 10.13

The Custom Color dialog box allows you to create and maintain a set of custom colors for your artwork.

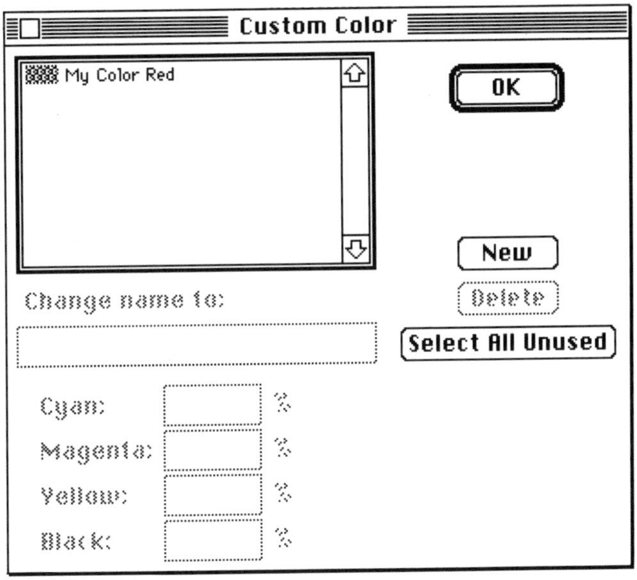

operation, simply select Custom Color and then choose the desired color from the scrolling list. All the custom colors that you define for your document are stored with the document, so you won't have to define them again when you reuse that document.

The issue of matching specific printed colors has been around about as long as color printing itself. One time-honored method of matching colors is the Pantone Matching System (PMS), which allows you to specify a specific color for your work by using a PMS color number. When you go to print, the printer will use a specific ink, provided by Pantone, which will match the color that you requested. You select the desired color by looking at a special color reference manual provided by Pantone. This manual lists all the Pantone colors along with their number and a color swatch that accurately represents what the color will look like when you print on coated (glossy) paper. In this way, you can specify an exact color and be sure that it will look the way you want every time you print.

Obviously, the PMS system is a natural for custom color definitions. However, with over 700 PMS colors to choose from, defining the ones that you want might get tricky. Luckily, Illustrator and Pantone have made using and specifying PMS colors very easy. The Custom Color dialog box allows you to create and maintain a set of custom colors for your artwork. Each copy of Illustrator ships with a Pantone application that installs a special document on your disk, called the Pantone Colors (coated paper) document. This document contains the definitions of over 700 Pantone colors which you can use in your own documents. When you want to specify a PMS color for your artwork, simply open up the document in Illustrator. This automatically adds all the Pantone color definitions to your work as custom colors. Then just use the Custom Color button and select the desired PMS color from the scrolling list. As long as you have the Pantone Colors document open, all the PMS color definitions will remain available to you. If you use one or more of these in your own document, those colors will remain with the document, like any other custom color definitions, even after the Pantone document is closed.

You can use this same technique yourself if you often use the same custom colors. Create a dummy document and define all your custom colors. Then save that document as a reference. Notice that you don't have to actually use the colors anywhere in the document; just define them while the document is open using Paint ➤ Custom Color. Then, whenever you want to use one of these colors, open this document. Custom colors—and patterns as well—that are defined in any open document are available in *all* documents. So you can simply select the correct color directly from the Paint Style dialog box, instead of having to recreate the colors for each document.

Although the Pantone system is the oldest and most widely used color matching system, it is not the only one. Your Illustrator application comes with TruMatch and TOYO91 color documents as well. Specification and use of these color systems in Illustrator works the same way as the Pantone system—although each system works differently once you get the artwork to your printer. Consult with your printing professional to determine which system will be most appropriate for your requirements.

Exercise 10.3: Setting a PMS Color as a Custom Color

Let's do a short example to see how this all works. This example uses the apple artwork that you should now be familiar with. You will tint this with red for the apple and green for the leaves and stem. To begin, open the *Modified Apple art* that you created in *Chapter 7*. For this exercise you can choose to use the template or not, as you wish. For the sake of clarity, we will dispense with the template background. Figure 10.14 shows you this artwork on your drawing surface.

Now you need to add the Pantone colors to your document. Go to File ➤ Open and choose the Pantone Colors (coated paper) document. This will take a few moments to open, since it has all of the Pantone colors defined in it. The document is visible as a single page of text on your drawing surface. Choose Window ➤ Modified Apple art (or whatever name your artwork has) to return to the apple artwork.

Now you are ready to set the first color. Select any part of the apple outline and then choose Paint ➤ Style to get the Paint Style dialog box. Notice that the Custom Color radio button is now active. Click on this button and you will see a scrolling list of Pantone colors appear, as shown in Figure 10.15.

Scroll down the list to the entry PANTONE 186 CV and select that. If you have a color monitor, you will see a small example of each color next to its

Figure 10.14

This is the modified apple artwork ready to have color added to it.

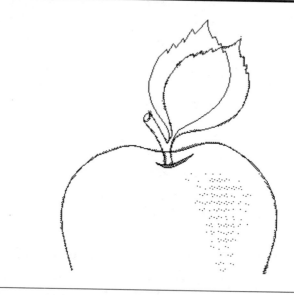

Figure 10.15

If you open the Pantone olor document, you will be able to access all the PMS colors.

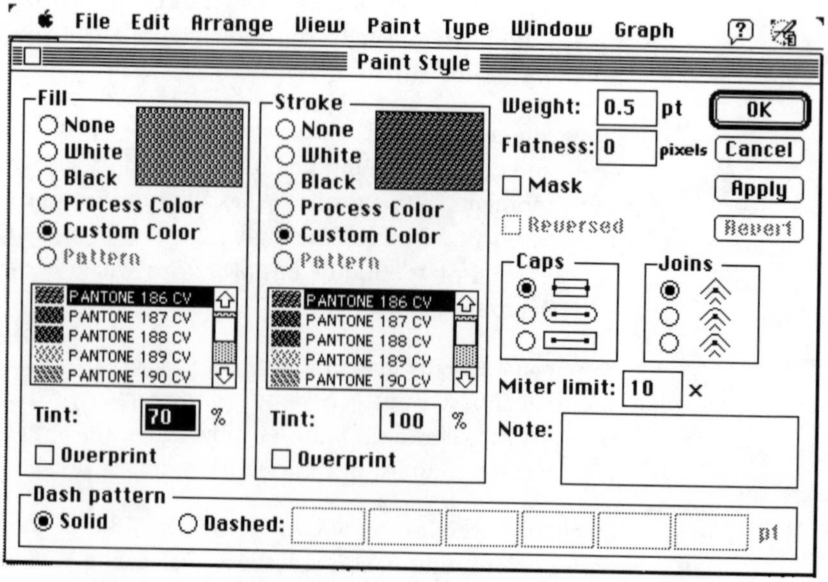

name; and when you select the color, the large demonstration swatch at the top of the Fill section also shows your selected color. If you are working in black and white, all the swatches will be in shades of gray. Set the Fill Tint to 70% and use the same Custom Color at 100% for the stroke. Set the stroke Weight to 0.5. This provides a slightly darker red as an outline to the apple itself. Click OK.

Now select the front leaf. For this, change the Paint Style to PANTONE 361 CV. Use a Tint of 50% for the Fill and a Stroke of 100% of the same color, with a line weight of 1. Set the back leaf to the same color, but with a Fill Tint of 80% and the same Stroke that you used on the first leaf. Finally, select the stem artwork and paint that with a Fill of 100% of PANTONE 361 CV, a Stroke of 100% Black and a line weight of 0.5.

If you print this in full color, it should look something like Plate 8.

As you see, the trick to using PMS colors is to open the Pantone document and leave it in the background. This allows you to access the entire range of Pantone colors as custom colors, without having to define them yourself.

Printing in Color

There are several possibilities when you print a colored document. First of all, of course, you may have colored your document but only be able to print it on a black-and-white device, such as a LaserWriter. In this case, as you saw earlier, the PostScript interpreter will convert your color instructions into shades of gray for output. This can be very useful for determining the placement of graphic elements and for general proofing of the artwork.

However, if you have gone to all the trouble of creating a colored document, you will probably want to see it in color at some point in the proofing process. You can use any PostScript color printer for this purpose. Since Illustrator stores all the color information with your document, you don't need to do anything more than select a color output device in the Chooser. Then, when you print, be sure to select the Color/Grayscale radio button for output (if it isn't already selected). The artwork will print in full color.

Such prints may be used as final output, if you only need one or two copies. However, color printers are generally rather slow—since they require three or four passes to produce a single sheet of output—and expensive. Therefore, the most common use of color printers is to provide full-color proofs of the artwork that you have created. Such proofs are more commonly known as *color comps*.

For multiple full-color copies, your color artwork must be converted into *color separations*. Color separations are separate prints of each color component in your artwork. Your printer uses these to create separate plates, one for each color, which are used for the printing process. Sometimes, for proofing purposes, each separation is printed on a transparent background in the correct color (generally cyan, magenta, yellow, and black). You will read all about making and using separations with Illustrator and Adobe Separator in the *Appendix*.

Summary

Remember that the colors that you see on color PostScript output may not exactly match the colors that you see on screen, and generally neither of these will match the colors that you get when you make color separations and print. This happens for a variety of reasons, but you should always make tests of your output as you work if you are looking for certain precise colors. As an alternative, you can use the PMS or other color matching mechanisms to ensure that you will get the correct color on your final output.

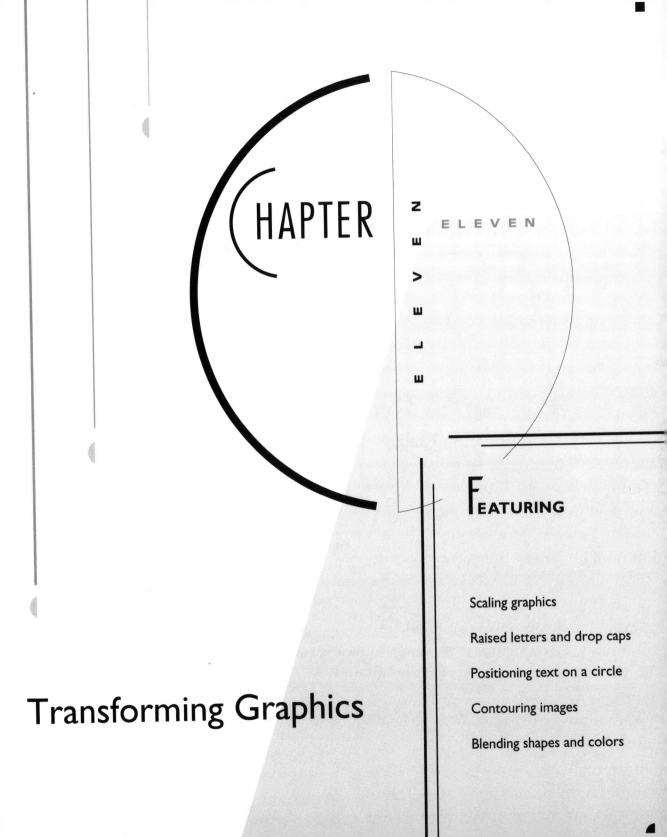

CHAPTER ELEVEN

Transforming Graphics

FEATURING

Scaling graphics

Raised letters and drop caps

Positioning text on a circle

Contouring images

Blending shapes and colors

THE TRANSFORMATION TOOLS

There are four transformation tools in Illustrator:

Scale tool	Reduces or enlarges selected objects proportionally
Rotate tool	Turns a selected object in a circle around a defined center of rotation
Reflect tool	Mirrors a selected object along a defined axis of reflection (which is a straight line)
Shear tool	Slants a selected object uniformly along a defined shear axis (which is a straight line)

Each of these tools provides a powerful transformation ability for Illustrator graphics. They can be used individually or in combination. They can be invoked repeatedly to generate some very unusual effects. Conveniently, the tools work in very similar ways. Once you know how to work one, the others will be much easier to understand and apply.

Basically, each of these tools requires that you select the object to be transformed, set a *control* point for the operation, and then drag or click to move the selected object to the desired location. All of these tools can be constrained to an axis that is a multiple of 45° by using them in conjunction with the Shift key. All of them have the same facility for duplicating an object by using the Option key when you complete the transformation. And, finally, all of them have the same optional dialog-box mechanism, controlled either by using the Option key when you invoke the transformation or by selecting the alternate dialog tool in the Toolbox.

There are two uses for the Option key during transformations. At the beginning of the process, when you are setting the control point, use the Option key to change to the dialog tool, invoking a dialog box that allows you to more precisely control the process. At the end of the transformation, use the

Option key to create a copy of the original object. You will see examples of both methods in these exercises.

Scaling Images

The Scale tool produces larger or smaller versions of the selected artwork. This operation is so common, so powerful, and so natural that you have already used it in several of the examples in earlier chapters. You used it to scale the logo artwork for the letterhead, and again to generate the concentric rings for the target artwork. You may not even have thought about it very much.

Before you start on the major examples using the Scale tool, you should undertake a few simple exercises to see how all the features work. Begin by opening a new document with no template. Select the Oval tool and create a circle on the left side of the drawing surface. You will use this artwork as the subject for the next series of scaling exercises. Now select the Scale tool. You see the cursor become a small cross (+) to mark the designated origin for the scaling operation. Click the cursor on the right edge anchor point of the circle. This sets the *origin* for the scaling, the point that all other points on the circle will be magnified or reduced around.

Now the cursor turns into the delta you have seen before in several contexts. Clicking the delta cursor allows you to drag the selected object in any direction. The distance you drag governs how much scaling is done to the object and the scaling is done relative to a fixed scaling origin—in this case, the right anchor point. First, click on the left anchor point, and drag the circle a small distance away from the original graphic. The result looks something like Figure 11.1.

Notice, as you move the circle, that it is quite easy to get very large movements of the graphic even when making really small movements. Remember that you can always return to the original artwork immediately after any transformation by selected the Edit ➤ Undo Scale (or whatever the transformation was). Finish this exercise by doing that to return to the original circle.

You see that the cursor has returned to the cross, showing you that it is once again ready to set a new origin for the scale process. Now select the center of the circle. Position the delta cursor on the top anchor point and drag downward. Notice here how the right and left edges of the circle stay in place while the others move. This happens because these two points lie along the x-axis of both the current figure and the scaling origin that was chosen. Therefore they don't move as you move the remainder of the figure. As you move around, the figure is quite a bit less sensitive than the first selection.

A typical arrangement is shown in Figure 11.2.

Figure 11.1

This shows how a circle looks when you perform a scaling operation using two anchor points.

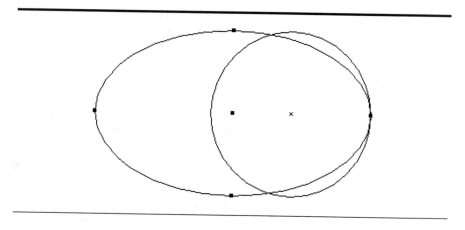

Figure 11.2

This shows another scale operation on a circle.

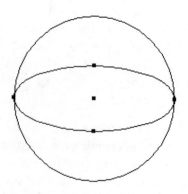

Select the center again and use the delta cursor on the upper-right edge of the circle, at about the two o'clock position. This time, the scale works on both axes, since you are positioned at an angle to both the *x* and *y* coordinates and you get a result that may look like Figure 11.3.

As a final exercise in scaling, show the rulers and select the point (36, 36) as the origin for the scaling operation. Then move the delta cursor to (24, 28) and click and drag the cursor toward the bottom-right corner of the drawing surface. You will get a result that looks something like Figure 11.4.

It isn't necessary to choose points that lie on the selected graphic for either the origin or for the position that you are scaling. Wherever you choose, the selected graphic will be scaled accordingly. This flexibility is tremendously powerful, but it is also the reason you must be sure you have selected the object that you desire before you start clicking and dragging. If you select the wrong object, you may get remarkable results that you really didn't want to have. If that ever happens, just be sure to immediately Undo the action to return to your original artwork.

Figure 11.3

Even scaling only comes when you don't use the anchor points for the scale operation on the circle.

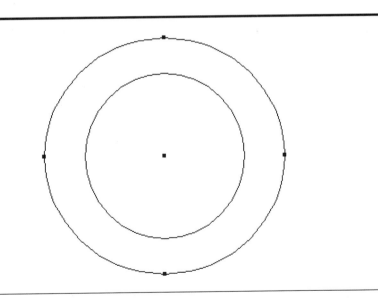

Figure II.4

*You can scale using points
entirely off the circle.*

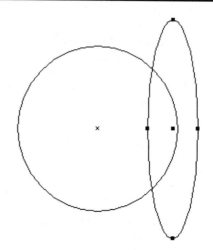

Exercise II.1: Scaling Text

The transformation tools can also be used to create a variety of text effects. In particular, the Scale tool provides some interesting possibilities when applied to letters.

To sample some of these, you will do an exercise that allows you to make changes to text and letters. The actual text and selection of font, point size and so on is not critical, so long as you use a Type 1 font that you have installed on your system. If you feel like experimenting, please go ahead. This exercise stands alone and will not become part of any succeeding exercise.

To start with, open a new document. Move to the left side of the drawing surface and, using the Text tool, create a letter R. This exercise uses the Times font in the Roman (regular) style, 36 point, left adjustment. For such large type, the Leading values chosen by Illustrator are ridiculous, so change the Leading from Auto to 38 points. Tracking and the other options are not relevant for this exercise. Return to the Toolbox and click on the Text tool to start a new text block. Next to the letter R, as a separate text block, enter another string of text, as follows:

aised capitals
can be very decorative

Notice that there is a line break after the word *capitals*. This is necessary because, at 36 points, the entire line of text will not fit on the page. For this string, leading is set to 36 (the same as the point size).

Now take the R and move it down to line up horizontally with the second line of the text, *can be very decorative*. Convert the R to an outline, using Type ➤ Convert Outlines as you did in *Chapter 10*. Then use the Scale tool to expand the capital R to fill the space next to the two lines of text. This can most easily be done by using the rulers and marking where the second line of text falls on them. Then maneuver the baseline for the R to match. When you scale the R, make the alignment point the origin for the scaling operation. As a final touch, return elect the R and then choose Paint ➤ Style. Besides setting the type style information for text, you can also set the painting values. In this case, set Fill to White and Stroke to 100% Black with a line Weight of 1.

In earlier versions of Illustrator, without ATM, the screen would not have done justice in any way to the printed output. Because of resolution limitations and font concerns, the resulting screen image, even in preview, would be only an approximation of the actual output. However, with ATM, the screen provides both placement information and a good idea of what the result will look like. Nevertheless, you will have to print the page to really see what it looks like.

You also see here some of the alterations that you can make to text by using the Paint Style dialog box choices. You can use this box to select any Fill or Stroke option, as you would for any other graphic. You can also combine fill and stroke to create various effects. These selections, combined with the scaling operation, can make letters that are truly unique.

As a simple example, use the same drawing surface to try another exercise. You will create multiple copies of a letter, one on top of the other, and change the painting characteristics of each version. Then the final layer is slightly offset from the others, to create a type of shaded outline.

To speed up this process, just select all of the previous text that you created and copy it down below the first exercise. Then select the first letter, the capital R. This will be the letter that you modify for this exercise.

Begin by setting the Fill and Stroke attributes for this letter; set Fill to None and set Stroke to 100% Black with a line weight of 2. Then choose Edit ➤ Copy. Select Edit ➤ Paste In Front to restore that copy directly in front of the first letter. Now set the Paint Style attributes for this letter as no Fill, Stroke in White, and a line Weight of 0.8 points. This layers a copy of the letter over the first copy, but outlines it in white, rather than black. Because the line weight of this copy is less than the preceding copy, the first copy of the letter will show behind the second as the difference in the line weights. So now you have one copy of the letter on top of the other; if you printed this now, you would get a letter that looks very much like the first outlined R.

Now you want to make another copy, using the same technique: Edit ➤ Copy, then Edit ➤ Paste In Front. This copy is automatically selected, so just go into the Paint Style dialog box and set Fill to 100% Black with Stroke set to None. This gives you a final copy of the letter, not stroked but just filled. Now you need to move this letter just a little bit to the right and up to create the shading effect that you want. In this case, you want to move such a small amount that you need to use a new technique. Hold down the Option key and go up and click on the Selection tool. You will see the Move dialog box.

Use this dialog box to move the last copy of the letter 2 points horizontally, and 1 point vertically. In this way you have offset the final, unstroked copy of the letter horizontally and vertically to create a outlined and shaded effect, as shown in Figure 11.5.

These two exercises should give you some additional familiarity with the Scale transformation. In particular, I hope that this last exercise sparks some ideas for transforming text in some interesting and imaginative ways. Remember that this is one area where the Preview is only of marginal help; the best things the screen is good for here is placement and some indication of what attributes you have set. For that reason, you might want to develop, by experimentation, and record some specific combinations of font, size, scale, and movement that give particularly nice results.

Figure 11.5

This is a magnified preview of the revised, shaded capital letter.

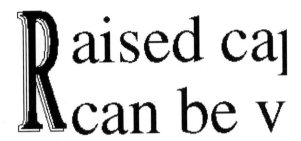

The Scale Dialog Tool

The Scale tool provides an optional dialog box for controlling the operation. Like all dialog boxes, it is accessed by holding down the Option key while you set the fixed point—in this case, the scale origin.

You have been introduced to this already, and you will see it again in later exercises. It is presented here to review and discuss all the various options in the box. To begin with, the default options are Uniform scale, with a default value of 100%—in other words, no change—and Preserve line weights. Each of these has an alternative. You may choose to scale the line weights with the object. This is especially important in cases where there is an outlined object that is being scaled down (such as a letter, for example) and you want to have the line weight change in proportion to the graphic image. This was an important issue in reducing the triangular logo graphic (in *Chapter 10*) to ensure that the line that formed the logo would not get too thick.

You can also choose to scale the object in a non-uniform way. In that case, you would click on the Non-uniform scale button and fill in the percentage that you wanted to scale the object in both the horizontal and vertical directions. This type of scaling can be used to produce short, fat objects or long, thin objects out of regular graphics. Uniform and Non-uniform scaling are mutually exclusive. Therefore, the Preserve line weights and Scale line weights radio buttons are not available when you are doing a non-uniform scale; when you scale something non-uniformly, the line weights are always preserved.

If the object that you are scaling is filled or stroked with a pattern, you can choose to scale the pattern tiles with the object by checking the Scale pattern tiles checkbox. The default is to leave the pattern at the current size.

Finally, you have the options of canceling the whole operation, which simply leaves without setting or doing anything, and of making a copy of the selected object with the current scaling values.

Exercise 11.2: Blending to Add Contours

In concept, the Blend tool works something like the scale tool. The blend tool transforms one artwork object into another in a series of regular steps. This is a very useful device, and can be used to generate some spectacular effects. One of the most common uses of the Blend tool is to add layers of gray or shades of color to produce the effect of a solid object. As a concrete example of this technique, we'll add contours, or dimensionality, to the apple artwork that you created earlier.

Start this exercise by opening any version of the apple that you have worked on. I have used the latest version, the one with two leaves on it; but you may choose any version that you want, since the leaves and stem artwork are not used in this exercise.

You will start by grouping the leaf and stem artwork to make these elements easier to work with later. Use the Selection tool and the Option key to select the base of the stem, then use the same technique, with the addition of the Shift key, to add the stem artwork to the selection. At this point, you will have both the stem and the base selected. Remember to add all the artwork pieces that make up the stem, including the small curve that forms part of the top of the stem. Choose Arrange ➤ Group (⌘–G) to make these objects into one unit.

Now you're ready to begin working on the apple itself. Use the Selection tool and the Option key to select the entire outline of the apple itself, not including the leaves and stem. The apple should be positioned in the center of the screen.

Now select the Scale tool and position the point selection cursor, the +, on the upper-right corner of the shoulder of the apple. This is indicated on the template by the slight shadow that has been placed there. The position at this point is shown in Figure 11.6.

Figure 11.6

*Set the Scale tool origin
at this position for
scaling the apple outline.*

Click on this point to set the scaling origin. Then move the cursor, which is now the familiar delta shape, down to the bottom of the apple and drag the outline up a short distance as shown in Figure 11.7. Hold down the Option key and release the mouse button to make a copy of the apple outline inside the original.

You could do all this with the Scale tool by pressing Option, setting the percentages of reduction, and clicking on copy. However, I don't think it gives as good an effect as making each contour by hand. The regularity of shape that this technique provides was quite appropriate for the target artwork, where you used the technique to good effect, but shadow and light are not so uniform.

While this new contour outline is still selected, you want to change the Fill and Stroke attributes. The current settings are 50% Black Fill and Stroke with a 100% Black line of 0.1 Weight. You want to shade this section of the apple as a highlight, almost white without any stroke around the outside edge. Use 5% Black Fill and set Stroke to None.

Figure 11.7

This shows you the interior contour for the apple.

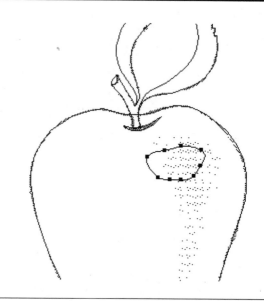

Now you will use the Blend tool to create a series of images between the outer apple outline and the inner copy that you just created. The Blend tool will make a regular series of steps between the two images, while also changing the gray level for each step.

Use the Selection tool to select the anchor point on the upper-left corner of the apple highlight image. Then select the matching anchor point on the apple outline, using the Shift key so that both points remain selected. The result should look like Figure 11.8.

The Blend tool works by making a series of steps between two selected anchor points. Be sure that both points are selected (colored black); otherwise you will get an error message when you try to use the Blend tool.

Select the Blend tool from the Toolbox. Click the blend cursor on the selected anchor point on the apple outline. The cursor changes to a sideways t form to indicate that you are continuing a blend operation. Now click on the selected anchor point on the inner apple highlight. You will see the Blend dialog box, shown in Figure 11.9.

This dialog box sets the number of steps between the two points and shows the transformation percentages that will be used to change from one gray level into the other. Obviously, the more steps you use, the finer the blend—up to the limits of the output device. However, more steps take longer to calculate and display, so you want to choose a number of steps that will give the desired effect but still run reasonably quickly. In this case, you will use a blend of 16 steps, which will provide about a 2.5% change in the gray

Figure 11.8

You must select both a starting and an ending anchor point for blending.

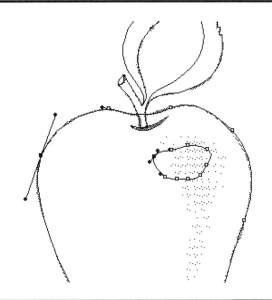

Figure 11.9

The Blend dialog box allows you to determine how many steps will be used in the blend.

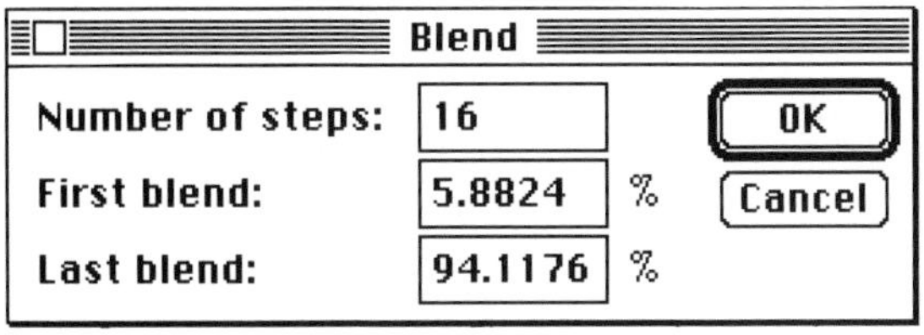

level at each step, because you're starting at 50% Black at the apple outline and ending at 5% Black in the highlight.

Enter 16 for the number of steps in the dialog box and click OK. You will see the change in the blend percentage factors. Note that these are the percent change in the existing color level, not the calculated new values. In other words, sixteen steps always gives you the same percentages, whether the starting gray level is 50%, 100%, or any other value. The actual gray level of each step is calculated as the levels are produced on the artwork.

After Illustrator calculates the necessary contours and gray levels, you will see the result on the screen, looking something like the image shown in Figure 11.10. You see that there are sixteen new layers, and exactly sixteen points between the two anchor points that you used for the transformation. However, Illustrator may add some points in individual layers to make a smooth transition from the outline to the highlight. Also notice that the resulting layers are automatically grouped as a unit.

Figure 11.10

When the 16 blend steps are added, the final apple contour artwork looks like this.

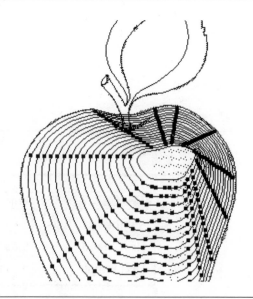

If you Preview this, however, you will see that there is still one small difficulty. Namely, the stem and base of the stem now paint behind the apple
contours, and so cannot be seen. This is remedied by cutting out the stem
and base and pasting them in front of the contour artwork. This is why
you grouped these objects at the beginning of the exercise.

Use the Selection tool to select the base of the stem. Because you grouped
these items earlier, they will all select as a unit. Use Edit ➤ Bring to Front to
move the selected artwork to paint in front of all the contours. The result will
Preview on the screen as shown in Figure 11.11 and prints as shown in Figure 11.12.

As you can see in the Preview, not all the levels that you added show on the
screen. This is because the LaserWriter and higher resolution devices will distinguish gray levels of 5% or less, but the screen display moves only in approximately 10% increments. That is, if you choose a value for the percentage
of black fill, the value chosen must be at least 10% different from the next
level to display as a distinct color on the screen.

Figure 11.11

This is the screen preview
of the apple with shading
added by contouring and
blending.

Figure 11.12

*Because the printer has
higher resolution than
the screen, the printed
output shows more detail.*

The 2.5% variation above will show on the screen, but it will be more of
a difference than you will see on the printed output. In fact, the value displayed on the screen for 45% Black will correspond to the gray scale for 40%
Black. The net result is that you will see only about seven levels on the screen,
since the gray levels are only 2.5% apart, but all of them will show on the
page output.

You can see the substantial differences between the shadings on these two
outputs, which points up the discussion earlier about the variation between
the screen version of an artwork and the printed version. When you are done
with this, please save the exercise as *Shaded Apple* art.

You should also be aware that all color levels shown on the screen are much
more dramatic than the variations on the printed output. This is a good demonstration of the fact that WYSIWYG (What You See Is What You Get) is really
a misnomer. You can't accurately reproduce a high resolution device on a low
resolution screen; the only way would be to reduce the resolution levels on
the higher device to correspond to what's available on the lower resolution
device. Illustrator allows you complete control of the output device and access

to the highest resolution available, but that leaves you with the display problem you see here. The only alternative is for you to understand the differences in resolution and to have some feel for the effect on the output. You can get some information from the screen, but don't rely on it entirely.

Exercise Summary

This exercise should have given you some good ideas about how to use scaling of a figure to create the effect of shading for a solid object. This is probably one of the most useful techniques that you will find; it is constantly used by many graphic artists using Illustrator. At this point, you should be very comfortable with a variety of ways to use the Scale tool. There remains one use which you still should see. This is the subject of the next exercise.

Exercise 11.3: Rotating Images

Like the scaling operations, you have already rotated images in previous chapters. Rotation is another of the most common and useful transformations that you have at your disposal. The Rotation tool is probably the easiest of the transformation tools to use, since it is quite easy to visualize how the control origin and the tool work together.

In the case of rotation, the fixed point that you set is the center of rotation and the selected object revolves around it. You used rotation to position the second leaf on the apple and to make the screw base on the light bulb.

In this exercise, we will set type around a circle. This is a good demonstration of a use of rotation that is quite unusual and difficult to do with many drawing programs. The exercise will set the name of a musical selection around a record label, with the composer's name inside it and the name of the orchestra on the bottom outside of the circle.

Start with a new document, and use the Oval tool to set a circle as a graphic and as a guide for the placement of the letters. You will set the title, *LA CETRA, Opus 9*, on the outside of this circle. Then you will set the name of the composer, *Antonio Vivaldi*, in such a way that the title and name appear to be on the same circle: the title outside above the visible circle and the composer's name outside below it. The visible circle should be about 16 picas wide. Make the circle using the techniques that you have learned previously, by holding down the Shift key, to constrain the figure to a true circle, and the Option key, which will allow you to draw the circle from the center. Center the circle in the drawing surface, leaving room for a row of letters around the top. Then paint the circle with Fill None and Stroke 100% Black and a Weight of 1.

The process of fitting the letters to the circle uses the Path Type tool from the Toolbox. To use this tool, it's easiest and most flexible to use a new path for the text. To generate one, select Edit ➤ Copy and then Edit ➤ Paste in Front. Now you have a copy of the first circle pasted in front of it; the copy is automatically selected. Now select the Path Type tool from the Toolbox—this is an alternate tool for the regular Type tool. You can tell that you have the Path Type tool by the name in the information box and the jagged line behind the text cursor. Move the Path Type tool to the top anchor point on the circle and click once. This changes the cursor to the familiar I-beam cursor for text entry.

Now set the Style characteristics for your text. For this exercise, you can use 16 point Helvetica Bold, with Alignment Centered. Type the line **LA CETRA, Opus 9**. At this stage, your screen should look like Figure 11.13.

Figure 11.13

The beginning of the circular text shows the title in position.

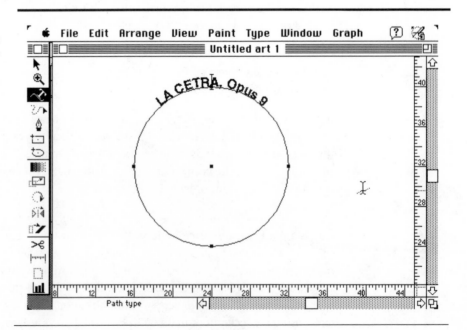

To set the remainder of the text, you are going to use a little trick, which is to copy the old text and paste it in front of this text, then change the text block to the composer's name. To do this, click once on the Path Type tool again. This selects the text you just entered and its associated path. Make a copy of this by using Edit ➤ Copy and then put it in front of the original text using Edit ➤ Paste in Front. The new copy is automatically selected.

Now for the hard part. Use the Path Type tool and click at the front end of the text block. This will move the text insertion point to the front of the text. Then drag to highlight and select the entire block of text.

Delete this text by selecting Edit ➤ Clear. Don't be surprised that the text appears to remain on the artwork; remember, you have an exact copy underneath this. In fact, if you can't see the text underneath this, there's some mistake in your artwork—select everything, delete it, and start again. The sign that you have correctly removed the top layer of text will be that the I-beam cursor reappears at the top of the circle. Then set the type Style for the new text block to Helvetica Regular, 14 point, still using Alignment Centered. Type the composer's name, **Antonio Vivaldi** along the path. You won't be able to see it very well, since it's lighter and smaller than the title text that shows through from the layer beneath.

Now go to the Toolbox and select the Rotate tool. Click on the center point of the circle (the small × in the center) to set the center of rotation; then click on the I-beam cursor at the top of the circle and drag the name text around the circle to the bottom. Don't worry too much, at this point, about the position of the entire block around the circle. Worry about creating the correct spacing between the words and the letters. You will not be able to change that relationship once you have placed the individual letters; you can however adjust the set of letters around the circle. You do that by selecting the entire block of text and then using the Rotate tool to revolve the entire block. In that way you can position the name so that it is correctly centered at the bottom of the circle. The end of the name placement should leave the screen looking something like Figure 11.14.

Now, of course, the name is upsidedown. To make the name read correctly you will have to reverse it by moving it inside the circle. Do this by using the Selection tool and double-clicking on the I-beam cursor in the middle of the name. This switches the name from the outside to the inside of the circle.

Figure 11.14

*When you have created
and rotated the
composer's name text,
the artwork will look
like this.*

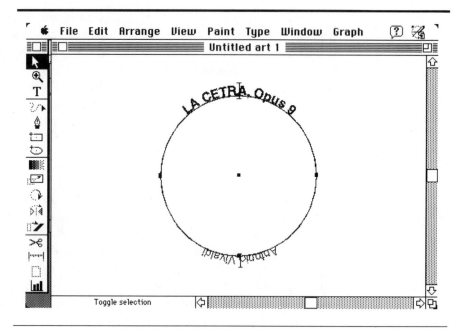

This still isn't quite what you want, since you want the name reading like this but on the outside of the circle. This is why you made a copy of the original path with text. Be sure that the name text and path are selected (they should still be selected from the previous operations.) Get the Scale tool from the Toolbox and click on the center of the circle. Now move to the lower right side of the circle, about the four o'clock position, and drag the text and its path out to expand the entire object until the text is correctly aligned with the inner circle. Recall the work you did earlier, when you were scaling ovals. Scale the text and path so that the name fits along the outer edge of the original circle, as shown in Figure 11.15.

There is only one drawback to this, as you will see if you Preview it now. The text for the title lies exactly on the inner circle, while the text for the composer lies a little outside it. This is almost inevitable, for two reasons: the letters are uneven on the top, and they were scaled by hand. To adjust for this you can move the name text up, off of the circle, by a small amount. Return

Figure 11.15

After you scale the name text and path, the final figure will look like this.

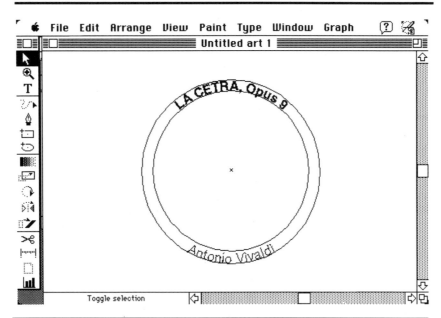

to the Text tool and select all of the name text again. Now select Type ➤ Style and enter a small value in the Vert. shift box. This will move the text the given number of points up from the text path. I used 4 points for this artwork, but the exact amount will depend on how far away your name text is from the inner circle, and your personal taste.

This actually consists of three elements: the painted circle; the text and circular path that contains the title of the record; and the outer text and path that contains the composer's name. The only circle that is actually visible is the first one that you created. The two circles that form the paths for the title and name text are invisible. If you select these, you will see that they are actually neither stroked nor filled. The Path Text tool automatically sets these attributes when you apply it to the paths and begin to add text. If you want to remove these from your artwork you can select View ➤ Hide Unpainted Objects, which will make the two text path circles disappear from the artwork views as well as from the Preview.

The Rotate Dialog Tool

The Rotate tool provides an alternate tool, the Rotate dialog tool, that displays an optional dialog box that allows you to specify the angle that you want to rotate the selected object. As is always true with Illustrator, positive values of the angle represent counterclockwise motion, and negative values are clockwise. The dialog box is shown in Figure 11.16.

Reflecting Images

The Reflect tool works like a mirror, moving the selected object through a line of reflection to a matching position on the other side. Each selected point on one side of the line, called the *axis of reflection*, is moved a corresponding distance on the other side of the line. If you think of the line as a mirror, the concept is quite straightforward.

The Reflect tool, unlike the other transformation tools, doesn't require any clicking and dragging to indicate how far you want to move. Once the line of reflection is established, all the selected points have exactly one mirror point that matches them; there is no other control necessary. For the Reflect tool, the choice comes in establishing the axis of reflection, the line that makes up the mirror for the selected object. This whole idea is illustrated by Figure 11.17, which shows the important factors in the reflection process.

Illustrator allows you to reflect the selected objects along any axis that you want; the axis is defined by the two clicks of the cursor that activate the reflection. The first click, with the cross cursor (+) sets one end of the axis of reflection; the next click, with the delta cursor, finishes the axis of reflection as the straight line connecting the two points.

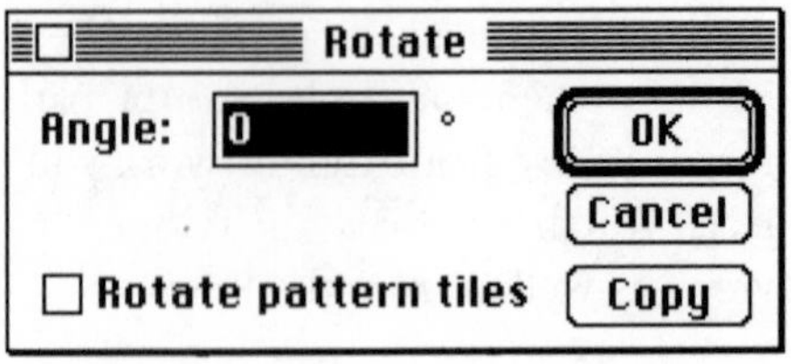

Figure 11.16

The Rotate dialog box allows you to set precise values for rotation of selected objects.

Figure 11.17

This illustrates the conceptual model for reflection of Illustrator graphics.

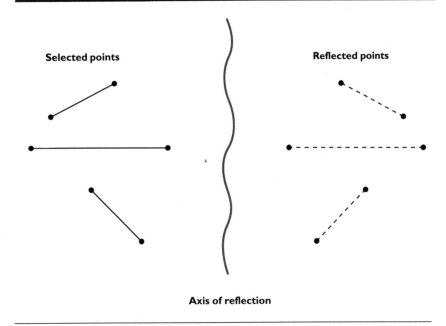

Selected points

Reflected points

Axis of reflection

The Reflect Dialog Tool

The Reflect tool also provides an optional dialog box, where you can specify the axis of reflection. The dialog box, shown in Figure 11.18, offers the option of using a horizontal, vertical, or angled axis. If you select the angled axis, you must specify the angle of the axis relative to the horizontal axis. As always, the angles are positive in the counterclockwise direction.

The process of reflection is very interesting and useful, and you will work with it in the next section, using this dialog box for part of the work.

Shearing Images

There still remains one last transformation for you to learn: the Shear tool. This transformation is probably the least intuitive of the group, and yet it can be one of the most dramatic in results. The real issue here is to get a thorough understanding of the parameters of the shear mechanism so that you can use it effectively.

Figure 11.18

The Reflect dialog box allows you to set precise values for reflection of selected objects.

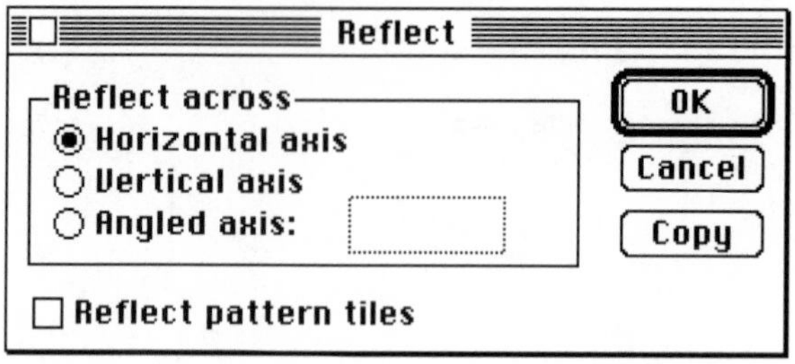

Reflect

Reflect across
- ● **Horizontal axis**
- ○ **Vertical axis**
- ○ **Angled axis:**

[OK]
[Cancel]
[Copy]

☐ **Reflect pattern tiles**

The easiest way to approach the shear is to consider the effect of the wind blowing a tree. The tree, bending in the wind, is a classic example of a sheared object. In that case, the shear is called a *horizontal* shear, because the wind is acting parallel to a horizontal surface, the ground. In my part of the world there are sometimes earthquakes; during an earthquake, the earth often moves in a *vertical* shear.

The important point here is that the shear motion occurs parallel to some plane, or line on the drawing surface, and the amount of shear is measured by the angle that the sheared object moves. Consider the tree again; the harder the wind blows, the more the tree leans. One good measure of the strength of the wind is the angle that the tree trunk makes with the *vertical* position it normally maintains. In other words, a 30° shear would bend the tree 30° from a vertical position.

Illustrator works the same way. You set a shear axis, then you use the familiar delta cursor to shear the selected object perpendicularly to the axis defined by the starting point of the shear. If that all seems a little unclear, don't worry; the axis of the shear is the line perpendicular to the line defined by the point that you click with the delta cursor and the first point that you set. This may prompt you to recall your high-school geometry: through any point there exists one, and only one, perpendicular to a given line. In this case, the perpendicular extends between the first point that you set and the point that you began the shear motion from. Figure 11.19 shows you the essential components of the shear transformation.

Figure 11.19

This diagram illustrates the concepts behind shearing Illustrator artwork.

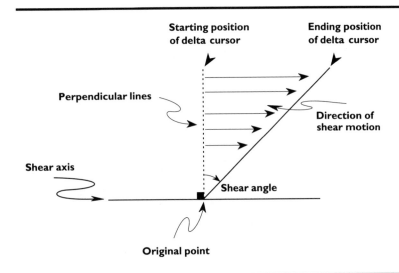

You can see on the figure each of the components of the shear: the original point, which is the one you fix first with the cross cursor; the starting point for the delta, which defines the perpendicular line to the original point and hence defines the shear axis; and the angle that measures the shear. The greater the value of the angle, the more pronounced the shear. In this case only, positive angles represent movement in a clockwise direction.

This applies to all angles in the shear; both the shear angle itself and the measurement of the angle of the shear axis to the horizontal axis. This is of most concern in using the shear dialog box, where an angle must be specified if you want to produce an angled shear. The angle of the axis is measured from the horizontal, or x-axis. Thus, for example, an angled shear with a setting of 90° is the equivalent of a vertical shear. Actually, in this case, the angle can be positive or negative and it will have no effect on the outcome; both axes are vertical. Similarly, angled shears of 180° or −180° are also identical in result, since both define the horizontal axis. However, for the angles in between, the sign makes a difference.

The Shear Dialog Tool

The Shear tool also has an alternate form, the Shear dialog tool; this one perhaps somewhat more difficult to understand than the others. Intuitively, a shear is like a tree being bent by the wind; the object is distorted in a regular way in the direction of the shear. Analytically, there are two components to a shear: the first is the axis along which the selected object is sheared and the second is the amount of the shear. This amount of shear is expressed as an angle.

The Shear dialog box, shown in Figure 11.20, allows you to specify each of these components. The shear axis can be specified as vertical, horizontal, or at some arbitrary angle. The most usual shears, of course, and the ones easiest to visualize, are either horizontal or vertical; but Illustrator will allow you to shear along any arbitrary angle.

The other value that you must specify is the amount of the shear, expressed as an angle. This angle is measured relative to a line perpendicular to the shear axis, and a positive angle *in this instance only* measures a clockwise movement. This is actually the intuitively correct approach, since the tree, bent to the right by the wind, would be sheared relative to the horizontal axis (the ground) and by some positive angular amount. If this isn't entirely clear, review the discussion and explanation earlier in the section, especially the diagram in Figure 11.19.

Figure 11.20

The Shear dialog box allows you to set precise values for shearing selected objects.

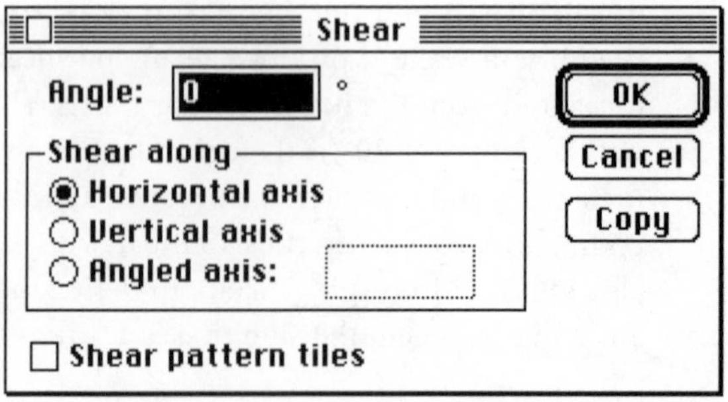

As further exercises, you may wish to repeat the movements demonstrated in the exercises, using the optional dialog box. The pair of lines, distinct and at right angles, makes it easier to visualize what the shear is doing. There is not room here for more of this type of practice, but I would encourage you to continue until you feel quite comfortable with the Shear tool and its alternate, the Shear dialog tool.

Text Shearing for Shadowing

You saw earlier how you could use the Scale tool to create certain shading effects from type. You can also use the Shear tool to create shading and shadow effects. If you think about it, any shadow is just a sort of sheared image of the original.

You will use the letterhead artwork that you prepared earlier for this exercise. Open it up, and scroll up so you can see the letterhead name and address. You are going to change this from Helvetica Bold Oblique to a standard Helvetica Bold, and then add a shadow effect behind it, so that it looks like it is coming from the sun on the logo.

First, select the line of text, CHESHIRE GROUP, and change the font to Helvetica Bold. This is the starting point for your work. First, click once on the Zoom in tool to magnify the line of type for the name. This will make it easier to see what you are doing to the type. Now make a copy of the original type on top of itself by choosing Edit ➤ Copy and then Edit ➤ Paste in Front. This gives you a new copy of the type to work with for the shadow effect. Now paint that type 30% Black. If you previewed at this point, it would look like you had just changed the line of type from 100% Black to 30% Black; actually, there is still a line of Black type behind the gray. This front copy of type is going to form the shadow effect for us.

You will place this shadow in front of the text, to make the effect more visible. To do that, select the Reflect dialog tool from the Toolbox. Click the reflection cursor on the type alignment point. For this line of type, that point is in the center of the type, under the front of the last E in CHESHIRE, and is shown by a filled-in black square. Set the dialog box to reflect across the horizontal axis (the default) and click OK. This creates a mirror image of the name, which should look something like Figure 11.21.

Now select the Shear tool and click on the same alignment point. Move the delta cursor directly down, below the mirrored type, press the Shift key to constrain the shear, and then click and drag horizontally to the right by a reasonable angle, less than 30°. Using the Shift key contrains the shear to the horizontal plane, and ensures that the bottoms of the letters stay in alignment.

Next you have to scale this type to make it look like a shadow. You do this by keeping the scale in the horizontal direction (since the base of the shadow will be unscaled), but changing the scale in the vertical direction. This is best done using the optional dialog box. Set the scale origin on the alignment point of the text while holding down the Option key. Set Non-uniform scale, with Horizontal as 100% and Vertical as 70%. Once this is done, your screen will look like Figure 11.22.

The only point that remains is to move the shadow to the back of the lettering. Right now, the shadow will paint in front of the letters because it was the

Figure 11.21

You start to add the shadow to the letterhead by creating a mirror image of the name.

Figure 11.22

Next you scale the sheared mirror image to create a shadowed letterhead name.

last object created. To move it behind the original lettering, select Edit ➤ Send to Back (⌘−−). This gives a nice, shadowed effect to the text as shown by the printed output shown in Figure 11.23.

There are, obviously, a wide variety of other effects that can be done using the Shear tool as well.

Figure 11.23

Print the revised letterhead.

CHESHIRE GROUP

6061 Van Ness, Suite 800 San Francisco CA 94111
TEL: (415) 555-7205   FAX: (415) 555-1212

CHAPTER

FEATURING

Creating cutaway drawings

Adding labels to artwork

Simulating motion in drawings

Repeating a drawing element

Masking graphics with text

Combining Tools and Effects

COMBINING TRANSFORMATION TOOLS

The tools that you have used to transform artwork are very powerful. These tools also can all be used in combination with one another or with other tools in Illustrator to generate some remarkable and powerful results. This chapter is devoted to exercises that will show you some of the ways you can combine the transformation tools to create the effects you want.

Combining Tools

When combining tools, you must define in your mind the sequence of tools needed to generate the result that you want. A good example of this is the up-side-down lettering of the diskette label in *Chapter 11*. The trick was to see that the reversed text is most easily and accurately positioned by using a double reflection: once through the horizontal and once through the vertical axis.

Much of what we do in this part of the chapter will be to expose you to various combinations of Illustrator tools, to generate various effects. You will undoubtedly find some of these self-evident. If so, just skip the exercise. I believe, though, that many of the examples will surprise and inspire you.

Exercise 12.1: Exploded Views

This exercise will use the now familiar apple artwork, cutting out a segment of it to make the traditional "exploded" or "cutaway" view of an object. Then we'll label the segment and the artwork for clarity. This is a good example of using the basic Illustrator tools to make a complex graphic image.

Begin by calling up the version of the apple graphic that you prepared with the two leaves. This isn't essential; any of the previous versions will work just as well, but the figures here reflect the version with two leaves. Position the artwork so that the body of the apple is a bit to the right of the center of the screen. Your screen should look something like Figure 12.1.

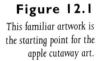

Figure 12.1

This familiar artwork is the starting point for the apple cutaway art.

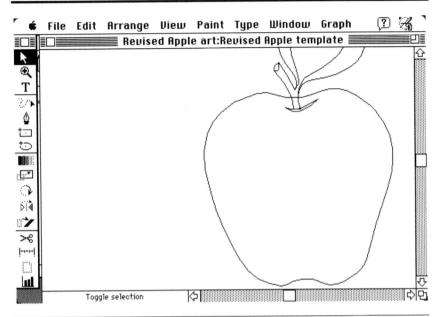

Since there is no template for this work, I recommend choosing View ➤ Artwork Only for these changes.

Now use the Split Path tool to cut the apple outline at the anchor point that is on the top, left-shoulder of the apple and at a point along the bottom-left curve. Select the cut segment and move it away from the apple outline, using the Option key to make it a duplicate. This segment will form the basis of the slice of the apple, as shown in Figure 12.2.

Now connect the top and bottom anchor points with a curved line that approximates the shape of the apple segment. This can easily be done by eye; I would recommend that you use one additional anchor point along the curve to define the shoulder of the apple. The result is shown in Figure 12.3.

Notice that the middle anchor point here is a mild form of a curved corner, to make the curve move away in a manner to suggest the shoulder of the apple. You don't need to set any painting attributes here because this segment inherits the paint characteristics of the apple outline, which is what you

Figure 12.2

This copy of the apple outline is the beginning segment of the cutaway.

Figure 12.3

This shows you the side of the apple cutaway segment.

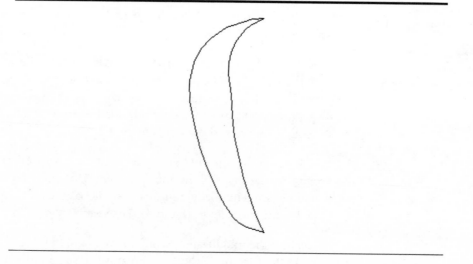

want. Finish off the segment by drawing a line from the top anchor point to the bottom one, 0.5 line weight and 80% Black, which will make it light but visible.

Now you need to complete the apple outline with the missing segment. Select the apple outline in its entirety, so you can see the anchor points. Make a new curved line, beginning at the depression in the center of the apple and extending down to the base of the apple; this represents one side of the cut. The curve arcs up from the center to cross over the top anchor point of the apple, then joins the cut segment of the apple outline at the top anchor point. Continue with the inner portion of the cut by making a corner anchor point at the bottom of the cut segment, moving back up toward the top of the apple, and rejoining the beginning point. The resulting curve looks like Figure 12.4.

This would be excellent, except that the two curves that make up the outline of the apple and the cut surface are partially distinct and partially joined. Preview the image and notice that the cut portion of the apple paints gray and the inner surface of the cut paints white, but the colors don't join correctly.

Figure 12.4

This shows you the completed slice and the matching cut apple outline.

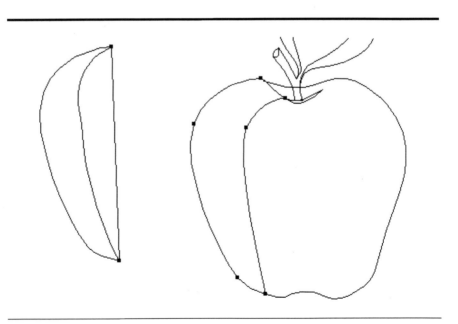

The outer surface of the apple is not closed, so the paint just stops along the straight line that goes from the top of the apple to the bottom. What you want is for the color to follow the shape of the inner cut. All the pieces are in place. How do you make it paint the way you want?

You need to create two outlines, one for the outside of the apple and another for the inner cut surface. The answer is to make two paths that share the one common line that forms the inner edge of the cut, and color one side white and the other with the current shade of gray. There is an easy way to do this with Illustrator.

Start by selecting the entire inner cut of the apple using the Object Selection tool. Then use Edit ➤ Copy to make a copy of this path. Finally, use Arrange ➤ Hide to hide the current inner cut and choose Edit ➤ Paste in Front to return your copy to the artwork.

Then use the Split Path tool to cut the apple outline (at the two anchor points at the base and at the top of the apple). When you do this, select the outer portion of the apple, and move it slightly away from the rest of the apple. You could do the remainder of the exercise with the cut portion in place, but selection of the correct points and visualization of what is going on becomes much more difficult. It is easier and faster to move the cut segment slightly out of the way and then to continue the work. Figure 12.5 shows the segment selected and moved.

Now use the Split Path tool to cut this segment at the top anchor point, which matches the top point of the apple artwork, and at the bottom anchor point as well. Then use the Selection tool to select the inner anchor points, as shown in Figure 12.6. Notice that the outer points, the ones that define the outer edge of the segment, are not selected.

Now use the Selection tool to move this curve back to match the apple outline. Select the remainder of the curve that you left behind and use Edit ➤ Clear to remove it. Position the inner curve so that the bottom anchor point is directly over the matching anchor point on the apple. This forms one piece of the common border. You still have to close up the two paths that make up the outer part of the apple so that it forms one continuous outline. If you check now, by using the select tool, you will see that the two outlines are quite separate still, even though their endpoints are exactly on top of one another.

Figure 12.5

You should move the
inner cut for easier
processing.

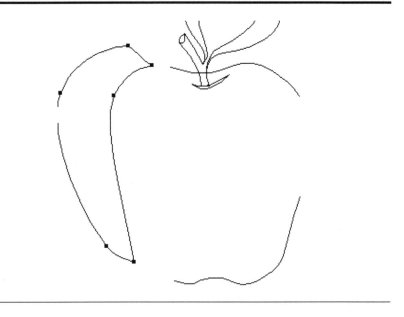

Figure 12.6

Select only the common,
inner segment of the
curve for replacement.

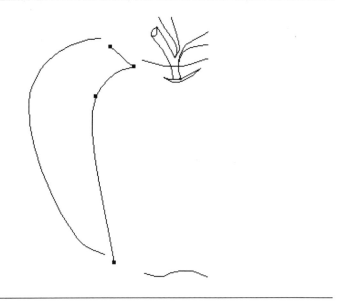

Use the selection marquee to select both points at the bottom of the apple. Now choose Arrange ➤ Join. You have selected two matching and overlapping endpoints; Join tells Illustrator to make them into one point and join the two curves that they represent. When you do that, the multiple direction points that you saw previously disappear, leaving only one anchor point and two direction points.

Now perform the same function on the two top endpoints. To get these to match exactly, you may have to move the top point of the cut surface down and in slightly to fall exactly over the apple. Do this now and then join these points. This completes the outer apple outline. If you select it while holding down Option, you should see something like Figure 12.7.

Now return the cut segment of the apple back to its original position by choosing Arrange ➤ Show All. This will match the curve of the outer portion precisely. Set the Fill to White and the Stroke to the same value as the outer segment; here, that's 0.2 line weight and 100% Black. Finally, adjust any features of the artwork that you think need to be adjusted. In the example, the

Figure 12.7

This completes the outer apple outline with the cut missing.

top of the cut was moved up, on top of the depression, to give a more realistic effect, and some changes were made to the cutaway segment to match the cutout more closely. At this point, the Preview version of this artwork paints like Figure 12.8.

You can make this more functional by adding two dotted lines that connect the cutaway segment and the cut portion of the apple. Do that as follows. Starting from the artwork shown above, draw a line from the top of the cutaway segment to the top of the apple. Set the Paint Style attributes as shown in Figure 12.9. Note that the Dashed option has been chosen, and the length of the dashes is 2 points, while the gap between them is 5 points. Generally, to create a real dashed effect, the gap has to be appreciably longer than the dash.

Check after you have created the line to be sure that you have not automatically been joined to the line that defines the front of the cutaway segment. You can check this by using the Selection tool and seeing if the Option shows more than just the line you have created. If it does, you can disconnect these

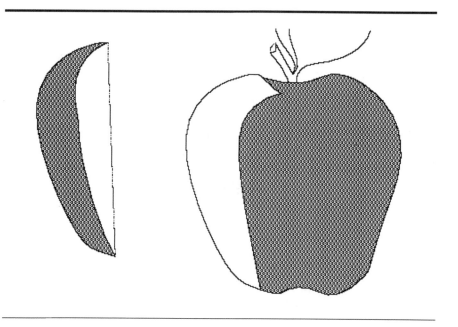

Figure 12.8

This is a preview image of the apple with the cutaway section missing.

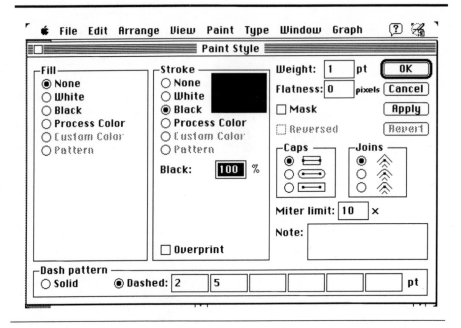

two lines by using the Split Path tool to cut the lines apart at the common point. Create the bottom dotted line in the same way and with the same attributes and precautions. The final result will preview like Figure 12.10.

You can finish this off by adding a small circular core section and a few seeds. These are quite straightforward. The core section is just a curve set onto the cutaway segment as shown in Figure 12.11. Set the Paint attribute to a solid line, 100% Black, and 0.5 line weight. The seeds can be added by using the Oval tool in the core area. Magnify the area so you can make small ovals for the seeds, and make several at random intervals over the core. Paint these with a Fill of 100% Black and no Stroke. The final result should look something like Figure 12.11.

Exercise Summary

This finishes the work with the apple cutaway for the time being. Save this artwork (⌘–S), because we'll be using it in the next section, where you'll add labels to the artwork and see how to move the exploded segment.

Figure 12.10

This is a preview of the cutaway apple artwork with dotted lines included.

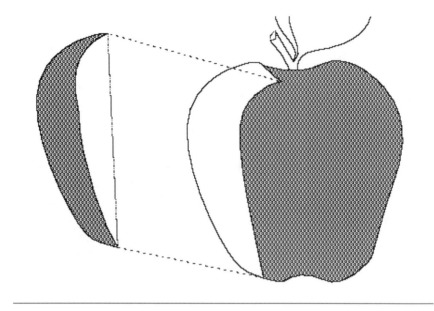

Figure 12.11

This is the final preview of the cutaway apple with core and seeds.

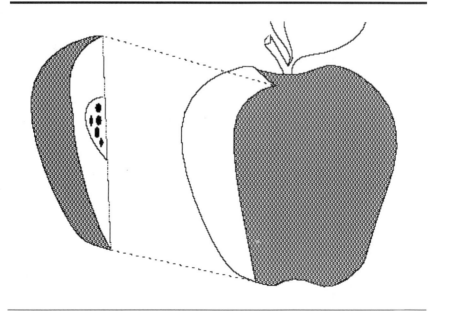

Exercise 12.2: Text and Graphics

You have already merged text with graphic images in several of the exercises. This example shows you additional ways to place and handle text and also discusses moving a graphic when necessary for text placement. The text to be added will be some captions for the apple cutaway art that you prepared in the previous exercise. As you will see, this involves moving the artwork around to provide room for the text.

Start by opening the version of the apple art that has the cutaway segment. The template has become mostly irrelevant and distracting at this point; display the artwork without the template or delete the association permanently. You can do that by temporarily renaming the template and choosing None when Illustrator asks you to choose a template to associate with the artwork. Then, when you save the artwork, there will no longer be any template associated with it. This has been done for this exercise, and the starting screen looks like Figure 12.12.

Figure 12.12

This is the starting graphic for your text and segment exercise.

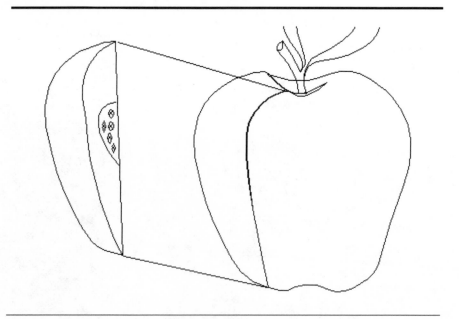

You commonly attach the label to a specific element by using an arrow to tie the label to the graphic. You will use the same method here. First, create a large version of the arrowhead that you want to use, which you can scale down later to an appropriate size. In this way, the arrow can be kept in constant proportion to the text size while also maintaining a correct look and shape.

Make an arrow that has the dimensions given in Figure 12.13.

Use 1 unit on the rulers for each unit on the plan. Then copy the arrow some distance away. Using the Scale dialog tool, make a copy of the arrow, setting the scale origin at the nose of the arrow, so the scale is completely symmetrical, and using the Scale line weights radio button. Use two 50% reductions to generate the result you see in Figure 12.14. The image is enlarged for greater clarity.

This small arrow is scaled so that the width of the arrowhead is about the size of 10-point type. You can check that, if you want to scale it by hand, by typing a small selection of characters and measuring the arrowhead against

Figure 12.13

These are the dimensions for the arrow graphic.

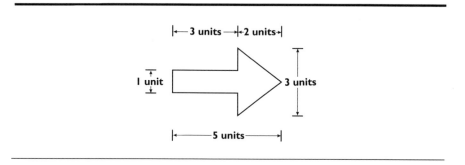

Figure 12.14

This shows you the actual arrow and the reduced arrow next to some sample text.

them. You should group the small arrow so that it can be moved and rotated without worrying about accidentally selecting only part of it.

Now, add the following text captions to the figure: *stem, leaf, segment,* and at the bottom *The Apple*. The basic captions should be in 10-point Times-Roman, and the name caption in 15-point Helvetica Bold. Place an arrow next to each caption, using the Rotation tool to position it in the correct orientation. Use the Option key to copy the arrow as you move it. The results on the exercise are shown in Figure 12.15.

In all cases, the arrows have been rotated, if required, by the bottom point on their tails.

It would be nice to add a label for the seeds; however, there isn't room between the cutaway segment and the main body of the apple to do so. The trick here is to move the segment out to make room for the label. This can be done by moving the segment as a unit (including the label for the segment and its associated arrow). This can best be accomplished by using the selection

Figure 12.15

Place the basic captions around the cutaway apple.

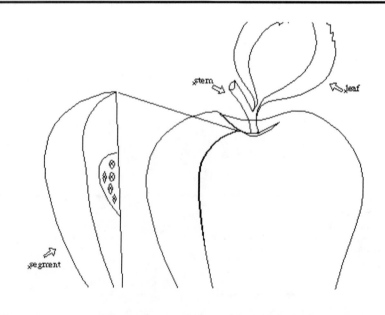

marquee to select the entire section of the page. The result of this is shown in Figure 12.16.

You might be tempted to group the results, so that you can be sure they will move together. Don't. Making a group out of this would add the far endpoints of the two dotted lines to the figure, which, you will notice, are not included in the selected points. You particularly want to exclude these points, since you want to only move one end of the dotted lines, not both. The ends at the apple need to stay fixed.

Now step back from the artwork by reducing it. Use the Selection tool to move the selected graphics up and to the left, as shown in Figure 12.17.

You can position this anywhere that you want and the dotted lines will follow the motion, since one end of the lines is moving while the other end is fixed at the apple. Reposition the cutaway segment, leaving enough room to place the label next to the seeds. The label position is shown in the preview version in Figure 12.18.

Figure 12.16

You want to select the entire segment, the label text, and the endpoints of the dashed lines for the move.

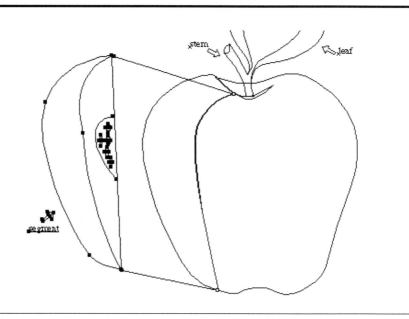

Figure 12.17

You can shift part of the cutaway apple without moving the rest.

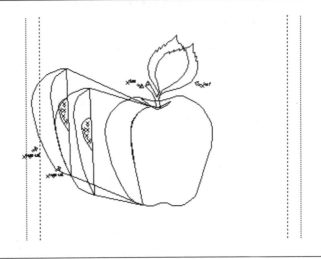

Figure 12.18

This is a preview of the cutaway showing the location of the new label.

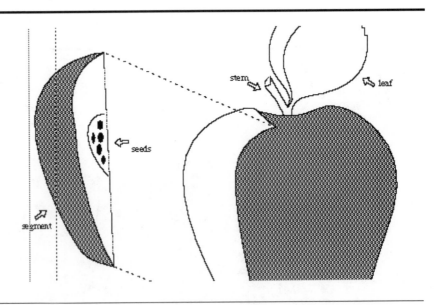

There remains one small problem; namely, that the artwork now spills over onto another page. Look back at Figure 12.17 and see how the slice runs off the printable page. There is a large part of the page on the right that is unused and it's easy to move Illustrator graphics around. So you could choose Edit ➤ Select All and move the entire graphic to a better position on the page. This approach has some drawbacks, however. First, it's hard to position such a large graphic accurately since all the lines tend to overlap one another; second, it is slow to move so many points.

There is an alternative; you can use the Page tool to reset the page to fit the graphic rather than the other way around. Just click on the Page tool and center the new page around the existing graphic. The result is shown in Figure 12.19 and the printed output looks like Figure 12.20.

Exercise 12.3: Multiple Copies

Another area where Illustrator is a great improvement over previous drawing programs is in creating multiple copies of the same or similar images. In this section you will do exercises on two fairly common types of repetition. The first is a strobe effect, where the same image is repeated in slightly different orientations to mimic motion. The second is a figure with a large number of repeated elements.

Figure 12.19

You can move the page orientation to get the complete cutaway apple on one page.

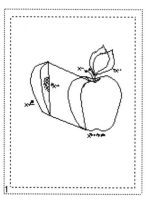

Figure 12.20

*This is the printed
output of the cutaway
apple with labels.*

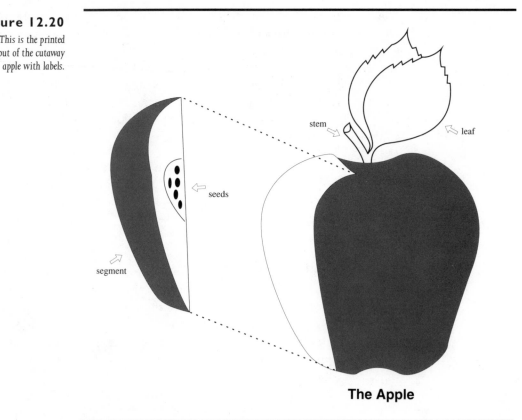

The Apple

Copying for Movement

The first exercise is to draw a falling tomahawk. There is no template for this, so open a new drawing surface with no template. Start by drawing the head of the tomahawk in the center of the surface, which is more or less the center of the page. The tomahawk blade looks like Figure 12.21.

Paint this with Black 10% fill and a stroke of Black 100% with a line Weight of 1 point. Next add a handle, which is most easily done by using the Rectangle tool. Paint this with 50% Black fill and 0.5 weight stroke of 100% Black. As a final touch, add two crossed thongs that hold the head onto the handle. There is a fast way to do this. Make one thong across the head and handle as a straight line. Paint it as Fill None and Stroke 100% Black with a line weight of 3 points, to make it stand out. Now select the entire line (both endpoints), as shown in Figure 12.22.

Now use the Reflection tool, positioned at the center of the thong, where you want the second thong to cross. Use the Option key to access the alternate Reflection dialog box and reflect the thong across the Horizontal axis as a copy. This will make a perfect second thong. You want to use horizontal rather than vertical reflection because the head, and therefore the thong, are not symmetrical vertically—the front is larger than the back.

Now group the entire tomahawk. The final result looks like Figure 12.23.

Figure 12.21

This is the tomahawk blade

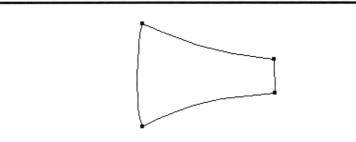

Figure 12.22

You can select the single thong and duplicate it to make another.

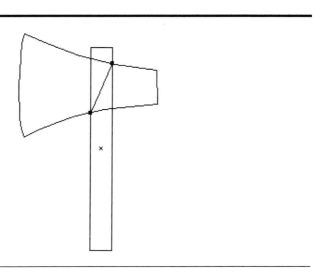

Figure 12.23

*This is the completed
tomahawk.*

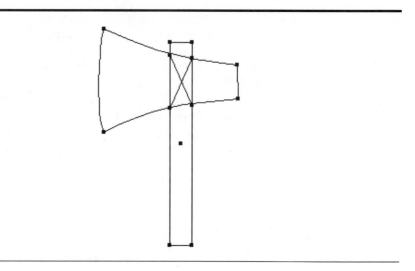

Now take the Rotation tool and rotate a copy of the entire image 20°. The exercise uses a center of rotation about 4 units below the bottom of the handle; you can use whatever distance looks best to you. After the rotation, the entire copy artwork is still selected. Select Paint ➤ Style. What you want to do here is make this entire copy much lighter and less "real" than the top version of the object. You can do this by setting the paint attributes in a global fashion. When you open the Paint Style dialog box, you will see that most of the information is blank. That happens whenever you have selected objects with differing attributes; Illustrator can't show them all, so it doesn't show any. Override these individual items by setting global values: Fill of None, Stroke 80% Black, and line weight of 0.5 points. This makes the copy quite a bit lighter than the original, giving the desired strobe effect. Do two more rotations, using angles of 30° and 40° respectively. This will result in Figure 12.24, which has the graphics reduced to allow you to see the entire image in Preview mode.

Copying Graphic Elements

Next you will do an exercise where you use repeated shapes to create a figure; in this case, a dinosaur with a row of spines down its back. This time there is a template, made up from a series of curves, lines and ovals in Illustrator itself. This was prepared by making the necessary outlines using Illustrator tools, previewing the outline, and then saving the screen in a Mac-Paint format. The screen was then edited to remove the extraneous elements. The template is shown in Figure 12.25.

Part of the advantage of making a template in this way is that you can always go back, modify the artwork, and create a new version of the template instantly.

Figure 12.24

This preview of the tomahawk art shows how you can create motion in Illustrator.

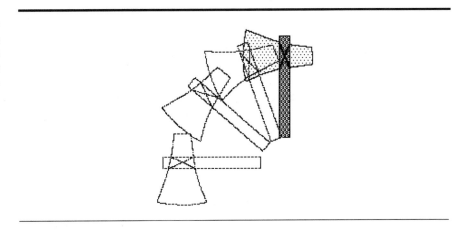

Figure 12.25

This is the template for the dinosaur art.

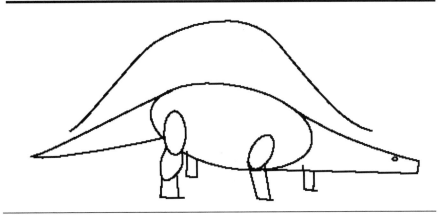

Start by outlining the body. Notice that the nose should not be quite so straight and flat; make it more pointed. Remember to make corners where required. Fill the body with 50% Black and stroke it with 100% Black and a line weight of 1.

Next add the legs. Although the template shows the thighs and legs as ovals, you should do them as open figures. The legs should be stroked and painted with the same attributes as the body. Then add two curves along the front of each thigh, to give some contour to the body. Now take a moment to add the eye, using the Oval tool. Use the Zoom in tool to help position the circle accurately; and paint the eye with the attributes Fill White and Stroke 100% Black with a line weight of 0.5 points. Finally, add a single line with a weight of 1.5 for the mouth. The artwork, at this stage, looks like Figure 12.26.

Also, when you make the two far legs, on the other side of the body, you want them to paint behind the body. This is most easily done by cutting each leg out after you create it, selecting the body of the dinosaur, and then choosing Edit ➤ Paste In Back. This paints the cutout directly behind the dinosaur's body. This is different from choosing Edit ➤ Send To Back, which simply sends the selected artwork to the rear of all other objects. The cut-and-paste method moves the cut artwork behind the selected object only. The entire product previews like Figure 12.27.

Now you need to add the spines down the dinosaur's back. The height and relative scale of the spikes is shown by the continuous curve that runs along the top of the dinosaur template. Also, the spines run in two rows, so the effect should be of alternating, front and back spines. As always, for painting order, you want to draw the back spines first.

Figure 12.26

The Dinosaur's body and legs

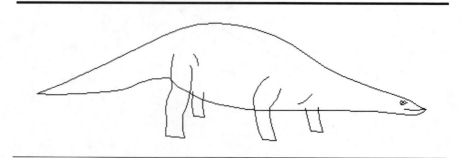

Draw the first spine at about the shoulder and up to the curve in height. The spines have a vaguely diamond shape, so you will have to make corners at the edges and top. (If you need a refresher on how to make corners, review the section on corners in *Chapter 6*.) Change the Paint Style attributes to Fill 30% Black to make the spines slightly lighter than the rest of the body. The first spine on the exercise is shown in Figure 12.28.

Now select the spine and move it forward, making a copy of it with a space between them of about one-half the width of the previous spine. Remember that you are going to come back and place another row of spines over this one. Now choose the Scale tool from the toolbox. Place the scale origin under the front anchor point of the spine and pull the top point down until it reaches the curved template line, forming the next spine. The result looks like Figure 12.29.

Figure 12.27

The preview shows how the legs will paint behind the dinosaur body.

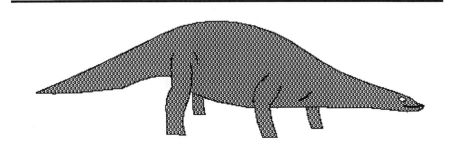

Figure 12.28

This shows you how to form the dinosaur spines.

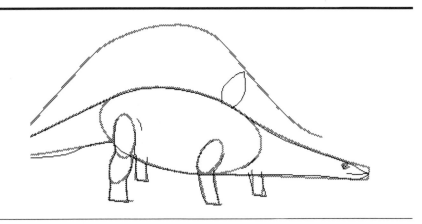

At this point, you could modify the spine form a little if you want, just as you did to the leaf tip earlier. Continue this process to make all the spines up and down the back. As you go over the top of the back, you will have to rotate the spines as well as enlarge them. Also, as you move toward the back, you will get better results from the Scale tool if the scale origin is at the back anchor point rather than the front, since the point that doesn't move is the one lower down the figure. After you are all done, the result should look something like Figure 12.30.

Figure 12.29

This shows you where to place the second spine on the dinosaur.

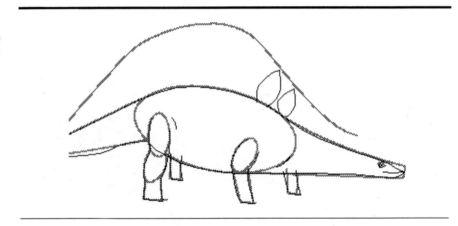

Figure 12.30

This shows you the dinosaur with one row of spines completed.

I have left the template visible in this figure so that you can see how the spines match up to the curve along the back.

Now you need to make the next row of spines, which overlaps and paints in front of the previous row. You can do this most easily by moving each scale forward or backward to create a matching overlapping scale. Use the Preview mode periodically to make sure that your spines are going in order.

The real caution here is to remember that whenever you move a spine, it automatically paints in front of the previous objects; therefore, if you want to adjust any of the spines in the back row, do it *before* you create the overlapping front spines. If you do get out of sequence, use Edit ➤ Send to Back or Edit ➤ Bring to Front to place the spines in their proper order again. Use the Zoom in tool at the back and front ends to help you place and adjust the spines. When you are done, the result should look something like Figure 12.31.

There still remain several things to be done. First, the dinosaur outline should paint in front of the spines. Now you can't just Cut and Paste In Front here; if you do, the legs will get all out of painting order. You need to use the Group function (⌘−G) to make the body and the legs one unit. This maintains the painting order within the group, which is what you want, while allowing you to paste the entire group in front of all the spines. Select all the components of the body, including the legs, eye, and mouth. You cannot use the selection marquee to pick all of the points because you will get some of the spines. You

Figure 12.31

This is the complete
row of spines.

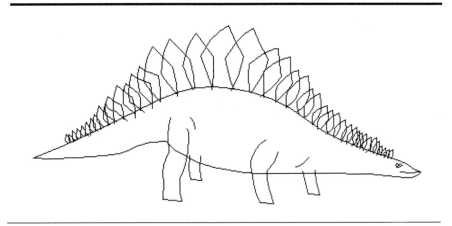

can, of course, use the Selection tool and the Shift key to select each piece individually. Is there some faster way? Yes, there is. You can use the selection marquee to select part of the work, then group that part, and then use the selection marquee to select another part, group that, and so on. This will allow you to get the entire range of artwork that you want grouped in about three steps.

When that's done, use Edit ➤ Bring To Front to paint the entire group in front of the spines. The legs, eye and so on will still paint in the original order, giving you the effect that you want.

There is one further item to add to this dinosaur. It should have a set of four spikes at the end of its tail. You can add these by making two sets of two tall, thin triangles. There are two sets because the spikes are in two rows, just like the spines. Don't close the triangles at the bottom; like the legs, you want these to blend into the body. Therefore set the same painting attributes for these as you have for the body. A quick way to do this is to select the body, click on ⌘-I (Paint ➤ Style) and immediately click 'OK'. This sets the paint attributes for the next object to the same as those for the body. Make one set of triangles, then copy them over themselves to make the next, overlapping set. You can use the same techniques that you used for the overlapping spines. The final result previews like Figure 12.32.

Figure 12.32

The final dinosaur art looks like this when you preview it.

Exercise Summary

This finishes the section of this chapter on repeated shapes and the various uses that you can make of them. Both kinds of repetition will occur many times as you work with Illustrator and, as you have seen, when they are combined with other Illustrator tools, they can be powerful and productive.

CONSTRAINING GRAPHICS

This section of the chapter deals with various ways to constrain movement. This form of constraint is very powerful; you have already used the most simple form of constraint—to keep lines straight, for example, or to make sure your circles are round—in many exercises, and I'm sure you found them easy to use.

Actually the Shift key does not constrain to horizontal and vertical lines; what it actually does is constrain according to the current x and y axes. These axes are normally horizontal and vertical, parallel to the sides of the desktop, and that is how you have used them so far. It is possible, however, to rotate these axes to any arbitrary angle. Effectively what you do is rotate the x axis to some defined angle relative to the horizontal. This is accomplished by using the Constrain Angle item in the Preferences dialog box, which you access by choosing Edit ➤ Preferences. When you select this item, you are presented with the Preferences dialog box shown in Figure 12.33.

When you use this dialog box to set constraints on the axes, it affects all the Shift functions that you use thereafter. Of course, a square is still a square and a circle, a circle; but the sides of the square will be at the defined angle, and the anchor points on the circle will also be at the defined angle. Any type that you set will run along the new x axis, just as it ran horizontally before. This makes setting captions or other type on an angle very easy indeed. In the same way, the constraint on squares and circles means that you can apply all the techniques that you have previously learned to any arbitrary angled perspective. For example, you can make precisely angled half-circles by using the technique of ungrouping a circle, which you learned earlier.

You can use the Constrain angle box and the Distance tool together to set axes at any angle. Select the Distance tool from the Toolbox. Click on any two points on the Illustrator desktop. This provides a precise measurement of the angle and distance and the horizontal and vertical displacement between the two points. This information is presented in the Measure dialog box, as shown in Figure 12.34.

Note the value shown next to Angle and then click OK. Choose Edit ➤ Preferences (⌘–K) and enter the value that was shown next to Angle in the Measure dialog box as the Constrain angle and click OK. This sets the new constrained axes to the given angle.

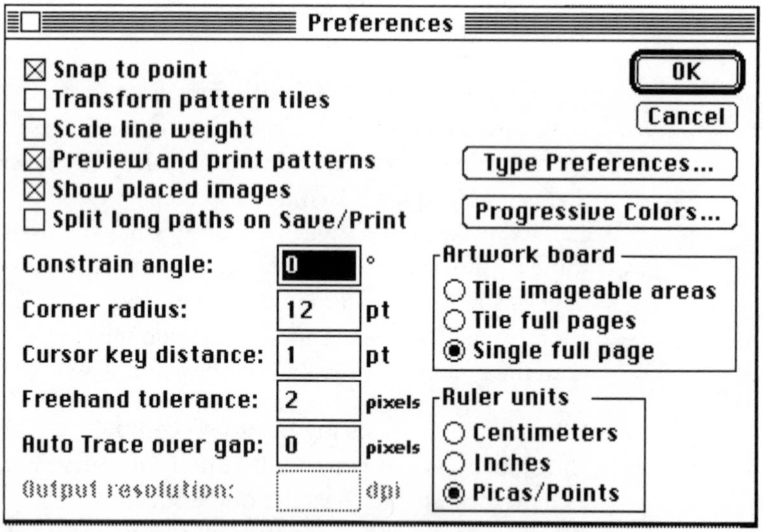

Figure 12.33

You use the Preferences dialog box to set the Constrain angle for the axes of your drawing.

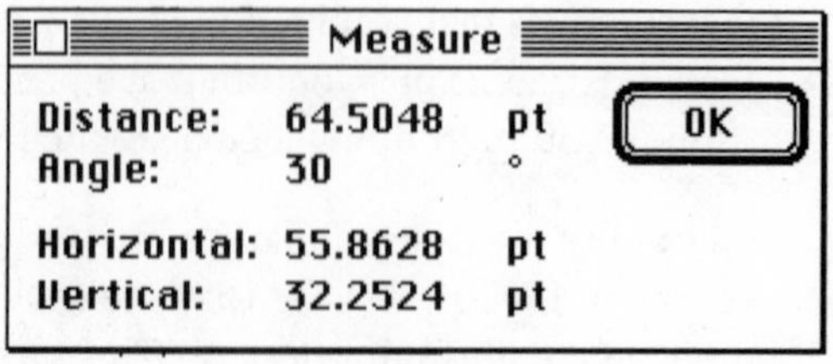

Figure 12.34

The Measure dialog box will show you the distance and angle between any two points.

Matching "Off-Axis" Templates

You will find the ability to set new constrained axes really helpful, indeed, possibly essential, for matching scanned templates exactly. If you use scanned images with any regularity, you will soon discover that they have one large potential problem: namely, that they may be scanned off axis. This is quite annoying if you are using the scanned image as a template for Illustrator. You can't alter the template with Illustrator; and, furthermore, scanned images usually are presented in MacPaint format, and MacPaint can only rotate by multiples of 90° because of the limitations of bit-mapped graphics. What to do?

You could, of course, continue scanning the document until you get the scanned image at exactly horizontal and vertical alignment, but that's tedious and time-consuming. Instead, you should constrain the artwork that you create to the axes of the drawing by picking any straight line, tracing it in Illustrator, selecting the line and then use the Preferences dialog's Constrain angle as described above. Now you can trace all the template with an exact match and rotate the final artwork back to horizontal and vertical when you're done. This is an elegant solution to a vexing problem.

Exercise 12.4: Isometric Drawing

Since it would be excessively optimistic, not to say unreasonable, to expect you to have a slightly skewed template to practice on, the next exercise uses the constraint mechanism in another typical fashion. The process of creating isometric drawings is quite common in engineering or architecture. In isometric drawings, the axis or axes of some figure are at a constant angle to the page (sound familiar?).

The exercise here will be quite simple: a ring and shaft arrangement that is angled to the page to provide an exploded, three-dimensional effect in the drawing.

All isometric drawings use the following four basic steps (using an angle of 30° as an example):

1. Draw the basic object full face on the drawing surface.

2. Scale the object in the vertical dimension only, leaving the horizontal dimension alone. The value for the scale of the vertical dimension is

exactly the tangent of the angle of the isometric axes (in this case 0.57735).

3. Rotate the figure clockwise through the complementary angle, that is, 90° minus the desired angle (in this case, 60°).

4. Now constrain the axes to the desired angle (in this case 30°).

And that will produce an isometric drawing with the isometric axes at 30° from the plane of the drawing surface.

Traditional isometric drawings are always done so that the x-axis is rotated 30° and the y-axis is rotated 60°, so that both appear to be at a 30° angle from the horizontal axis in the drawing. Therefore, you may often see directions for creating isometric artwork that use certain "magic numbers" to produce their effect. Actually, these numbers are simply trigonometric functions (the tangent or cosine) of 30°. Although you will use the standard angle in this exercise, you can substitute any other angle quite easily by simply using that angle in the steps given here and using the appropriate trigonometric values when you create your artwork.

Let's work this through using the standard angle of 30°. Then the tangent of 30° (as you can easily determine from a table of trigonometric functions or your trusty trig calculator) is .57735. This means you will scale the figure by 57.735% vertically and 100% horizontally to get the effect you want. The complement of 30° is 60°. So the work proceeds as follows.

Start with a new drawing surface with no template. In the center of the surface, draw three concentric circles as shown in Figure 12.35.

Set the Paint Style for all of these as Fill with None, Stroke 100% Black, with a line weight of 1. You may want to change these for various effects when you are doing more sophisticated work; for now, however, let's just use the simple outline to make the clearest example possible. This is the first step in the outline.

Select all the artwork on the drawing surface by using Edit ➤ Select All (⌘–A). Group all the points for convenience in operations. Now select the Scale Option tool to get the dialog box and position the scale origin under the bottom point of the circles. Set the scale values in the dialog box to Non-uniform scale with Horizontal set to 100% and Vertical to 57.735%, as we discussed above. Then click OK; the resulting figure is shown in Figure 12.36.

This completes the second step of the outline above.

Now use the Rotate tool to move the circles into position for the isometric view. Remember that you want to rotate them clockwise through the complement of the angle of the axes. That means that you subtract the angle from 90° to get the complementary angle. For 30°, the complement is 60°. Then

Figure 12.35

Start with these concentric circles to create your isometric artwork.

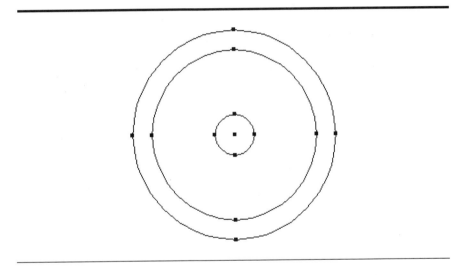

Figure 12.36

These are the scaled circles for your isometric artwork.

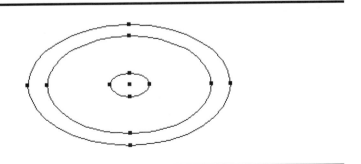

you use that angle as a negative value in the rotation dialog box. Remember, positive angles in Illustrator move counterclockwise. The center of the rotation should again be the bottom of the circles. The result looks like Figure 12.37.

The circles have been rotated clockwise to the right, angling the line of the centers of the circles up to the right at 30°. This completes the third step of the outline.

Now choose Edit ➤ Preferences and set the Constrain angle to 30°. This sets the artwork for the rest of the isometric exercise and completes the outline above. Let's see how this works.

Use the Pen tool to draw a line up and to the right from the top point of the center circle. This will represent the axle from the disc, which will be represented by two versions of the circles you drew earlier. Use the Shift key to constrain the lines along the axes you set previously. The result looks like Figure 12.38.

Now do another line the same way from the bottom anchor point of the inner circle, making it about the same length. Next use the Selection tool with both the Shift and Option keys to move a copy of the circles up a small distance to show the other side of the disc. Finally, ungroup one set of circles and copy the small, inner circle out to the end of the axle. The result looks like Figure 12.39.

Figure 12.37

Now you have rotated and scaled the circles for your isometric artwork.

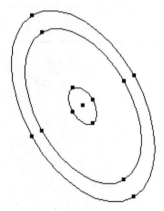

Figure 12.38

Once you have set the constraints, you can easily draw along the new axes.

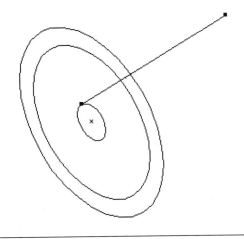

Figure 12.39

This is the completed isometric artwork.

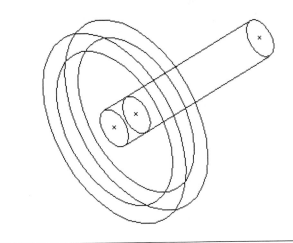

Exercise Summary

I'm sure that you can find many more advanced examples of isometric drawings if you work on them. I have deliberately kept the elements of this drawing to a minimum to reduce this process to the bare essentials. You can use the basic constraining techniques discussed here, along with the other advanced techniques that you have learned, to produce very complex drawings.

Exercise 12.5: Masking Graphics

Illustrator also has the capability to confine the printing of artwork to a defined region of a page. This region is called a *clipping region*, and is defined by drawing the region with standard Illustrator tools and then setting the Mask checkbox in the Paint Style dialog box. A clipping region's function is similar to a stencil's: only marks that are painted inside the region show on the page.

This is easier shown than said, so, as a simple example, we'll define a clipping region, draw some ovals, and preview the result. This will allow you to see how a clipping region is constructed, what is required to make the clipping work, and how to order artwork to include or exclude it from the region. Open a blank Illustrator desktop without a template. If you are continuing work from the previous exercise, be sure to select Edit ➤ Preferences and set the Constrain angle back to 0 degrees. Use the Rectangle tool to create a large rectangle on the desktop. This rectangle will define the clipping region that you will use to mask off other artwork.

With the rectangle selected, choose Arrange ➤ Ungroup. It is essential that the clipping region be an ungrouped, closed figure in order for the Mask setting to function correctly. Next, select the center point of the rectangle and use Edit ➤ Clear to delete it. The lone center point of the rectangle must be removed before using the rectangle's path as a clipping mask. This gives you a simple figure of four lines, as shown in Figure 12.40.

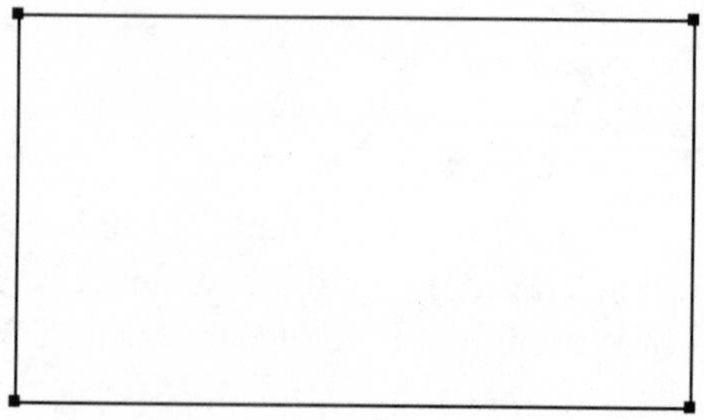

Figure 12.40

You can use this rectangular path (or any other closed Illustrator path) to make a clipping mask.

Select the remaining portion of the rectangle using the Object Selection tool. Use Paint ➤ Style to bring up the Paint Style dialog and set Fill to None, Stroke to Black 100% with a line Weight of 0.1 and click in the Mask checkbox to turn it on. The Mask option sets the rectangle as a clipping region. We have also stroked the rectangle so it will show the outline of the selected area. Figure 12.41 shows you these setting in the dialog box.

Now we will create some circles and ovals inside, overlapping, and outside the rectangle. Use the Oval tool and draw some ovals and rectangles on your artwork. Paint these ovals with 100% Black Fill and no Stroke. Be sure that some of the objects that you draw are entirely inside the rectangle, some overlapping the edges of the rectangle, and at least one completely outside the rectangle. Figure 12.42 shows you how this might look.

At this point, you have drawn a series of ovals which will paint *after* the rectangle since they were drawn after it. As you remember from the previous exercises, this means that the ovals are all *on top* of the rectangle. This is an important rule for using masks: the only objects that are masked are those

Figure 12.41

Use these settings to transform your path into a clipping region.

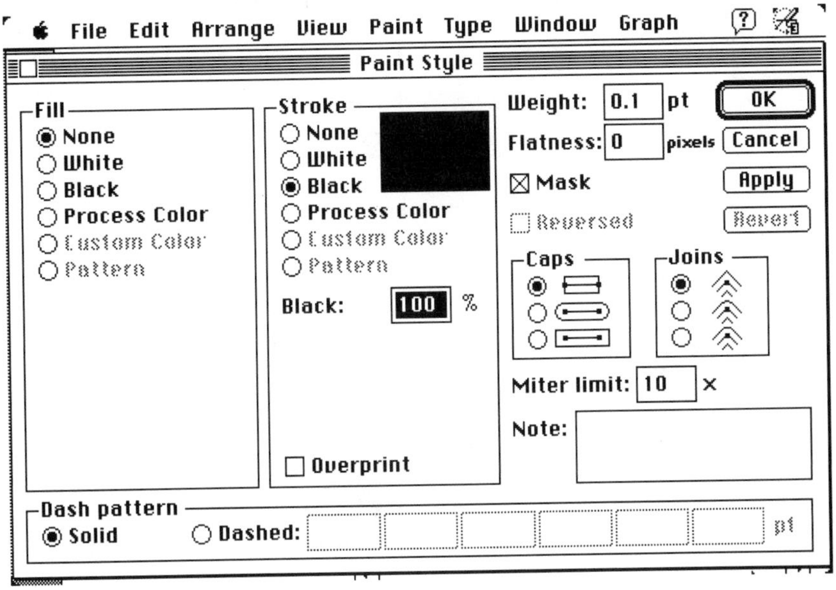

painted after the clipping region. To see how this looks, use View ➤ Preview Illustration. Your screen should look something like Figure 12.43.

No part of the ovals that falls outside of the mask rectangle is painted, including the oval in the upper-left corner, which is entirely outside of the rectangle.

However, if you move any object behind the rectangle, thereby painting it before the rectangle, all of that object will be visible, regardless of whether it is inside or outside the clipping region. As an example, select the oval in the lower-left corner of the artwork. Now choose Edit ➤ Send To Back to move that oval behind the rectangle. Select View ➤ Preview Illustration to see the effect of this change, which looks like Figure 12.44.

Figure 12.42

Draw a variety of ovals both inside and outside the clipping rectangle for this exercise.

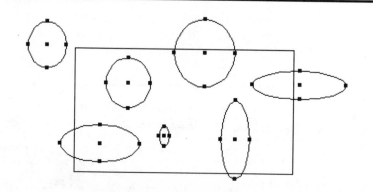

Figure 12.43

This shows you how the clipping region prevents anything outside its boundaries from painting on output.

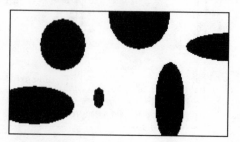

This is one way to allow objects to print over a masked region. Simply move the object that you want to show behind the mask object.

There is another way to control how the mask interacts with your artwork, without having to mess about with the layers in the artwork. This is to group the objects that you want masked with the mask itself. If the mask is part of a group, it will mask only objects in the group. Any objects not in the group, whether painted before or after the mask, will show completely. As an example, select all the objects in this artwork except the oval in the upper-left corner, which is entirely outside of the rectangle. The easy way to do this is to select all of the objects by using ⌘-A (Edit ➤ Select All) and then using the Selection tool with Shift to *deselect* the top-left oval. Then make the remaining selected objects into a group by pressing ⌘-G. Preview this now and you will see something like Figure 12.45.

Figure 12.44

You can control what is clipped by moving the objects into different layers.

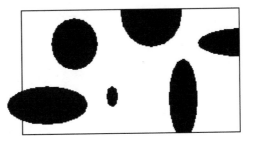

Figure 12.45

You can group objects with a mask to limit which objects get clipped.

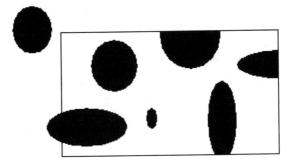

Now the single oval that is outside the group shows clearly, even though it is painted after the mask and the other objects. Notice also that the oval that you moved to the back earlier still prints outside the mask, even though it is part of the group. It isn't enough to simply group objects with the mask. The objects in the group must paint after the mask if they are to be clipped.

Using Text as a Mask

You can use this same technique with paths that are not as simple as a rectangle. For example, you can use text characters as a mask. This follows the same basic process you saw above, but with some important twists.

Let's use the text and graphic exercise that you did in *Chapter 10.* In that exercise, you changed the word *PARADE* into text outlines and then distorted them to make a graphic statement, adding a series of wavy gray lines behind them for effect. Now you can clip the gray lines to your text and make another common and interesting effect.

Begin by calling up the previous exercise. Select all of the characters from the line of text and use Edit ➤ Copy. Then start a new drawing surface and use Edit ➤ Paste to place the text onto it. This will give you something like Figure 12.46.

Your first inclination might be to simply select all of the letters, check Mask, and then proceed. However, that doesn't work. Each letter is a separate path and, as a result, only the first letter P will show when you Preview; all the subsequent letters will be clipped out of the display. You must make all the letters into a compound path to make them one path for masking, then make them into a mask object. Select all of the letterforms on the artwork with ⌘-A and then use Paint ➤ Make Compound (⌘-Option-G) to make them all part of a compound path. Now return to your earlier artwork and select the wavy line

Figure 12.46

Letter shapes can be used as a mask once they are converted to outlines.

background. Copy this and paste it onto the new artwork. This automatically places it in front of the text mask, making it paint after the mask where it will be clipped by the text outlines. The result should look something like Figure 12.47.

Figure 12.47

Once you make the character outlines into a compound path, you can make them an effective mask for any other object.

Exercise Summary

Remember that using complex paths, like text characters, can cause your artwork not to print if its complexity exceeds the limits of your output device. If that happens, you can use this trick to simplify your artwork: Cut your background—here, the wavy lines—into one segment for each letter. Then release the letters from the compound path by using Paint ➤ Release Compound. Make just the path for the first letter into a compound path, using Paint ➤ Make Compound and then make it a mask. Group it with one segment of the background, making sure that the background paints after the mask. Repeat this process for each letter that you want to use. This technique makes each letter and background a separate object, and so escapes the limit problems that occur when too many letters are placed into a single mask path.

Summary

Whew! This chapter is filled with a lot of different and complex work. This just shows you how much you can do with Illustrator as you become proficient with its tools and techniques. In this chapter, you have begun to combine tools and use various techniques to make some typical Illustrator artwork. As you have seen, these combinations are practically unlimited in their power and versatility.

We began this chapter by using several tools to create an exploded view of the apple artwork. This is a good example of how you might use sections of existing artwork as components in an exploded view. Next, you added text to this artwork for labels. This gave you a chance to use the scale and text tools and to reorient the page for easier output. Next you used several tools to create two different types of repeating graphics. First, you created the illusion of movement by repeating a complete figure in different positions, then you repeated a single graphic element in an artwork, using scale and movement to make the copies slightly different for each repetition.

Finally, the chapter concluded with some of the most advanced features of Illustrator. You learned how to use the constraint preference, and you used it to create some simple isometric artwork. You also learned how to use the Autotrace and Freehand tools to make your drawing work easier and faster. Lastly, you created and used a pattern as a fill for your artwork. All of these techniques will help you get the most out of Illustrator.

CHAPTER THIRTEEN

FEATURING

Using the Graph tool

Choosing graph options

Editing graphs for clarity

Using specialized designs
for columns and markers

Charting
with Illustrator

WHY VISUAL PRESENTATION?

Numbers are everywhere in this society. In business and science, in politics and education, the new tools created for the personal computer have spawned a plethora of numeric information. After all, numbers are the computer's basic language, and numbers have a real power. For better or worse, the compelling force of numeric data is clear to all of us every time we balance our checkbook.

Unfortunately, people working with data occasionally suffer from the same myopia that often affects scientists and computer programmers: they feel that the information is almost self-evident. When you have been working with a set of numbers long enough, even those old line-printer sheets of data seem eloquent. However, communicating that information to others who have not spent time analyzing and understanding its nuances requires a more effective method of presentation. Here is where graphs become important. Indeed, your choice of a graph may make or break the vital flow of information to those who must use it to make policy decisions, for example, or to change investment plans. Once you have the numbers, the presentation becomes the critical factor. The whole point of using Illustrator is to make the process of turning your numbers into graphs easy and quick.

Visual Factors

Keep in mind that some elements are more clear than others. Here are the elements that most audiences can see, ordered from the easiest to the hardest to differentiate:

1. Line length

2. Angle

3. Area

4. Volume

5. Color (hue, saturation, or shading)

Use those measurements that people find easiest for your data whenever possible, and to be careful as you move down the list to be sure that you don't lose your audience.

CHOOSING THE CORRECT FORMAT

The correct format for your graph depends upon two things: the data and your purpose in making the graph. The choice of chart type begins with your data. As you work with numbers, you will find that numbers depend on one another in how they should be organized. Choosing a graph depends directly on your data analysis and your requirements for the presentation.

There are five reasons to use a graph: description, exploration, tabulation, persuasion, or decoration. Different reasons indicate different types of graphs. If you are trying to show conclusions and additional insights, then scatter graphs can be of great help. You would be unlikely to use a pie or bar chart in those circumstances, because those types of graph are more useful to tabulate or describe data. Also, to make a good graph, you must understand your audience.

Just as you edit text to convey the crispest and clearest meaning, so you must edit your graph to create the clearest and most effective display that you can.

All types of graphs do some things better than others. It is quite easy to slip into using just a few types of graphs just because they are familiar and comfortable. Here you have an opportunity to review a variety of charts, and learn when a given type is appropriate. This chapter should help you arm yourself with some new ideas about the various types of charts and graphs.

CHART TYPES

In this section we are going to explore some of the most common types of charts and graphs. The intention is to show you how to create graphs, what the strengths and weaknesses of Illustrator are when you're using the Graph tools, and how and when you might modify these graphs.

Exercise 13.1: A Grouped Column Graph

One of the most common types of graph is the *column*, or *bar graph*. In a bar graph the dependent (changing) variable is shown by the length of a bar rising from the scale line which measures the independent variable. Generally, the independent variable is horizontal and the bars are vertical. This is a good method for showing relative amounts since the eye is very good at measuring lengths, particularly from a common baseline. Figure 13.1 shows you a basic bar chart, such as you might use in a report, as generated by Illustrator after some customization.

This shows the annual sales in dollars for four divisions of a company. The divisions are listed along the bottom of the chart, while the sales are mapped along the vertical scale. This chart is quite clear about the results; it shows the audience what each division has contributed to the overall revenue of the company.

Let's create this graph in Illustrator. Begin with an empty drawing surface and choose the Grouped Column Graph tool from the Toolbox. Move the cursor out onto the drawing surface and click at about (12, 44) and drag the resulting rectangle to about the point (40, 28). This rectangle defines the area where your graph will be placed.

Figure 13.1

A bar graph is good for showing relative amounts.

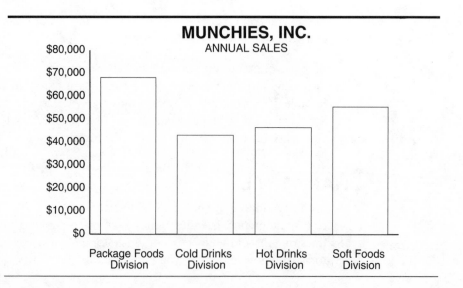

As soon as you release the mouse button, the graph is drawn on the desktop, using default values, and the Graph Data dialog box, shown in Figure 13.2, is displayed.

You use this dialog box to enter data into your graph. There are three methods of entering data: you can type the data into the spreadsheet cells in this dialog, you can cut the data from some other graph or application and paste it in here, or you can import data from another application using the Import button at the top of the dialog.

Data that is entered from another application must be in screen or text format. Each line forms a row in the data matrix, and each entry must be separated by tabs. Cutting and pasting are quite straightforward; they work just as they do in any other Macintosh application. Cut the desired data out of your source application; remember that each line will be a row of data and that each column is separated by a tab. For data import, save the data from the exporting application (such as Excel) in text format, again with each line

Figure 13.2

You can enter or import data for your graph in the Graph Data dialog box.

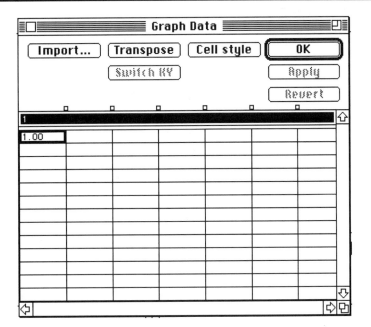

representing a row of data and each column separated by tabs—this is the natural format used by most spreadsheet applications when you save in text format.

Let's begin this graph by entering the following data directly into the cells in the dialog box.

Package Foods Division	68100
Cold Drinks Division	43120
Hot Drinks Division	46470
Soft Foods Division	55450

Be sure not to use any commas in your numbers. If you do, Illustrator will think that they are labels and will try to place them on the graph that way instead of using them as numbers. Illustrator does understand decimal points. If you have decimal values, go ahead and put them in. These figures give you a graph that looks something like Figure 13.3.

The first thing to notice about this graph (and all Illustrator graphs) is that all the graph elements are grouped. A graph in Illustrator must be grouped for you to use the Graph menu item. This is a critical point. If you ungroup the

Figure 13.3

This is the basic bar graph as generated by Illustrator.

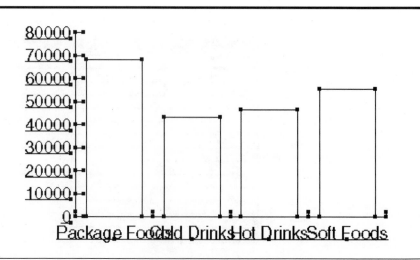

graph, Illustrator will no longer recognize it as a graph, and will delete all the graph data and style features. The result will be that you have a pretty picture, but no graph. Moreover, you *cannot regroup it as a graph* by using Arrange ➤ Group. So be *very* careful with graphs and the Ungroup command. You probably will never want to disassociate a graph into its component elements. To access the individual elements, like labels, areas, and so on, use the Direct Selection tool to reach inside the graph for the elements that you want.

Let's now make some modifications to this graph. There are obviously several things wrong with this graph, beginning with the size of the font used for the labels. Illustrator always uses Helvetica for labels, scaling it according to the size of the graph rectangle. For large graph rectangles, this results in fairly large type. You can easily change this, however, by selecting the labels and making them into the style, size, and so on that you want.

Begin by selecting the Direct Selection tool from the Toolbox. Use the Direct Selection cursor to draw a selection marquee around the anchor points of the numbers on the left. Then change these to 12-point Helvetica. When you do that, notice that the alignment of the labels with the tick marks is lost. Move the labels up slightly to realign them. Use the Shift key to constrain the move-ment to the vertical direction, and magnify the left side to ensure that the labels line up correctly.

Next select the labels along the bottom of the graph in the same way and set these also to 12-point Helvetica. This resolves the confusion at the bottom somewhat, but the labels still run into one another. To solve this, simply make your labels two lines. Select the entire graph using Edit ➤ Select All. Then select Graph ➤ Graph Data. This returns you to the Graph Data dialog box, where you can edit your labels. Select the

> Package Foods Division

cell and change it to

> Package Foods | Division

The vertical bar is a signal to Illustrator to insert a return into your label text. This will move the word *Division* down one line below the words *Package Foods*. Make the same change to the other labels, always before the word *Division*, and click OK. The labels now occupy two lines and don't run into one another. As a final touch, select these labels again with the Direct Selection tool and change the leading from Auto to 12. This moves the labels slightly closer together and makes them more readable. Figure 13.4 shows you the graph at this point.

Now you need to clean up the tick marks on the graph and add a dollar sign in front of the numbers on the vertical scale. To do this, select the entire graph again and choose Graph ➤ Graph Style. This brings up the Graph Style dialog box, shown in Figure 13.5.

This dialog box allows you to set specific parameters for each type of graph, as well as determining the type of graph itself. The top-left group allows you to set any one of the six types of graph for the data that you have entered. These correspond to the different graph type tools in the Toolbox. If you select a different type, the graph is automatically changed to that type, using the data that you have already entered.

The top-right box changes with every type. For both grouped-column and stacked-column graphs, this box allows you to set the width of individual columns and groups of columns, which Illustrator calls *clusters*, as a percentage of the basic column width. The basic column width for the graph is determined by the number of rows of data that you have entered in the Graph Data dialog box, and the size that you made the graph when you created it.

Figure 13.4

The labels on the edited graph are easier to read than before.

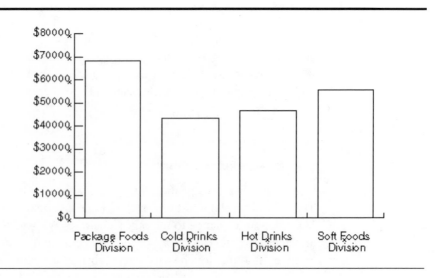

Figure 13.5

The Graph Style dialog box allows you to set a variety of parameters for each type of graph.

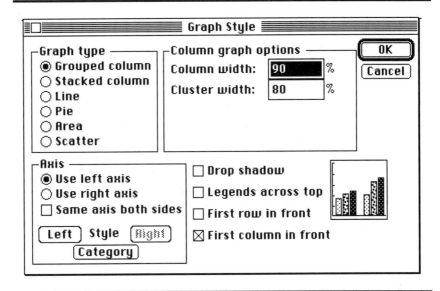

The default values of 90% for the column width and 80% for cluster width ensure a small space between columns and clusters, with a slightly greater space for cluster groups than for columns, Generally, this will give you good results.

Below the Column graph options group are a series of checkboxes. These allow you to set various options for your graph. The Drop Shadow checkbox adds a drop shadow to the bars on the graph. Although this checkbox is available with all graph types, it is obviously more appropriate for some, like column graphs, than others, like line graphs. Legends across top moves the legend from the side of the graph (the default) to the top of the graph, which changes the legend from vertical to horizontal. The First row in front and First column in front options control which columns display in front when the columns overlap. If you select First column in front, then the columns representing the first column of data in the Graph Data dialog are displayed first; if this is not checked, the last column displays first. If you have organized your data by rows instead of columns, then the First row in front performs the same function. Notice that the small window to the right of these checkboxes shows you a small icon representing the type of graph that you are using.

The Axis group controls how the axes of the graph are labeled and displayed. The radio buttons allow you to set the vertical axis on the right or left, as you choose. If you check the Same axis both side checkbox, then the vertical axis is displayed on both sides of the graph. The buttons at the bottom allow you to control setting for the left or right vertical axis and the horizontal axis independently.

Click on the Left button to display the Graph Axis Style dialog box, shown in Figure 13.6.

There are two groups in this dialog box: Axis label and tick line values and Axis tick lines and marks. The top group is used to set the number of labels along the axis. You can allow Illustrator to calculate these for you, as we have here, by selecting the Calculate radio button. Alternatively, you can force a range of values by choosing the Use manual axis values button and entering the maximum, minimum, and number of units between labels in the appropriate boxes. Finally, this group allows you to enter text values to be inserted before of after the labels on the graph. For this graph, you want to enter dollar signs before the labels, so enter **$** in the Labels before text box.

Figure 13.6

The Graph Axis Style dialog allows you to set display options for the vertical or horizontal axis.

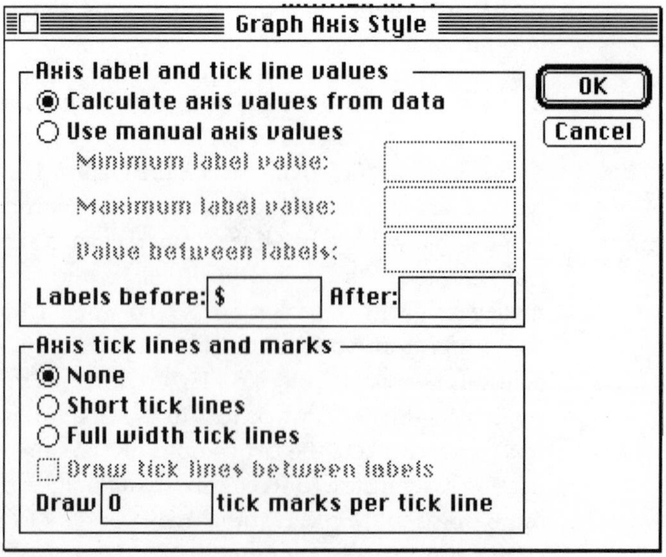

The bottom group, Axis tick lines and marks, controls the actual display of the tick marks on the graph. The three options here are None, to display no tick marks whatsoever, Short tick lines (the default), which uses short lines; and Full width tick lines, which extends the tick lines all the way across the graph. For this graph select None. Generally you should use labels instead of tick marks in column graphs. Click OK to return to the Graph Style dialog box.

Next, choose the Category button. This displays the same dialog box for the horizontal axis; the only difference is that the Draw tick lines between label checkbox is now available and checked. This box is only available for the Category axis, and it is automatically selected. When checked, it places tick marks between the clusters on your graph. This is completely unnecessary chartjunk that should almost always be removed. Click on the box to deselect it, and click on None to remove the tick marks within the columns. Now click OK to return to the Graph Style dialog and click OK again to return to the graph itself. At this point, the graph looks like Figure 13.7, much better than the original, but not yet finished.

The last touch to this is to change the color of the columns themselves. Illustrator defaults to a 100% Black bar for this graph. This is too dark and overpowers the graph itself. You want to change this to a lighter color, or

Figure 13.7

When you have edited the labels and tick marks, the graph looks like this.

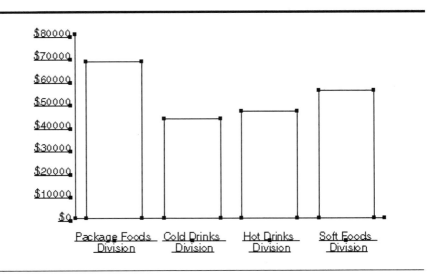

even to remove all color from the columns. To do this, use the Direct Selection tool again and select all of the columns. You don't need to select all of the points in each column; in fact, you don't need to select any points. Draw a selection marquee across the columns at any point that touches all of the columns and nothing else. Then select Paint ➤ Style and change the Fill from 100% Black to 10% Black (or whatever you want). This sets the fill values for all the columns at once, which is the most efficient way to handle this problem.

Finally, you can use the Text tool to add a heading to the graph. You can also use the Text tool to edit the label values to add commas in the dollar values if you want. Your graph should ultimately look something like Figure 13.1. Note, however, that any change to the graph, either the data or the style, will remove the text changes to the labels, since the graph labels will be rewritten from the graph data and the style will revert to the default. Therefore, you don't want to make style changes until you're all finished with the graph. Save this graph for use in the next exercise.

Exercise Summary

Another common form of the bar graph occurs when time is the independent variable. When time is an axis it is almost always the independent variable and plotted along the horizontal scale line. For example, instead of plotting sales by division, as in Figure 13.1, you might have presented sales by quarter. Such a graph would show each quarter on the independent horizontal scale, while the dependent variable is once again the sales.

Exercise 13.2: Multiple Column Graphs

Graphs like Figure 13.1 are very simple bar charts, and really contribute very little to the understanding of the audience. If you want to give the audience something that uses more of the graph's power, you can add more information. In our example, this might be the previous year's sales and next year's projected sales, as shown in Figure 13.8.

This graph has the kind of concentrated information that makes graphs compelling. Here your audience can see both the past performance and the projected future performance at a glance.

Let's create this graph as you did the previous one.

Figure 13.8

This example includes sales by division over a three-year period.

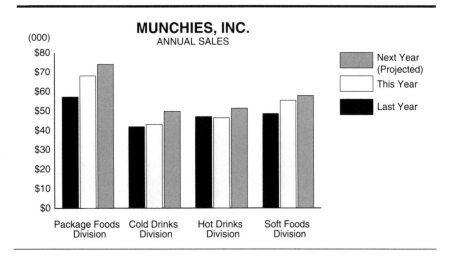

Begin by opening your previous graph and choosing Edit ➤ Select All (⌘-A). Then choose Graph ➤ Graph Data to get the Graph Data dialog box. Select all of the data in the dialog box—the two rows and four columns—and choose Edit ➤ Copy (⌘-C) to place the data on the Clipboard.

Now open a new drawing surface and create a grouped-column graph in a rectangle about 28 picas wide and 16 picas high; that is, from about (12, 44) to (40, 28), as in the last exercise. When the Graph Data dialog box opens, move to the second row, first column position and choose Edit ➤ Paste (⌘-V) to paste in the data that you copied from the previous graph. Enter the label

    This Year

in the first row, second column, as a label for the data row. Select all of this column and choose Edit ➤ Cut (⌘-X). Move over one column and use ⌘-V to repaste the information in that column. Then enter the following data.

Last Year	Next Year|(Projected)
57240	74100
41970	49800

Last Year	Next Year|(Projected)
47120	51400
48620	57900

Don't forget the return code (|) in *Next Year | (Projected)*. When you're done, the Graph Data box should look like Figure 13.9.

Notice that the upper-left cell, row one column one, is left vacant. This allows you to have label data going both across and down, which will translate into appropriate labels on the graph.

You can make the same edits on this graph as you did on the previous one to generate the output shown in Figure 13.8. There are two differences here. First, the vertical scale has been edited to remove the extra zeros, with a legend placed at the top of the vertical axis. Second, I have used File ➤ Page Setup to set the output to a landscape format for output.

Figure 13.9

This is how your Graph Data dialog box should look when you enter your data.

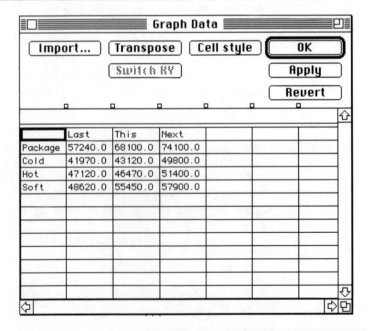

Exercise Summary

If you wanted to make the graph even more useful, you could add an additional line across the actual sales figures, showing the previously projected sales for that period. This would give your audience several items to chew on. First of all, seasonal variation would be taken into account by seeing the previous year's performance. Second, the accuracy of previous sales forecasts would be clearly shown by the visible variation of actual sales from projected sales. The bias, if any, could then be factored into the projections for next year.

You can also use sideways bars, making the independent variable vertical and the dependent variable horizontal. This is useful when the data is clear and where you need to use a relatively long name but don't want to use legends or codes. If you have only a few bars, you can place the labels beneath them, next to them, or on top of them, to create a clear picture without extraneous coding. You should avoid vertical labels on the bars, though, because they are hard to read and difficult to interpret.

USING SPECIAL GRAPHIC DESIGNS

One reason why bar charts are so useful is that the actual column or bar may be drawn in almost any way. You might use stacks of coins for a money variable, or small rolls of carpet or other output unit as a measure of production. You can also color the bars, to emphasize a specific one, if you want to make a particular comparison. But you must be sure that your visual enhancements do not detract from the data.

Illustrator provides excellent tools for such enhancements. You can draw any graphic object in Illustrator and then convert it into a column design for use in any column in a graph. You can also use such a design as a label for a data point in a line graph. The process is very similar to creating a pattern.

Let's use this feature with the data that you just entered to generate a new graph. Figure 13.10 shows you four simple designs to match each of the four divisions of Munchies, Inc.: an ice cream cone for the Soft Foods Division, a cookie for the Package Foods Division, a soft-drink bottle for the Cold Drinks Division, and a cup for the Hot Drinks Division.

Figure 13.10

You can use these four
artwork objects for
columns in your
multicolumn graph.

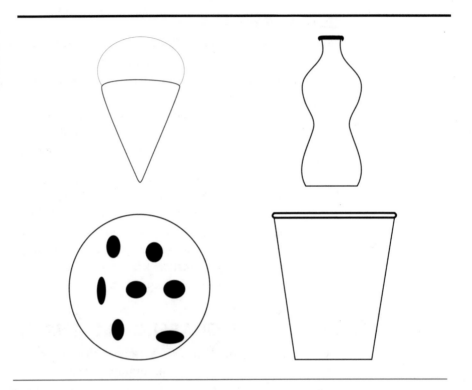

Note that these graphics are all the same height—in this case, 156 points.
The exact height is not important, just be sure they are all the same height
for use together in the graph columns.

You can use these steps to make an object into a column design. For example,
let's use the soft-drink bottle artwork. First, you create the desired design
using the standard drawing tools. Create the design at any appropriate size
that you want to use; Illustrator will later scale the graphic to your graph's
requirements. Second, use the Rectangle tool to draw a rectangle that encloses the design. This rectangle will be the actual area that Illustrator uses for
filling the graph. If the rectangle cuts off any part of the design, that part will
not be in the column; on the other hand, if the rectangle extends past the
design, the white space around the rectangle will be included in the column.
In this case, make the rectangle just fit the bottle artwork. Then send the rectangle behind the artwork, using Edit ➤ Send To Back (⌘––). Now select

both the object and the rectangle. Both objects must be selected; only the selected objects become part of the graph design, so be particularly attentive to this step. Now select Graph ➤ Define Graph Design. This brings up the Design dialog box as shown in Figure 13.11.

Select the New button and Illustrator provides a default name for your new design (*New Design* 1) and a preview of the design itself in the bottom right corner of the dialog. If the preview looks different from your artwork or if there is no preview you probably have not selected the correct objects— remember, both the rectangle and the artwork must be selected. Type the name that you want to use over the default name. This design was called *coke bottle*. Then click OK. This defines the design for use in any open document, just like patterns or custom colors.

Use the same techniques to define the other three designs for your graph. Figure 13.11 shows you that I had already done that, using the names *cone*, *cookie*, and *coffee cup* for the other designs. Save these designs and their artwork in a separate document. I named this one *Graph designs*.

You can rename or delete a design in the Design dialog box. Note, however, that deleting or renaming a design will automatically delete the design from

Figure 13.11

The Design dialog box allows you to make art-work into a graph design.

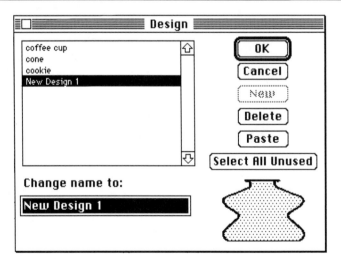

any open artwork that uses it. It will not affect any unopened artwork that uses the design, though.

Defining the design is only half the battle; the other half is using it in your graph. Let's look at how to do that. Open the graph that looks like Figure 13.8. We could simply use the new graphics for the arrangement on this graph, but that would simply be cutesy and not add any real value to the graph. Let's change the graph around, so that the three time periods are on the horizontal axis. In that orientation, the data for the divisions will be shown side-by-side for the same period. In that format, the column designs will have a positive impact, since they will let the audience see immediately how each division was doing. Since we have selected designs that are easily tied to the divisions themselves, the designs will allow viewers to make comparisons without reference to the legend.

Luckily, changing the display from division to period is quite easy in Illustrator. Select all of the graph. Then select Graph ➤ Graph Data to bring up the Graph Data dialog box. Click on the Transpose button at the top of the dialog box. This reverses the rows and columns in your data, which makes the periods the horizontal axis and the divisions the coded data. Click OK.

Now you need to substitute the designs that you made for the present columns. To do this, use the Direct Selection tool again. Click once off of the graph to deselect everything. Now click on the first column (the Package Foods Division column) in each of the three periods, using the Option and Shift keys to select all of these columns together. Still using the Option and Shift keys, click on the box representing the Package Foods Division encoding on the right side of the graph. At this point, your screen should look like Figure 13.12.

This represents all the columns and the legend that you want to fill with the cookie design. Make sure that you have the Graph Design artwork open and available so that the column designs can be added to your graph. If you have the designs available, all the entries on the Graph menu should be available and not dimmed. Select Graph ➤ Use Column Design. This brings up the Graph Column Design dialog box.

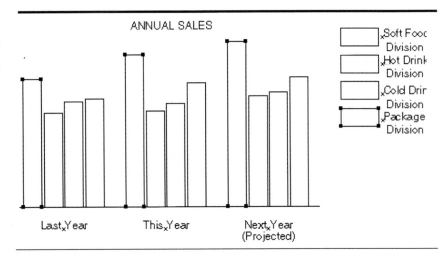

Figure 13.12

You must select all of the columns and the legend for one group before changing the design.

Click on the Repeating radio button in the Column design type group. This group allows you to use your designs in several ways. Select Repeating. This means the design will be repeated along the column for the required distance. This also does two other things: it activates the Repeated designs group and it displays a scrolling list of available designs in the Column design name list. Select *cookie* from this list. Now you need to tell Illustrator how to use the repeating design by setting the required values in the Repeated design group. The first requirement is to define how much of the column each cookie represents, in column units. Since the columns are a maximum of 80000 in height, enter **20000** here. This means that each column will be no more than four cookies high and each cookie will represent about one quarter of a column. Next, choose the Chop design fraction radio button. Obviously, a column isn't likely to be exactly a uniform number of cookies in height. These two radio buttons, Chop design fraction and Scale design fraction, govern how partial designs are displayed. The two options are fairly clear from the labels on the buttons: you can either chop off the part of the design that doesn't fit or you can scale the design so that it fits. I think that chopping off the fraction is better than scaling, because scaled objects are harder to compare than simple distances. Finally, click on the Rotate legend design checkbox to deselect it. This checkbox, if selected, rotates the design that you are using onto its side for the legend display. Again, I think this is a bad idea, since it requires your audience to perform some mental gyrations to rotate the design back into the display orientation used in the column. However, if space is limited, this may be necessary. The final result should be a Graph Column Design dialog box that looks like Figure 13.13.

Click on OK to apply these setting to the graph. This returns you to the graph itself, which should look like Figure 13.14.

As you can see, this has widened the column significantly, since the cookie design is wider than the column it replaces. However, before correcting that, let's continue and replace all of the other columns with their respective designs: Cold Drinks Division with coke bottle; Hot Drinks Division with coffee cup; and Soft Foods Division with cone. In each case, you should use the Repeating design type and make each design represent the same number of units—in this case, 20000. This was why you made each design the same height, so that when the design is inserted into the graph, each will represent the same number of units and each will look about the same size.

When you are done, all the columns will overlap to some degree. You need to change that so that the graph data is easily visible and comprehensible.

Figure 13.13

These are the correct entries to select the cookie design for the Package Foods Division columns on your graph.

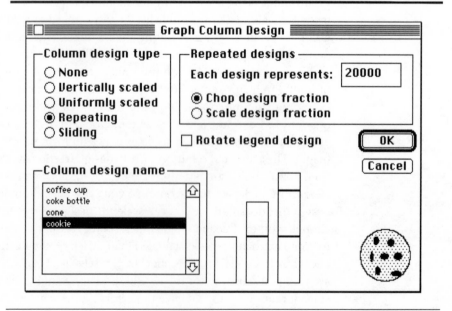

Figure 13.14

The graph looks like this after you have set the new design into the columns.

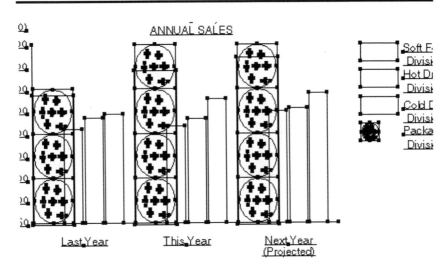

Otherwise all this fancy design work would only have made the graph worse, not improved it. To do this, select all of the graph again and choose Graph ➤ Graph Style. The Column graph options group sets the size of the columns and clusters for the graph. Change the Column width to 60% and the Cluster width to 80% and click OK. This reduces the size of the columns and of the clusters as a whole, so that each design shows clearly. The result prints as shown in Figure 13.15.

I also cleaned up the legend on the right side, making the symbols all line up vertically and adjusting the leading on the text to make the overall effect that you see in the figure.

When you preview or print this file, you will notice a significant pause while your Macintosh or LaserWriter works through all of the pieces of this graph, so be prepared for a small wait. This occurs because each column, besides now having a series of designs to render instead of a single, shaded bar, must also clip the design at the top of the bar. If you look closely at the artwork displayed on your screen, you will see that both the design and the bar are still part of the graph.

Figure 13.15

The printed graph output when you use column designs for the graph.

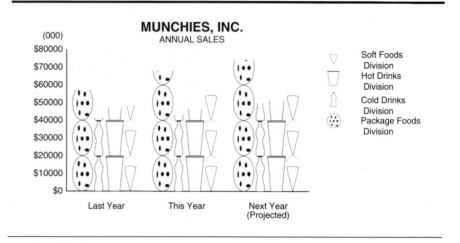

Overall, specialized column designs should be used sparingly, and only when they add something to the data display on the graph. As you saw in the exercise, this can mean reducing the amount of work the viewer does by making the encoding of some of the data easier to see. In addition, you should probably confine yourself to using the Repeating or, occasionally, the Vertically scaled or Sliding options for display. In all cases, remember the data and your audience and graph accordingly.

OTHER GRAPH TYPES

Illustrator provides several other types of graphs, including pie graphs, area graphs, and scatter graphs. Each of these is suitable for specific types of data and specific situations. Although creating these graph types is essentially the same as the graphs you have already done, let's look briefly at each of these types.

Stacked Column Graphs

The bar graph can also be created in a stack, to show both the components and the total of some value. This is a useful technique, if you don't push it too far. A bar graph gives some feeling for the breakdown of the data and provides some additional feedback for your audience. However, it makes comparisons quite difficult, because your eye has a harder time assessing lengths that are not along a baseline. For this reason, the changes may be connected by lines.

If the lengths to be compared are not along a common baseline, move the bars to a common baseline by using the grouped column graph format for the data.

Line Graphs

Another common form of chart is the simple line graph. In this chart, the data is presented as a series of points, which are connected by a line. Line charts are particularly useful to show several data sets at once. They do, however, present several problems.

It is sometimes difficult for the eye to follow the lines across the page. Making a separate legend is one solution, but it creates a special problem, because matching the line types or sizes with the graph can be quite difficult if there are several types.

Pie Graphs

The pie graph is one of the most often used types of graph, and it is the simplest. Since childhood, we all have an image of a pie as a unit, and of pieces cut from the pie as segments of a whole. This is what pie charts are used for: to represent the portions of a whole.

The basic pie chart represents only one set of numbers, and they must all be shown as percentages of a total.

A pie chart does not convey much more information than a simple table, but it is more graphically compelling and catches the viewer's attention. You can display actual numbers on the chart, so that the viewer does not have to guess at the amounts as presented. The graph shows quite graphically the relationships of the various slices. You can even separate a particular segment out for emphasis—presumably, this would be a focus of the accompanying presentation.

You should avoid pie charts when you have a number of small segments in the display. Small segments in a pie are almost indecipherable. When you have a number of small data values that will translate into small slices, you should either lump them together, or consider an alternative chart format, such as a bar chart, where the numbers will not be lost. Remember that the eye has quite a bit of trouble making angle judgements; don't try to force it to estimate small, acute angles.

Area Graphs

You can make a line chart more interesting and visually compelling by filling in the areas underneath the lines. This type of chart is called an *area graph*. The result gives an impression of solidity and a strong visual presence to the graph; it may also make the data easier to see and follow.

This technique is frequently used when showing a set of numbers that adds up to some total; the individual data sets are shown as filled areas and the top becomes the total. This approach has some good features, but requires careful handling and analysis to work properly. It is important that the data be sufficiently distinct so that the areas can all be seen clearly. If you are making the data cumulative, you also must ensure that the overall picture is as visible as the individual elements, and vice versa.

Scatter Graphs

One of the best ways to examine and understand data is to plot it. For this type of work, scientists and others who wish to understand a variety of data traditionally plot the information as points on a graph. This type of graph is called a *scatter graph*. A typical use of scatter graphs is to explore the relationship of two distinct sets of data; for example, you might use it to plot the relationship of the sales of lemonade to the daily high temperature.

When you use a scatter graph, you must take notice of which variable you place on which axis. If you were plotting lemonade sales against temperature, you would normally place the temperature along the horizontal axis, making it the independent variable. The graph would be equally accurate if you flipped the axes, but it would give a strange impression. The natural feeling of the audience is that the variable graphed along the vertical axis depends in some manner on the variable that is plotted along the horizontal one.

Although the mathematical relationships do not change if you alter the axes, the visual and psychological ones do.

In this example, it is clear that the temperature cannot depend on sales; the dependence must be the other way around. Obviously, not every data set will provide such a clear-cut relationship; if you were plotting clouds against wind speed, for example, you might theorize either way on which one depended on the other. Nevertheless, even when the dependence relationship is not clear, as in that example, you should remember that your viewer will assume that the variable plotted along the vertical axis depends in some fashion on the one on the horizontal.

Summary

This completes our survey of types of charts and graphs. We have, to a great extent, stayed with those formats that can be prepared directly from Illustrator with a few keystrokes and some minor editing. As you have seen in this chapter, you can easily import or paste data from other applications into Illustrator for exciting and dynamic graphic output.

CHAPTER FOURTEEN

FOURTEEN

Importing and Exporting Graphics

FEATURING

Using Illustrator
output formats

Sharing files with earlier
versions of Illustrator

Creating Encapsulated
PostScript files

Placing artwork
in Illustrator

Using Illustrator
printing options

ILLUSTRATOR OUTPUT FORMATS

Once you've created your artwork, you have to save it. Throughout this book, we've asked you to save artwork so you can reuse it. Up to now, this simple type of storage is all that you've used. However, there are a variety of methods for saving Illustrator documents. This section of the chapter looks at all of these in some detail, so that you'll know which ones to choose and why to choose one over another. In particular, you will be introduced to Encapsulated PostScript (EPS) files and how you can use them to communicate images between Illustrator and other applications, like Aldus PageMaker, QuarkXPress, and Microsoft Word.

Native Illustrator 3.2 Formats

Your choice of output format implies certain choices in the use of that output. Since the choice made affects both use and storage size, you need to be sure that you understand what each of these options means. Here you will see why you choose one over another.

Even in the default output format, which you have been using up to now, there are some new wrinkles to be investigated. There are several things you can do to control the size of your PostScript output that require no direct knowledge of the PostScript language itself but that do require some understanding of the structure of Illustrator output.

Save Options

When you choose File ➤ Save for unnamed artwork or File ➤ Save As for any artwork, you are presented with a standard file selection dialog as shown in Figure 14.1.

Figure 14.1

This dialog box allows
you to save your artwork
in one of several formats.

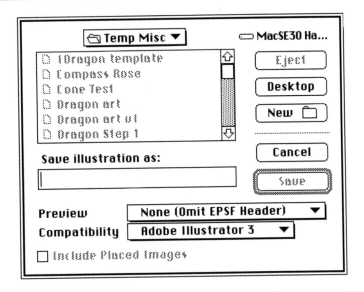

Besides the standard file selection display, this dialog box has two important
menus: the Preview pop-up menu and the Compatibility pop-up menu. The
selections you make here determine the final format used to save your
Illustrator file.

There are five options in the Preview menu and three in the Compatibility
menu. The options in these two menus are complementary, so that the
choices in one do not exclude or force any choices in the other. Let's look
at the Preview list first.

The default Preview option is the one that you have been using up to now:
None (Omit EPSF Header). This saves the file in standard Illustrator 3 format,
which can be read and understood by any version of Illustrator from 3.0 on.
However, this format does not have any of the data required by other applications for including Illustrator artwork. In order to use Illustrator files in other
applications, you need to save your file in one of the Encapsulated PostScript
(EPSF) formats. The default format cannot be used by earlier versions of Illustrator, such as Illustrator 1 or Illustrator 88.

This saves the file as a text file, which can be transferred and printed on any other computer system. Of course, you must use appropriate transmission software that understands the Macintosh file format to do the transfer.

Compatibility Options

No matter what Preview format you select, you can make your Illustrator file compatible with an earlier version of Illustrator. Generally, you don't want to do that since there are some features of Illustrator 3 that are not available in earlier versions. When you save a file in one of the earlier formats, Illustrator presents you with an alert dialog box that reminds you of this fact.

You select the compatibility format by choosing one of the three options in the Compatibility pop-up menu. Besides standard Adobe Illustrator 3 compatibility, you can choose either Adobe Illustrator 88 or Adobe Illustrator 1.1 compatibility. When you change the Compatibility setting, Illustrator automatically changes the Preview selection to None (Include EPSF Header). This makes the file complete, since it includes the correct set of Illustrator procedures to print or place the file. Under normal circumstances, you should stay with this Preview selection, but you can change to any other of the Preview items.

ENCAPSULATED POSTSCRIPT

Encapsulated PostScript (EPS) is a PostScript file that has a special structure. This structure was designed to allow other programs, most notably other application programs that produce PostScript output, to view a PostScript graphic and manipulate it in certain limited ways. Here we will look at some of the important aspects of EPS without getting into too many technical details of exactly how these files are structured.

In the following discussion, let's call the program or person that creates the EPS file the *source* and the application that uses the file the *destination*. Note that this format is not limited to Macintosh systems; EPS files can be used on a wide variety of computer systems.

The EPS format always consists of two distinct parts. The first contains the PostScript program created by the source that will generate the desired image on the output device; the second part contains a bitmapped image of the resulting graphic itself. The bitmapped image is used by the destination application for screen-display purposes, while the PostScript code is used for printed output. The PostScript program's text contains additional information and follows a rigid structure that allows the destination application to translate, rotate and scale the final image as required for the new output.

As the name implies, EPS files are intended to be used as separate *capsules* of graphics and not interact in most ways with the rest of the destination application's output. The significant deviations from this are the ability of the destination application to position the graphic on a page at any point, and to crop, scale, or rotate the graphic as required for correct placement and viewing on the output page. It is the destination application's responsibility to create the necessary changes in the output environment to ensure that this occurs correctly and to restore the original environment when it's done.

Notice that the destination application cannot change the image internally. For example, if you save the apple artwork as an EPS file, the other application can't change the apple to add leaves. It can, however, take the apple and scale it to fit into a defined space. Generally, the destination application uses information provided in the structure of the EPS file to determine the proportions of the graphic being used.

EPS File Format Options

There are four options when you want to save your Illustrator artwork in one of the EPS formats. Let's look at each of these in turn.

The first selection on the list is labeled None (Include EPSF Header). This selection adds the required PostScript code and structure to your file but does not add any PICT graphic to the file. In this case, the file will have the necessary PostScript format to be used by other applications, but it will not have a preview image that you can see on the screen.

Because PostScript files are entirely text characters, it is possible to move an EPS file generated with this option over to any system, such as a workstation or a mainframe, and still use the file once it has been converted so that it can be read. In that case, no EPS image will show on the screen since no preview image was included; only a gray box of the correct size will show. Usually, however, this is often sufficient to give you placement and control information, and the image will still print perfectly correctly on any PostScript device. This EPS format is also the smallest of the EPS formats in terms of disk or other media storage space.

For display on Macintosh systems, you have the choice of using a color or a black-and-white preview image. These are selected by the next two items in the Preview list: Black&White Macintosh and Color Macintosh. The color preview image is larger than the black-and-white one, even for artwork that only uses black or shades of gray. The color preview also converts some grays to black to allow for color display. For these reasons, you should use the Color preview only if color is part of your artwork.

There are two basic forms of EPS files, because of the requirement for a bit-mapped screen image. Since the IBM and the Macintosh have quite different approaches to screen graphics, source applications must use two separate file types to generate the required screen graphic and link it correctly to the Post-Script output if they are going to support both graphic formats. This is what the last option in the Preview list, IBM-PC, allows you to do. The IBM format of an EPS file uses the Aldus/Microsoft TIFF graphic format to store the image rather than the Macintosh PICT format, and any destination application that wishes to display the image must be able to read and display that format. This is an important distinction that you should note carefully: when you choose the IBM-PC EPS format, you are creating a file that can be read directly by an IBM or IBM-compatible personal computer only. Do note, however, that your Illustrator application can still read and modify files stored in this format, even though other Macintosh applications cannot.

ILLUSTRATOR AND OTHER APPLICATIONS

This whole format process may be made clearer by an example. This is not precisely an exercise, because it discusses taking an EPS file from Illustrator back into Illustrator itself, which you normally wouldn't do. The basic process that you will use here for importing EPS graphic files into Illustrator will be the same for other applications (including how it handles placed graphics).

Start by calling up the apple artwork with leaves that you created into Illustrator. I used the file Modified Apple art, but you can use any of your saved documents. Save the artwork using File ➤ Save As and choose a new name for the file; the example uses *Apple EPS*. Then save the file with a Preview selected for Black&White Macintosh and click Save. Return to the artwork and select File ➤ Close. This gives you a new file in EPS format with the name *Apple EPS*. This is the file you will import back into Illustrator.

Before you move on to the next step, return to the Finder and look at these two files. The file Modified Apple art takes up 6K but the file Apple EPS requires 26K. The difference is the inclusion of the additional PostScript commands (the EPSF Header) in the file and the preview image. Keep this difference in mind when you save files; it points out why you only want to use the EPS formats when you need them.

Next return to Illustrator and choose File ➤ New. This gives you a new, untitled drawing surface. Now select File ➤ Place Art. This displays a standard file-selection dialog box, showing all the Illustrator or EPS files in your folder. Select Apple EPS and click Open. The result is shown in Figure 14.2.

Figure 14.2

The Apple EPS file placed back into Illustrator

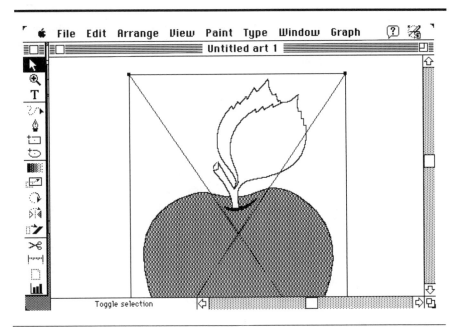

What appears on your drawing surface is a preview image of the apple artwork, enclosed in a rectangle with diagonal lines connecting the opposite corners, like an x through it. The rectangle represents the *bounding box* for the artwork. The bounding box is a rectangle that just encloses all of the marks on the artwork; it is the smallest area that the artwork requires. Notice that the placed EPS artwork looks like a preview image, even though you are still in Artwork Only mode. The image that you see within the rectangle is the bit-mapped screen image that you saved with the artwork; it is not the artwork it-self. Therefore, for example, you cannot use any of the tools to select or move parts of the graphic. When you actually print, the PostScript file will be used, not the bitmapped image.

You can use some of the Illustrator tools to make simple changes to the graphic by using the rectangle that encloses it. You can reposition or trans-form this imported graphic by using the functions provided. Figure 14.3 shows the image after it has been shrunk vertically and expanded horizon-tally with the Scale tool and moved to the top-left corner of the page with the Selection tool.

Figure 14.3

This is the placed EPS graphic scaled and moved, but otherwise unchanged.

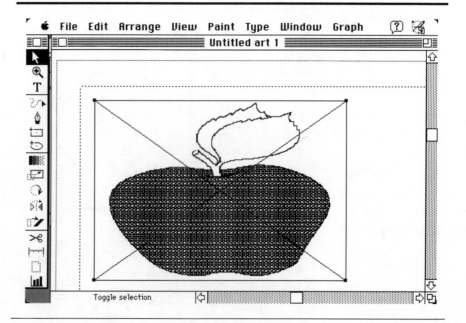

Note that this change has not redefined any details of the image. It simply transforms the image like a distorting mirror in a fun house, expanding or contracting each dimension as requested. Destination applications can perform this type of change on the EPS file because they can interpret certain information that is provided by the file format about size and shape. They don't have to understand the PostScript code itself. The destination application—in this case, Illustrator itself—is not using the PostScript code to generate the screen image and has not interpreted the PostScript code that goes with this image. In fact, if you had used an edit program that could access the Post-Script portion of the EPS file, you might have changed it to produce some other graphic and Illustrator would still show you the same image of an apple here.

As you can see, for this process to work smoothly requires a lot of coordination between the two applications. There are two essential points to take away from this discussion. First, the exchange of graphic information between cooperating applications using the EPS file format is quite simple from the user's point of view. Second, the placement and transformation of such imported graphics within the destination application is always limited to a fairly basic set of options. Therefore, the role and work of each application is quite well-defined.

Placed Graphics

When you import an EPS file into your Illustrator artwork, Illustrator positions the graphic inside the bounding box rectangle that is displayed on your screen. If the file has a screen image stored with it, Illustrator displays that inside the rectangle. This is, as you saw above, just like the preview image that you would normally see on your screen. Like a preview, it can take some time to display. If you don't want the image displayed, you can choose Edit ➤ Preference (⌘-K) and turn off the checkbox marked Show placed images. Of course, the image is only displayed if it is present and in a Macintosh format. If you saved the file with the EPSF header but without a preview, or if the image was prepared or saved in an IBM PC format, only the rectangle will show, no matter what you have set as the preference option.

When Illustrator displays this rectangle on your screen, it does not actually access or change the PostScript data in the EPS file. The rectangle is like a frame for the EPS file data; Illustrator can change or distort the frame but it can't change the picture. The actual picture data remains in the file that you selected when you placed the image. This file is associated with your artwork in much the same way that a template file is; that is, Illustrator keeps track of the file for you. As long as you don't move or rename it, Illustrator will display it correctly on your screen.

When you save the file, things get a little more complex. If you save the file in a native Illustrator format, then Illustrator remembers the placed file name and location and keeps track of the connection, just as it would for a template. If you save the file in an EPS format, however, there are two ways to handle placed artwork. First, you can simply save your file, as discussed above, and not save the placed file. In this case, if you want to print your new file, you must be sure to keep any placed files with the new artwork, so that Illustrator can combine them when it goes to print.

The alternative is to keep the full data for the file with your current Illustrator file. This increases the size of the file substantially, but it means that you don't need to keep the placed artwork with your new file. In this case, the new file automatically contains all of the placed artwork as well. This is particularly useful if you are going to take your Illustrator EPS file and place it into another application, such as a page-layout program.

To keep your placed artwork with your current file, you must do two things. First, you must save the current file in one of the EPS formats. Second, you must select the checkbox marked Include Placed Images. This tells Illustrator to copy the placed artwork files into your Illustrator file when saving it.

Considerations of Speed and Efficiency

In the course of saving these files, you saw how large the EPS files are relative to the basic Illustrator ones. That isn't really surprising, since these files have a graphic image associated with them along with the EPS header information as well as having the basic PostScript file. Looking at these files raises the question of how you can minimize size of PostScript files for transmission and processing in those environments where size becomes an important factor. This might be a concern, for example, if you often transmit files between users over communications lines or if you are processing over a serial port to your output device.

The best method for reducing file size is to keep the number of anchor points to the minimum required to generate the figure that you want. This is a direct outgrowth of the rules that you learned earlier, the stride rule in particular. Each point that you create requires at least two numbers and possibly six numbers to be placed into the PostScript output. Since each PostScript coordinate position number generally has three digits before the decimal point and as many as four after, excess anchor points can eat up a lot of file space.

PRINTING ILLUSTRATOR FILES

Printing from Illustrator, like printing from any Macintosh application, is quite easy. You can simply select File ➤ Print, which brings you the Print dialog box shown in Figure 14.4.

To complete printing, make any changes that are required to the dialog box and then click Print. This gives you the most basic printing options, using the default page settings of your printer. Unlike some applications, Illustrator adds no additional selections or options to the Print dialog box. Generally, the default values in the Print dialog box will be fine for your Illustrator output.

Most of the settings here are quite straightforward, and are the same as those used for all other Macintosh applications, so we don't need to review them here. However, there are two items that I would like to mention before we

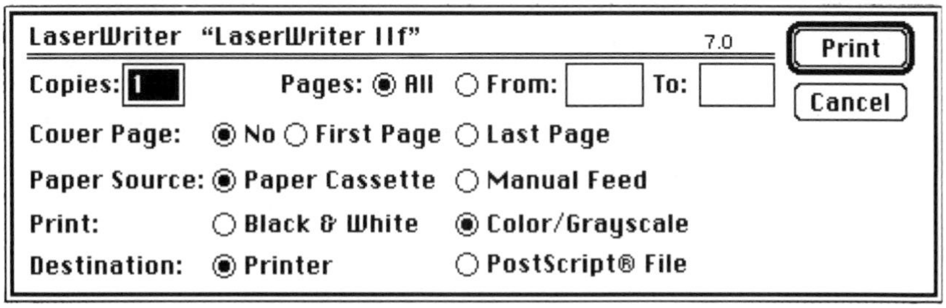

Figure 14.4

The Print dialog box allows you to set some options for printing.

```
LaserWriter  "LaserWriter IIf"                      7.0    [ Print ]

Copies:[1]        Pages: ◉ All  ○ From:[    ] To:[    ]   [ Cancel ]

Cover Page:    ◉ No ○ First Page ○ Last Page

Paper Source: ◉ Paper Cassette ○ Manual Feed

Print:         ○ Black & White   ◉ Color/Grayscale

Destination:   ◉ Printer         ○ PostScript® File
```

move on: the Print and the Destination radio groups. The Print radio group allows you to print either Black&White or Color/Grayscale images. This does not govern how your output is printed from Illustrator itself; if you have color defined in your Illustrator document, it still will print (as color on a color printer and as gray tones on a black-and-white printer) no matter how you set this. You should check the Color/Grayscale button when printing from Illustrator to a LaserWriter IIf or IIg; this enables higher quality output for color or grayscale images. Although it generally will not have much effect on Illustrator output, it can be useful. For other devices, this will not usually have any effect.

The other important option is the Destination radio group. Normally, you will leave this on the standard Printer selection. This prints your artwork to the current printer. However, sometimes it is important to get your output as a PostScript file. Although the Illustrator file itself is PostScript, there is additional code that is required to print your document. This comes from the printer driver that you have selected in the Chooser; usually, this is the Laser-Writer file, but it may be different depending on the printer that you use. If you need to capture a complete, print-ready file in PostScript format, click on the button marked PostScript File. When you select this, the default button changes from Print to Save. Clicking Save will bring up a standard file selection dialog that allows you to name the output file and place it where you want. Once you have done that, your document is stored under the selected file name with all the information required to print. This can be important if you want to send your file for remote printing or processing, as we will discuss later.

Page Setup

When you print from Illustrator there are some things that may change each time you print and some that remain much the same. The Macintosh system has collected the ones that change regularly into the Print dialog box that we discussed above; things like number of copies, page selection, printing to a file, and so on. The other options are things like page size and orientation, and so on. These don't generally change once you have set them for a particular document, so they are collected in the Page Setup dialog box, shown in Figure 14.5, which you access by selecting File ➤ Page Setup.

Figure 14.5

*The Page Setup dialog
box allows you to set
several important
parameters for your
document.*

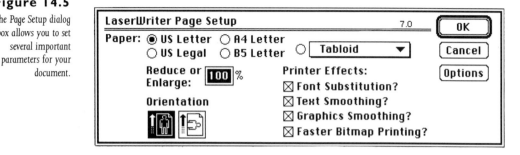

The most important items for an Illustrator user in this dialog box are the
Paper size selections and the Orientation. The Paper group allows you to
select a paper size for your output. Each page size that is available on your
printer or other output device is listed here, either as a radio button or as an
item in the pop-up menu list that is selected by the last button in the group.
If you have a special printer that will produce unusual sized pages, for example, these will be listed in the pop-up menu.

In the same way, you can select portrait or landscape orientation for your
artwork. You do this by clicking on one or the other of the two orientation
icons in the bottom-left corner of the dialog box. The one on the left is the
normal, portrait orientation where the top of the artwork lies along the short
end of the page; the one on the right is the landscape orientation, where the
top of the artwork lies along the long edge of the page.

When you select these options here, the exact dimensions of the page, its
orientation, and its margins are communicated to Illustrator. Illustrator then
uses that information to set the page size and orientation that you see on the
desktop. This helps to ensure that, when you print, you do get what you see
on the screen.

Page Setup Options

The Page Setup dialog box has an Options button in addition to the two
standard OK and Cancel buttons. Pressing this button brings up the Options
dialog box shown in Figure 14.6.

Figure 14.6

The Options dialog box allows you to set additional Page information for your output.

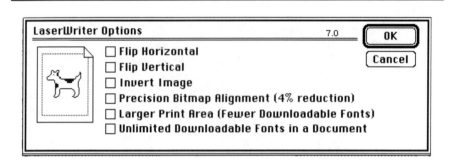

This consists of a series of checkboxes and a small icon. The icon displays the result of the current settings in the checkboxes. Of all of these options, the only one that is directly related to your Illustrator output is the one labeled Larger Print Area (Fewer Downloadable Fonts). This option allows you to print closer to the edge of the page. If you select this option, you will see the icon margins change. You can see the same change in Illustrator when you return; choose View ➤ Fit In Window to see the new page and margins.

Every PostScript printer uses its internal memory for several purposes: font storage, working storage, and image storage, to name three of the most important. When you increase the size of your page image by selecting this option, you use up memory that could be used for font storage. That's why there is a notation in the label for this checkbox that selecting this results in fewer downloadable fonts. Each font that you download to your printer typically uses between 30 and 80K bytes of memory (some especially fancy fonts may require more). The larger page size requires about 150K of memory; slightly more than the room required for two fonts. If you are not using a lot of downloaded fonts in your Illustrator artwork (and you probably shouldn't be), then having the larger page size is a useful and valuable tradeoff.

Creating Output for Remote Printing

There are several ways to prepare your output for printing on another system. If the other system is a Macintosh and has Illustrator installed, you can simply save your file in a format compatible with that version of Illustrator.

Then the other user can open your file, edit it if desired, and print directly from his copy of Illustrator.

If the other system is not a Macintosh or does not have Illustrator, then you have two options. First, you can save your artwork in one of the EPS file formats, choosing the preview option that suits the other system. An EPS file can be imported by most word processing or page-layout programs. Once the file is imported into another application, you can then print from that application. The EPS file that you prepared in Illustrator will print correctly to any PostScript output device. This is the best option if you want to combine the artwork with other text or graphic information.

The second option is to print the artwork from Illustrator to a file rather than to the printer, When you do this, you get a PostScript output file that is exactly like the file that is sent to your printer. This file is ready to print, and can be transferred to any other system and printed on any PostScript output device by downloading it directly to the printer. However, the file cannot be imported into another application since it is not an EPS file.

There are two additional issues to be concerned with when you send a file for remote printing. These are the fonts used in your artwork and any placed graphics that you have used. In both cases, the concern is to have the required information—font or graphic—available when you go to print on the remote system. If you save your file as a PostScript file, both placed graphics and downloaded fonts will be included in the file. If you save your file as an EPS file, then you can use the Include Placed Images checkbox, which we discussed above, to ensure that any placed graphics are included in the file. If you save your file in EPS format, the beginning of the file will have a comment line that names the fonts that are used in the file; you should also know what fonts are in the file, of course. You need to be sure that the destination system has these fonts available, both for screen display and especially for printing. If they are not available, then you may have problems displaying your artwork and you will certainly have problems printing.

SUMMARY

This chapter gives you an insight in how to set up your artwork for sharing with other applications or for printing. It also covers how to import properly formatted graphics into your own artwork. The basic mechanism for sharing is the Encapsulated PostScript (EPS) format. Files in this format can be used in other applications, and even moved to other computer systems, such as an IBM-PC or a Unix system, and still be used successfully for output. When you create EPS output for other systems, you need to control the use of placed graphics and the use of fonts in your own artwork to be sure that these are available on the new system.

Printing is quite easy from Illustrator. There are only a few options that you need to be aware of when you print. Of these, page size and orientation should be set when you start your artwork. When you go to print you have the option of printing on your normal printer or to a file. Printing to a file can be useful, but you need to keep a few points in mind about file size, complexity, and included items like fonts and graphics.

APPENDIX

APPENDIX

APPENDIX

FEATURING

What are color separations?

Creating separations from your Illustrator files

Using Adobe Separator options and controls

Making spot-color and process-color separations

Separating Color Images
with Adobe Separator

Adobe separator

As you read in *Chapter 10*, color printing generates all the colors that we see by using combinations of four process colors: cyan, magenta, yellow, and black—usually abbreviated CMYK. In order to print in full color, your Illustrator artwork must be broken down into each of these four components. In each case, when you print in color, your printer must ultimately run the drawing through the press one time for each color. The result is that each finished drawing is composed of four layers of ink, one lying on top of another, mixed to give you the colors that you want. The same breakdown and printing process must also be used if you use a custom color in your artwork and wish to print in only two or three colors.

The output from this process of dividing your colored artwork into sections, each of which corresponds to one of the primary colors, is a set of four separations. Each separation represents all of your drawing that is in one of the primary colors. Plate 2 of the color Insert shows you the four separations of the book cover shown in full color in Plate 3. As you see, the color separations work together to create all the colors in the final output.

Although you assign the color values to your artwork in Illustrator, this process of breaking down a piece of artwork into the primary colors is not done in Illustrator itself. Instead, Adobe ships with Illustrator a separate utility program called Adobe Separator, which can be used to separate Illustrator color files. Separator reads your Illustrator output file and analyzes the colors in it. Then it creates one output file for each color component in the input. It also allows you control over several variables that are important when you are creating color separation files.

Using Separator

Adobe Separator and its auxiliary files install as part of the normal Illustrator installation process. Separator itself is installed in the same folder as Illustrator.

The auxiliary files, called PPD files—which stands for PostScript Printer Description files—are installed in a separate folder called the PPD Folder inside the Illustrator folder.

PPD files, as the name implies, provide detailed information about the Post-Script printer or imagesetter that you will use to print your final color separations, including things like page size, color support features, fonts that are installed, correct color screens, and so on. Separator needs to know several of these items about a device in order to generate the separations correctly. It could get the required information by asking you, through a dialog box, or it could query the device itself, if you have it available. However, the PPD file provides all the required information without taxing your memory, or tying up the actual device, in fact, without requiring the device at all. Illustrator ships with a large set of PPD files for many of the most common and widely-used output devices. If your individual device is not in this group, you should get a PPD for your device from the device manufacturer. If you are planning to run your output at a service bureau, check with them to be sure that you have the correct PPD for their specific output device; if you don't, they should give you a copy. PPDs are not application software and copying a PPD file or using a copy of a PPD file is completely legal.

Separator is designed to work with EPS output. The best way to prepare a file for use with Separator is to save it in Adobe Illustrator 3 format with a Color Macintosh preview. This gives you the most information and best display when you are working in Separator. However, Separator can work well with any of the EPS formats, including the IBM preview format.

Although you can use standard Illustrator files with Separator, they may not print correctly. Separator issues two warning messages if you attempt to open an Illustrator file that is not in EPS format. You generally should always use an EPS format file for input into Separator. This guarantees that the program will work optimally with your artwork. Also, if your EPS file has a preview image associated with it, Separator will display that as you work, which allows you to see exactly what you are doing to the image. In the cases where you have chosen either None (Include EPSF Header) or the IBM PC preview format, Separator will separate the file but cannot display the preview. In such cases, for example, placed EPS images in Illustrator itself, the artwork is displayed as a gray box of the appropriate dimensions with an X through it.

Separator Display

When you launch Separator, it asks you to locate an Illustrator or EPS format file. Select an EPS file and open it. Next, Separator will ask you to select a PPD file. You should select the PPD file for the printer or imagesetter that your final output will be on, not your current printer—unless they're the same, of course. The names of the PPD files are quite cryptic, usually involving a short-hand of the device name and the PostScript level of the device. For example, there are two PPD files for the popular Linotronic 300 imagesetter, called L300_471.PPD and L300_493.PPD. The numbers after the underscore represent the version number of the PostScript interpreter in the L300. If you are running at a service bureau, be sure to check with them about which PPD is the best to use for their specific device. If you aren't sure about which PPD to use, use L300_471.PPD as a standard for imagesetters and use LWNT_470.PPD for any laser printer. These won't be perfect, but they'll get you close.

Once you have selected both your artwork and a PPD file, Separator displays a control screen as shown in Figure A.1.

Figure A.1

Separator has many sophisticated controls to allow you to separate your color artwork correctly.

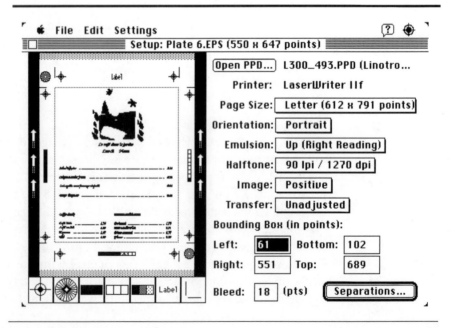

This shows you the preview image of the artwork on the left, including a number of useful items that Separator has added to the edges of the artwork. In order from left to right, these are as follows:

Cross-hair registration target	Registration marks allow your printer to align each color separation exactly over one another so that the image prints correctly.
Star registration target	Registration marks allow your printer to align each color separation exactly over one another so that the image prints correctly.
Black overprint color bar	Color bars allow the printer to identify the correct color balance of your separations during printing.
Standard color bar	Color bars allow the printer to identify the correct color balance of your separations during printing.
Gradient tint bar	The gradient tint bar allows the printer to determine if the color processing has changed over time.
Separation labels	The separation labels show the name of the color being separated, the name of the file, and the current line screen and angle for the color.
Crop marks	The crop marks show the exact edge of the page that is being printed. These are used to cut the film correctly for printing.

Illustrator defaults to positioning these along the edges of the output as shown in Figure A.1. Generally, the default placement and use of these will be satisfactory. You can move or remove any of these features from the output simply by clicking on the item that you want to change and moving it where you want it or moving it off the page to remove it entirely. Note that the arrows along the sides of the image tell you the direction that the output page is moving. This can be important when printing to imagesetters, since you may want to control the amount of material that is used for output.

Separator Controls

Separator provides a series of controls that allows you to set many options for your color separations. These are listed down the right side of the Separator window shown in Figure A.1. Let's look at each of these in turn.

Open PPD
: This button allows you to select a new PPD file. The name of the current PPD is shown next to the button. Pressing the button brings up the standard file-selection dialog box that allows you to choose a new PPD file. The output device that you select here is called the *target printer* and controls many of the other settings in Separator.

Printer
: This static text display shows you the name of the printer that is currently chosen in your system. Note that this is the printer that you have set with the Chooser, often called the *proofing printer*. This does not reflect the target printer that you set with the PPD, and it doesn't affect any of the settings in Separator. However, this is the printer that you will print on when you select any printing option from the File menu.

Page Size
: This pop-up menu allows you to select any page size that is supported by the output device set by the PPD. These names and dimensions come directly from the PPD. If your selected output device supports variable page sizes, you can use the Other size, listed in the pop-up, to define any size output that your device can handle.

Orientation
: This pop-up menu allows you to set the orientation of your output to either Portrait or Landscape. Some imagesetters have a Transverse output option that you can choose in the Page Size. Do not confuse Transverse with Landscape. The Transverse option simply prints your page rotated 90° to save film; it does not alter the image orientation. Landscape, on the other hand, does alter the image orientation.

Emulsion
: This pop-up menu allows you to choose Up or Down as the direction for printing. This is important when you are printing on film. On paper, the correct setting is always Up; using Down reverses the printing as though you had used a mirror. For film, however, it is important to set the direction correctly; check with your printer as to what setting will work best.

Halftone
: This pop-up menu allows you to set the lines-per-inch (lpi) and dots-per-inch (dpi) being used in your output device. This setting controls how halftone images look in your output. The values available in this pop-up menu are derived directly from the PPD that you choose.

Image
: This pop-up menu allows you to set whether the output is printed in Positive or Negative format. Positive is what you normally use when you print on paper; negative is more common on film.

Transfer

This pop-up menu with a dialog box allows you to adjust the color tints in your separated artwork to compensate for color changes in the final printing. Normally you will leave this as Unadjusted. The Adjust tints selection brings up a dialog box that allows you to enter adjustment values for all the process colors and for one custom color as well. You use this with the Densitometer Control Chart document. Use of these adjustments is highly technical; review your Illustrator documentation and work with your printer before making any changes here.

Bounding
Box
(in points)

These four edit text boxes—Left, Right, Bottom, and Top—allow you to enter the position of each of the corners of your artwork. Separator automatically positions the image on the page size that you selected in the best position it can, using the size of the image as set by Illustrator when you saved it. Changing the bounding box coordinates here moves the edge of the visible output area; it does not scale or change your image. If you make the area too small, some of the image will be cut off. The maximum and minimum values for these settings are determined by the page size that you have selected. Generally, you cannot set an image outside the edges of your page and you cannot define an area smaller than 72 points by 72 points (1" by 1").

Bleed	This edit text box allows you to specify additional room around the actual page being printed. The bleed area is added around your image as an aid to the printer. Note that the registration marks, label, and so on all fall outside the image area plus the bleed. If the image area plus the bleed exceeds the page size, some of these may move off of the output and will not print. The preview shows you what will or will not print. The maximum bleed is the difference between the image bounding box and the page size; you cannot exceed the page size.
Separations	This button allows you to select individual separations to be printed. Pressing this button brings up the Separation dialog box (this can also be displayed by selecting File ➤ Separations). The dialog box allows you to select any of the process colors that are used in the artwork and allows you to set the label for that separation. If your artwork has custom colors, this dialog also allows you to print these individually or convert them to process colors.

Separation Examples

Figure A.1 shows you the data from Plate 6 of the color insert, which was saved in EPS format and then opened in Separator using PPD file named L300_471.PPD, for the Linotronic 300 imagesetter. To print color separations for this artwork, select File ➤ Print All Separations (⌘-P). This will print separations for each color included in the artwork; in this case, that is every process color. If you only want to print selected separations, choose File ➤ Print Selected Separations. This will only be available in the menu if you have selected one or more separation colors in the Separations dialog box. All printed output comes out on your proofing printer, which you select in the Chooser.

Finally, you can print your artwork as a color composite by choosing File ➤ Print Composite. This is much the same as printing from Illustrator itself, except that it takes into account the setting and additions that you have made in Separator. If you have selected a color printer, then you will get full color output; if you have selected a black-and-white device, the colors will be transformed into shades of gray. Since Separator has set the area for printing according to the selected page size on your target printer, the actual printout may not match the page size in the proofing printer.

If you are going to print your output at a service bureau or other remote site, you will probably want to save the separations as files rather than print them. You can do this by choosing either File ➤ Save All Separations or File ➤ Save Selected Separations, if you have selected certain separations for processing. In either case, Separator presents you with a dialog box that allows you to direct where to save the file. This dialog box uses a suggested name for the file, consisting of the artwork file name and a period, followed by the name of the current color. You can change this in the dialog box if you want to.

If you are sending your separations out for processing, your service bureau will want to know several things about your artwork: what size it is, what fonts it uses, if it has any additional patterns or EPS file in it, and so on. To help you prepare for this, Separator will display selected information about your file if you choose File ➤ Get Info. This displays a window listing a variety of information about your file. Figure A.2 shows you the information list for Plate 6. You can print this information by clicking on Print in the dialog box.

Menu Artwork Example

The menu artwork shown in Plate 6 is a good example of basic color artwork. It uses a variety of process colors and tints to give a very pleasing effect to a simple lunch menu for a cafe.

The design at the top uses a deep purple-blue color (80% Cyan and 30% Magenta) for the table top. The same color is repeated in the shadow of the folded menu. The exterior of the menu is painted with a light (30%) Magenta tint. The coffee in the cup is a simple oval, filled with 40% Cyan and 30% Magenta to give a more purple effect. The two leaves are painted with 70%

Figure A.2

The Get Info dialog box shows you several important types of information about your artwork.

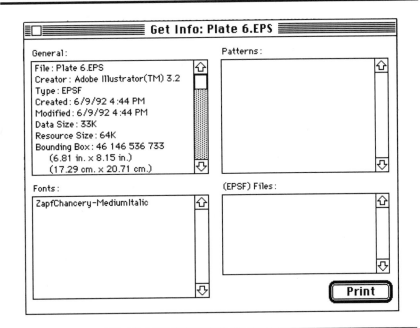

Magenta. The entire effect is to use various combinations of Cyan and Magenta to tie the overall design together. The coffee cup and the saucer ring are painted using 50% Yellow and 5% Magenta, for a medium yellow effect. The accent rings between the text and between the leaves is pure 50% Yellow, making it a little brighter than the cup itself. The entire design is framed and completed by the black leaf shapes on the sides of the design.

The text is all in Zapf Chancery. Guidelines were used to help align the left and right columns of text and prices. The only trick to note in the text is the use of dashed lines to connect the menu items and the prices. These were drawn from right to left—instead of the more usual left to right—so that the dashes line up correctly. By drawing the line from the right, the first dash for each line is just before the price and the succeeding dashes are laid out correctly back to the menu items. Line lengths were adjusted to ensure that no partial dashes were visible.

Color Wheels Artwork Example

Plate 4 of the color insert shows you two sets of simple color wheels. These two sets of color wheels demonstrate an important Illustrator option when you are creating color artwork. The wheels themselves are simply three overlapping circles, each filled with 100% of one of the primary colors: Cyan, then Magenta, then Yellow. The top wheel is standard Illustrator output. As you can see, each color overlaps the next as you would expect, with the last color, Yellow, completely covering the other circles beneath it, even though it is the lightest color.

The bottom circles, however, show a different appearance. In this case, each color was painted in the same way as the top set, but the Overprint checkbox in the Paint Style dialog box was checked. This allows the colors to be combined when they are separated and printed, resulting in a mixing of the colored inks and the combination pattern that you see in the bottom color wheels. To get this, you must follow two steps. First, you must check the Overprint box in the Print Style dialog box. This tells Illustrator that you want to allow the colors to mix. Then you must separate the artwork using Separator. If you print the artwork directly from Illustrator, you will still have each circle printing separately, regardless of whether you have selected Overprint. Separator, however, can separate the inks and allows them to print one on top of the other. Plate 5 shows you the Cyan separation from Plate 4. As you see, the Cyan wheel on the top is cut out, like a moon, so that the inks from the other two colors will not combine with it. On the bottom, however, the full circle prints, allowing the other colors to print over it and make the combined colors you see in Plate 4.

Notice that this overprinting occurs only when you make color separations. It does not occur when you print from Illustrator, even if you have checked Overprint and print on a color output device.

Separating Custom Colors

You may choose to use custom colors in your Illustrator artwork for two reasons. First, because there is a specific color that you want to reproduce. This is the motivation for selecting a Pantone color or one of the other predefined colors that come with Illustrator. Second, you may simply want to gather all of a single color into one place. In this case, you have defined the color as a set of process color values, and used it repeatedly in your artwork. This makes using the color more convenient than typing in the process color values repeatedly, and it makes it possible for you to change or adjust the color in a global fashion.

In the same way, when you use custom colors in your artwork, you have two options for separations. First, you can convert the custom colors into their process color components and print using process colors. This will get you the custom color that you have chosen. Alternatively, you can make a separation for each custom color and print with that color ink for that separation.

If you are doing traditional spot colors, where you have selected a specific color from a color table, you will probably want to make an individual separation for your custom colors. In such cases, you may get more or less than four separations, depending on how many colors you have used in your artwork. For example, if you have selected a single Pantone color, you will probably get the best results from printing your artwork using an individual separation for that color and then printing using the appropriate Pantone ink. This gives you the closest match to the color that you selected from your Pantone guide.

However, if you simply have used custom colors as a convenient way to group colors, you probably will want to make process color separations. This allows you to combine all of your colors into only four separations, at maximum.

Book Cover Artwork Example

The book cover artwork in Plate 7 of the color insert is an example of artwork that uses custom colors and then converts them to process colors for output. In this artwork, the artist has defined seven custom colors as follows:

Dark Green	80% Cyan, 0% Magenta, 100% Yellow, 0% Black
Light Green	20% Cyan, 0% Magenta, 100% Yellow, 0% Black
Light Blue	50% Cyan, 5% Magenta, 0% Yellow, 5% Black
Maroon	0% Cyan, 100% Magenta, 10% Yellow, 10% Black
Orange	0% Cyan, 70% Magenta, 80% Yellow, 0% Black

| Purple | 80% Cyan, 80% Magenta, 0% Yellow, 0% Black |
| Tan | 0% Cyan, 10% Magenta, 60% Yellow, 5% Black |

The artwork itself is built in multiple layers, to create the final effect that you see in Plate 7. The first layer is a simple background rectangle, painted with a 50% tint of Purple. The next layer consists of two smaller background rectangles, representing sky and water, painted Light Blue. (Unless otherwise stated, all colors are painted at 100%.) The top hill was drawn next and painted Dark Green, followed by the lower hill which is Light Green. The moon is a simple white oval. The bird was drawn and made into a group: the body is Purple; the beak is painted Orange with a black teardrop shape placed over it, and the eye is a white ellipse with a black circle on it. The hat consists of two ovals, both filled with 65% Tan and stroked with 65% Light Blue, with one oval for the ribbon in between the two. The ribbon itself is more complex and consists of several parts. The part of the ribbon around the top of the hat is simply an oval, matching the oval of the top of the hat and placed behind it, filled with Maroon and stroked 100% Light Blue. The remainder of the ribbon is drawn over the hat, and is filled with Maroon and stroked with 75% Purple. The bow is drawn over the ribbon, filled with 75% Maroon and stroked with 75% Purple.

The type is placed on the page last. All the type is Times Bold, except the author's name, which is Times Bold Italic. The title of the book is done in three segments. All of the type in the title is right aligned. The first type segment is the single ampersand which is 200 points. This is filled with white and stroked with Light Blue. The second segment consists of the three lines "The Bird... the Hat... Moon" which were in three lines with 70 point leading. All of this type could be set as a unit since the leading was constant for the three lines. The T in the first *The* is 80 points, while the *he* is reduced to 60 points. The entire word was then selected and painted 20% Light Blue. The *Bird...* is all 80 point type, painted 100% Purple. The second *the* is again 60 points, and painted 60% Purple. The *Hat...* is 80 point type painted 100% Orange. The last word in this type segment, *Moon,* is all 94 point type filled white and stroked with 100% Purple. To change the type's color, use the Type tool and select the desired type elements, then use Paint ➤ Style to set the correct fill and stroke values. The last segment is the final *the* placed over the ampersand. This is 60 point type, painted 100% Dark Green.

The author's name is left aligned, in 24 point Times Bold Italic, and painted Purple. The publisher's name is left aligned, 20 point Times Bold, and filled with white. No stroke is used because stroking a reverse type, like this type, which paints white over the background rectangle, coarsens the type outline without adding any detail to the image.

You can see here why the artist has used custom colors. Most of the colors were used several times, in varying parts of artwork. Defining the colors once and then reusing them is much easier than re-entering the process color values. Also, using custom colors like this allows the artist to change the color values without modifying the artwork. For example, if you wanted to change the color of the ribbon to red, you could add more Yellow. Changing the custom color definition would change all of the ribbon parts at once, including the bow, which uses a percentage tint of the ribbon color.

Once this artwork is created, and saved in EPS format, you can separate it with Separator. When you open it in Separator, use the Separations button (or File ➤ Separations) to see the custom colors; this is shown in Figure A.3.

As you see, each of the custom colors is listed in the Custom Colors scrolling list with a checkbox next to it. If you wanted to process separations based on each custom color individually, as you would do if you were printing spot

Figure A.3

The Separations dialog box shows you all the custom colors in your Illustrator file

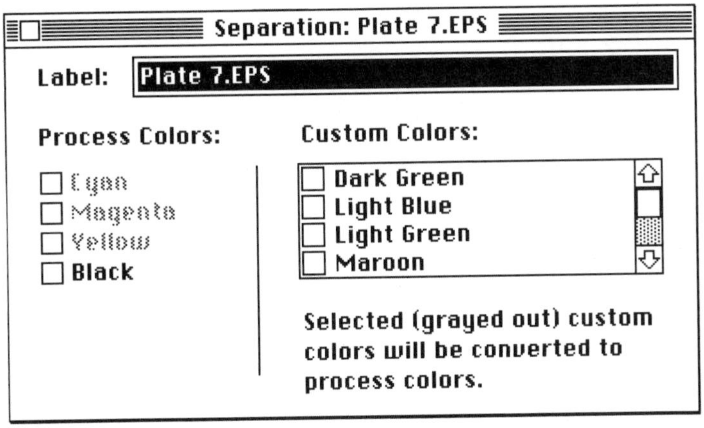

Separation: Plate 7.EPS

Label: Plate 7.EPS

Process Colors:

☐ Cyan
☐ Magenta
☐ Yellow
☐ Black

Custom Colors:

☐ Dark Green
☐ Light Blue
☐ Light Green
☐ Maroon

Selected (grayed out) custom colors will be converted to process colors.

colors, you could simply check the box next to the custom color that you want to print. These colors work exactly like the process color boxes on the left.

However, in this case, you would like to separate these custom colors into their process-color components. To do this, simply click on each custom color in turn. As you do, the custom color name and box will be grayed out, and the process-color boxes will become active. Each custom color that you check will now be converted into a set of process colors. From this point on, all the separation processing is exactly like any other separation.

SUMMARY

Adobe Separator is a useful utility that allows you to separate your EPS files into process colors or into spot colors for further processing and printing. Separator allows you to designate both a target output device and a proofing device. This enables you to set a variety of important device features, like page size and resolution, even though you don't have the device immediately available. Using Separator, you can create high quality output that is ready for printing on high-speed color presses.

INDEX

Special Characters

G

H

I

Selections from The SYBEX Library

APPLE/MACINTOSH

Desktop Publishing with Microsoft Word on the Macintosh (Second Edition)
Tim Erickson
William Finzer
525pp. Ref. 601-4

The authors have woven a murder mystery through the text, using the sample publications as clues. Explanations of page layout, headings, fonts and styles, columnar text, and graphics are interwoven within the mystery theme of this exciting teaching method. For Version 4.0.

Encyclopedia Macintosh
Craig Danuloff
Deke McClelland
650pp. Ref. 628-6

Just what every Mac user needs—a complete reference to Macintosh concepts and tips on system software, hardware, applications, and troubleshooting. Instead of chapters, each section is presented in A-Z format with user-friendly icons leading the way.

Encyclopedia Macintosh Software Instant Reference
Craig Danuloff
Deke McClelland
243pp. Ref.753-3

Help yourself to complete keyboard shortcut charts, menu maps, and tip lists for all popular Macintosh applications. This handy reference guide is divided into functional software categories, including painting, drawing, page layout, spreadsheets, word processors, and more.

Introduction to Macintosh System 7
Marvin Bryan
250pp; Ref. 868-8

An engaging, plain-language introduction to the exciting new Macintosh system, for first-time users and upgraders. Step-by-step tutorials feature dozens of screen illustrations and helpful examples drawn from both business and personal computing. Covers the Desktop, working with programs, printing, customization, special accessories, and sharing information.

Mastering Adobe Illustrator
David A. Holzgang
330pp. Ref. 463-1

This text provides a complete introduction to Adobe Illustrator, bringing new sophistication to artists using computer-aided graphics and page design technology. Includes a look at PostScript, the page composition language used by Illustrator.

Mastering Microsoft Word on the Macintosh
Michael J. Young
447pp. Ref. 541-7

This comprehensive, step-by-step guide shows the reader through WORD's extensive capabilities, from basic editing to custom formats and desktop publishing. Keyboard and mouse instructions and practice exercises are included. For Release 4.0.

Mastering PageMaker 4 on the Macintosh
Greg Harvey
Shane Gearing
421pp. Ref.433-X

A complete introduction to desktop

publishing—from planning to printing—with emphasis on business projects. Explore the tools, concepts and techniques of page design, while learning to use PageMaker. Practical examples include newsletters, forms, books, manuals, logos, and more.

Mastering Ready, Set, Go!
David A. Kater
482pp. Ref. 536-0

This hands-on introduction to the popular desktop publishing package for the Macintosh allows readers to produce professional-looking reports, brochures, and flyers. Written for Version 4, this title has been endorsed by Letraset, the Ready, Set, Go! software publisher.

PageMaker 4.0 Macintosh Version Instant Reference
Louis Columbus
120pp. Ref. 788-6

Here's a concise, plain-language reference, offering fast access to details on all PageMaker 4.0 features and commands. Entries are organized by function—perfect for on-the-job use—and provide exact keystrokes, options, and cross-references, and instructions for all essential desktop publishing operations.

Up & Running with the Mac Classic
Tom Cuthbertson
160pp; Ref. 881-5

A fast, breezy introduction to computing with the Mac Classic. In just 20 steps, you get the fundamental information you need—without the details you don't. Each step takes only 15 minutes to an hour to complete, making this book a real timesaver.

Up & Running with Macintosh System 7
Craig Danuloff
140pp; Ref. 1000-2

Learn the new Mac System 7 in record time. This 20-step tutorial is perfect for computer-literate users who are new to System 7. Each concise step takes no more than 15 minutes to an hour to complete, and provides needed skills without unnecessary detail.

Up & Running with PageMaker on the Macintosh
Craig Danuloff
134pp. Ref. 695-2

Ideal for computer-literate users who need to learn PageMaker fast. In just twenty steps, readers learn to import text, format characters and paragraphs, create graphics, use style sheets, work with color, and more.

Up & Running with Norton Utilities on the Macintosh
Peter Dyson
146pp. Ref. 823-8

In just 20 lessons, you can be up and running with Norton Utilities for the Macintosh. You'll soon learn to retrieve accidentally erased files, reconstruct damaged files, find "lost files," unformat accidentally formatted disks, and make your system work faster.

Using the Macintosh Toolbox with C (Second Edition)
Fred A. Huxham
David Burnard
Jim Takatsuka
525pp. Ref. 572-7

Learn to program with the latest versions of Macintosh Toolbox using this clear and succinct introduction. This popular title has been revised and expanded to include dozens of new programming examples for windows, menus, controls, alert boxes, and disk I/O. Includes hierarchical file system, Lightspeed C, Resource files, and R Maker.

DESKTOP PUBLISHING

The ABC's of the New Print Shop
Vivian Dubrovin
340pp. Ref. 640-4

This beginner's guide stresses fun, practicality and original ideas. Hands-on tutorials show how to create greeting cards, invitations, signs, flyers, letterheads, banners, and calendars.

The ABC's of Ventura
Robert Cowart
Steve Cummings
390pp. Ref. 537-9
Created especially for new desktop publishers, this is an easy introduction to a complex program. Cowart provides details on using the mouse, the Ventura side bar, and page layout, with careful explanations of publishing terminology. The new Ventura menus are all carefully explained. For Version 2.

Desktop Publishing with WordPerfect 5.1
Rita Belserene
418pp. Ref. 481-X
A practical guide to using the desktop publishing capabilities of versions 5.0 and 5.1. Topics include graphic design concepts, hardware necessities, installing and using fonts, columns, lines, and boxes, illustrations, multi-page layouts, Style Sheets, and integrating with other software.

Mastering CorelDRAW 2
Steve Rimmer
500pp. Ref. 814-9
This comprehensive tutorial and design guide features complete instruction in creating spectacular graphic effects with CorelDRAW 2. The book also offers a primer on commercial image and page design, including how to use printers and print-house facilities for optimum results.

Mastering Micrografx Designer
Peter Kent
400pp. Ref. 694-4
A complete guide to using this sophisticated illustration package. Readers begin by importing and modifying clip art, and progress to creating original drawings, working with text, printing and plotting, creating slide shows, producing color separations, and exporting art.

Mastering PageMaker 4 on the IBM PC
Rebecca Bridges Altman, with Rick Altman
509pp. Ref. 773-8
A step-by-step guide to the essentials of desktop publishing and graphic design. Tutorials and hands-on examples explore every aspect of working with text, graphics, styles, templates, and more, to design and produce a wide range of publications. Includes a publication "cookbook" and notes on using Windows 3.0.

Mastering Ventura for Windows *(For Version 3.0)*
Rick Altman
600pp, Ref. 758-4
This engaging, hands-on treatment is for the desktop publisher learning and using the Windows edition of Ventura. It covers everything from working with the Windows interface, to designing and printing sophisticated publications using Ventura's most advanced features. Understand and work with frames, graphics, fonts, tables and columns, and much more.

Mastering Ventura 3.0 Gem Edition
Matthew Holtz
650pp, Ref. 703-7
The complete hands-on guide to desktop publishing with Xerox Ventura Publisher—now in an up-to-date new edition featuring Ventura version 3.0, with the GEM windowing environment. Tutorials cover every aspect of the software, with examples ranging from correspondence and press releases, to newsletters, technical documents, and more.

Understanding Desktop Publishing
Robert W. Harris
300pp. Ref. 789-4
At last, a practical design handbook, written especially for PC users who are not design professionals, but who do have desktop publishing duties. How can publications be made attractive, understandable, persuasive, and memorable? Topics include type, graphics, and page design; technical and physiological aspects of creating and conveying a message.

Understanding PFS: First Publisher
Gerry Litton
463pp. Ref. 712-6

This new edition of the popular guide to First Publisher covers software features in a practical introduction to desktop publishing. Topics include text-handling, working with graphics, effective page design, and optimizing print quality. With examples of flyers, brochures, newsletters, and more.

Understanding PostScript Programming (Second Edition)
David A. Holzgang
472pp. Ref. 566-2

In-depth treatment of PostScript for programmers and advanced users working on custom desktop publishing tasks. Hands-on development of programs for font creation, integrating graphics, printer implementations and more.

Up & Running with CorelDRAW 2
Len Gilbert
140pp; Ref. 887-4

Learn CorelDRAW 2 in record time. This 20-step tutorial is perfect for computer-literate users who are new to CorelDRAW or upgrading from an earlier version. Each concise step takes no more than 15 minutes to an hour to complete, and provides needed skills without unnecessary detail.

Up & Running with PageMaker 4 on the PC
Marvin Bryan
140pp. Ref. 781-9

An overview of PageMaker 4.0 in just 20 steps. Perfect for evaluating the software before purchase—or for newcomers who are impatient to get to work. Topics include installation, adding typefaces, text and drawing tools, graphics, reusing layouts, using layers, working in color, printing, and more.

Your HP LaserJet Handbook
Alan R. Neibauer
564pp. Ref. 618-9

Get the most from your printer with this step-by-step instruction book for using LaserJet text and graphics features such as cartridge and soft fonts, type selection, memory and processor enhancements, PCL programming, and PostScript solutions. This hands-on guide provides specific instructions for working with a variety of software.

DESKTOP PRESENTATION

Harvard Graphics Instant Reference
Gerald E. Jones
154pp. Ref. 726-6

This handy reference is a quick, non-technical answer manual to questions about Harvard's onscreen menus and help displays. Provides specific information on each of the program's major features, including Draw Partner. A must for business professionals and graphic artists who create charts and graphs for presentation.

Harvard Graphics 3 Instant Reference (Second Edition)
Gerald E. Jones
200pp; ref. 871-8

This handy, compact volume is the single complete source for quick answers on all of Harvard's menu options and features. It's small enough to keep on hand while you work—and fast enough to let you keep working while you look up concise explanations and exact instructions for using Harvard commands.

Mastering Animator
Mitch Gould
300pp. Ref.688-X

A hands-on guide to creating dynamic multimedia presentations. From simple animation to Hollywood-style special effects, from planning a presentation to bringing it all to life—it's all you need to know, in straightforward, easy-to-follow terms.

SYBEX

FREE BROCHURE!

Complete this form today, and we'll send you a full-color brochure of Sybex bestsellers.

Please supply the name of the Sybex book purchased.

_____

How would you rate it?

_____ Excellent   _____ Very Good   _____ Average   _____ Poor

Why did you select this particular book?

_____ Recommended to me by a friend

_____ Recommended to me by store personnel

_____ Saw an advertisement in _____

_____ Author's reputation

_____ Saw in Sybex catalog

_____ Required textbook

_____ Sybex reputation

_____ Read book review in _____

_____ In-store display

_____ Other _____

Where did you buy it?

_____ Bookstore

_____ Computer Store or Software Store

_____ Catalog (name: _____)

_____ Direct from Sybex

_____ Other: _____

Did you buy this book with your personal funds?

_____Yes   _____No

About how many computer books do you buy each year?

_____ 1-3   _____ 3-5   _____ 5-7   _____ 7-9   _____ 10+

About how many Sybex books do you own?

_____ 1-3   _____ 3-5   _____ 5-7   _____ 7-9   _____ 10+

Please indicate your level of experience with the software covered in this book:

_____ Beginner   _____ Intermediate   _____ Advanced

Which types of software packages do you use regularly?

_____ Accounting	_____ Databases	_____ Networks
_____ Amiga	_____ Desktop Publishing	_____ Operating Systems
_____ Apple/Mac	_____ File Utilities	_____ Spreadsheets
_____ CAD	_____ Money Management	_____ Word Processing
_____ Communications	_____ Languages	_____ Other _____ (please specify)

Which of the following best describes your job title?

_____ Administrative/Secretarial   _____ President/CEO

_____ Director   _____ Manager/Supervisor

_____ Engineer/Technician   _____ Other _____

(please specify)

Comments on the weaknesses/strengths of this book: _____

_____

_____

_____

_____

Name _____

Street _____

City/State/Zip _____

Phone _____

PLEASE FOLD, SEAL, AND MAIL TO SYBEX

SYBEX, INC.
Department M
2021 CHALLENGER DR.
ALAMEDA, CALIFORNIA USA
94501

SYBEX

SEAL

TOOLS *(continued)*

Icon	Name	Use
	Pen	Draws curves or lines by setting anchor points
	Rectangle	Draws rectangles and squares
	Centered Rectangle	Draws rectangles and squares from center point instead of top-left corner
	Rounded Rectangle	Draws rectangles with rounded corners instead of square corners
	Centered Rounded Rectangle	Draws a round-cornered rectangle or square from center point
	Oval	Draws ovals and circles
	Centered Oval	Draws ovals from center point of oval instead of upper-left
	Blend	Transforms one selected shape or color into another
	Scale	Magnifies or reduces selected objects
	Scale dialog	Same as the Scale tool, but presents dialog box
	Rotate	Rotates selected objects